Small Books
and
Pleasant Histories

Small Books
and
Pleasant Histories

POPULAR FICTION AND ITS READERSHIP
IN SEVENTEENTH-CENTURY ENGLAND

Margaret Spufford

THE UNIVERSITY OF GEORGIA PRESS
ATHENS, GEORGIA

Published in 1982 in the United States of America
by the University of Georgia Press, Athens, Georgia 30602

Phototypeset in Linotron 202 Garamond
Printed in the United States of America

ISBN: 0-8203-0595-2

Library of Congress Cataloging in Publication Data
81-11684

'The beautiful Sentiment of Terence

"HOMO SUM, HUMANI NIHIL À ME ALIENUM PUTO"

may be adapted therefore in this Place, to persuade us that nothing can be foreign to our Enquiry, which concerns the smallest of the Vulgar; of those *little ones*, who occupy the lowest Place in the Political Arrangement of Human Beings.'

John Brand, AB, late Fellow of the Society of Antiquaries, introducing his amended edition of 1776 of Henry Bourne's Antiquitates Vulgares, *which was the first English work recording popular custom, published in 1725.*

Contents

❦

Illustrations

❧

The quality of the reproduction of these woodcut illustrations accurately reflects the condition
of the originals. Note, for instance, that the

bottom of the title page was often cut off by the collector (see p. 179).

Abbreviations

Samuel Pepys's collection of 'small godly' and 'small merry' books is bound up into the single volume of *Penny Godlinesses* (referred to in the text as '*PG*') and the three volumes of *Penny Merriments* (referred to in the text as '*PM*'). His 'pleasant histories' are bound up in the volume which he called *Vulgaria*. All these are in the Pepys Library, Magdalene College, Cambridge. They have simply been cited in the text as '*PG*', '*PM*' and '*Vulgaria*'.

Anthony Wood's collection is in the Bodleian Library, Oxford. Items from it have been referred to as 'Wood' with the appropriate reference.

The Lauriston Castle collection of chapbooks is in the National Library of Scotland. Items from it are referred to as 'LC', together with the call number.

Acknowledgements

The author and the publishers would like to thank the following for permission to reproduce copyright material:

The Master and Fellows, Magdalene College, Cambridge, for the many illustrations from the Pepys Collection in Magdalene College Library.

Bodleian Library, Oxford, for illustrations from the Wood Collection (126, 254(14), 321(3)).

The Trustees of the National Library of Scotland, for illustrations from the Lauriston Castle Collection.

The Trustees, The Wallace Collection, London, for 'The Strolling Ballad Singers' by K. du Jardin, Wallace Collection no. 641.

The Keeper of the Oils Section, The National Gallery of Scotland, for 'A School for Boys and Girls' by Jan Steen.

Bethnal Green Museum (Crown copyright reserved) for the female pedlar doll (Misc. 48–1924) and the pedlar stall (Misc. 48–1925).

Faber & Faber (Publishers) Ltd, for the poem, 'Complaint of the dying peasantry', reprinted from Edwin Muir (1960) *Collected Poems.* The copyright holder in the USA is Oxford University Press, Inc.

The Syndics of Cambridge University Library, for the illustration of the petty chapman from Jost Amman and Hans Sachs (1568) *The Book of Trades.*

FOR PETER
AND
FRANCIS AND BRIDGET

Preface

❧

This enquiry began when I first questioned in *Contrasting Communities*[1] the degree to which the non-gentle parishioner was open, in the century and a half after the Reformation, to suggestions and religious influences brought to bear on him, or her, apart from the obvious pressures stemming from the pulpit. My conclusion, which startled me, that the laity, at least in the diocese of Ely, were far from being the docile material which their ministers no doubt desired, coincided with my increased awareness of a range of documentary evidence which showed that cheap print did indeed reach the villages. In some cases it demonstrably influenced the religious beliefs of individuals. This evidence opened with an account of a man offering to show a scurrilous ballad entitled 'maistres mass' in an alehouse in the village of Orwell in 1553. It continued with the tantalizing account of a pedlar selling 'lytle books' to, amongst other people, a patcher of old clothes in the outlying village of Balsham in 1578. Six years earlier the devotees of the Family of Love, who were spread out across Cambridgeshire and the Isle of Ely, had been reading their tracts in secret. In the late 1580s and 1590s a Jesuit, gaoled in Wisbech, was horrified to observe large groups of Puritans, including women and children, following texts in their Bibles. The struggle between the sects during and after the Civil War spawned a mass of sectarian propaganda which was written and printed with only this one diocese of Ely in mind, since it was full of local personalities. The Quakers were shown to be circulating their printed paper in Balsham, and the Congregationalist, Francis Holcroft, encountered a critical audience in south Cambridgeshire which corrected his text from their Bibles as he read it, in the manner of the Wisbech Puritans years before. The Open Baptists disciplined their rural members of both sexes by letter. Most strikingly of all, a deaf fen-woman who had been an Open Baptist, and was certainly of mean background, since she earned her living by day-labour in her widowhood, was converted to Quakerism by reading Quaker tracts.

This evidence suggested that the historians of literacy were probably being far too conservative in their estimates of the spread of reading ability. One authority phrased his question on the possible effect of literate skills on religious history in the form 'Did the eighteenth-century masses have direct access to the New Testament independently of what they were told of it by the clergy?'[2] The evidence available to me suggested that there had already been direct access by the relatively humble to religious ideas expressed not only in the Bible, but also in a multiplicity of printed tracts, from at least the beginning of the seventeenth century. It therefore seemed worthwhile pursuing a further enquiry, along two lines. How wide was the spread of reading ability in the countryside? Were the examples of the non-grammar school educated readers I had collected likely to be typical or atypical? My first object, therefore, was to search for sources which might throw at least a little light on this murky unquantifiable subject of the social diffusion of reading ability. Secondly, what was available in print at a reasonable price for my hypothetical humble reader to buy, apart from the Bible and this sectarian religious pamphlet literature? What, in fact, were the 'little books' sold by the pedlar in Balsham in 1578? My initial enquiry spread and widened into a general curiosity about the possible nature of the mental furniture of the English peasantry and the printed influences at work on the non-gentle reader before 1700. As it did so, it became evident that the subject was now far too wide; the different influences brought to bear by the printing presses in the shape of ballads, little books, almanacs, religious and sectarian print, and political pamphlets and news books were far too many and diverse, and, indeed, each the subject of particular enquiry. It is evident that the seventeenth-century parishioner, far from being almost immune from external pressures apart from oral ones, as I initially supposed, was, if he could read, as over a tenth even of agricultural labourers could, exposed to a steady hail of printed pamphlets of news, political and religious propaganda, astrological prediction and advice, songs, sensation, sex and fantasy. At this point, I read Professor Mandrou's *De la Culture Populaire aux 17ᵉ et 18ᵉ Siècles* (Paris, 1964, 1975), and became curious about whether a comparable English study could be constructed. I have therefore limited the part of my enquiry concerned with cheap print to the contents of that bag of 'little books' peddled in Balsham and villages like it, from at least the 1570s onwards. This is possible because the group of men who dominated the ballad trade in England, in whose names the ballads were registered with the Stationers' Company, also developed a line in 'little books', or, in the words of a seventeenth-century trade-list, 'Small Godly Books, Small Merry Books, Double-Books, and Histories'. This small book trade developed by the Ballad Partners compared with its French equivalent has therefore, along with the diffusion of reading ability, been my concern.

I have taken the collection of chapbooks made by Samuel Pepys as a basis for this comparison. Pepys was collecting between 1661 and 1688, and most omnivorously in the single decade of the 1680s. Of course, other seventeenth, and indeed, sixteenth-century small books survive. The collection of Pepys's contemporary, Anthony Wood, now in the Bodleian Library, contains at least sixty-five titles of works that might be described as chapbooks, including over a score dated before 1660. A couple of these are sixteenth century. The very large Lauriston Castle collection now in the National Library of Scotland contains at least thirty chapbooks dated before 1700 amongst the mass of eighteenth- and nineteenth-century items. However, these collections do not contain a sufficiently large sample of the output of the specialist publishers before 1660 to permit the reader, excited by the survival of an extremely rare piece of cheap print, to be confident that this is in any way representative of the chapbooks produced before the Restoration. I have therefore eschewed the temptation of running the surviving chapbooks printed before 1700 together in my analysis, in favour of an analysis based solely on Pepys's collection, and the trade-lists of the main publishers contained in it. It seemed to me that I would be more likely to give a balanced picture of their output if I based it in this way, rather than if I took the small books that happened to survive from the whole period at random, and therefore included distortions based both on accidents of survival, and on the whims and fancies of more than one collector over different periods of time.

Samuel Pepys's motives for making his chapbook collection remain obscure. The *Diary* stops before the bulk of the collection was made. He was the son of a London tailor who happened to be educated at a Huntingdonshire grammar school. His immediate family spread from country gentry and impecunious millers in the countryside on the one hand, to London tradesmen and schoolboys on the other. The collection seems to reflect the eclecticism of his own family and social connections. It is such a thorough piece of work, and he collected the productions of all the main publishers so assiduously, that it is tempting to think that his attention had been caught by a new impetus in a trade that the documents show had already been flowering by 1664. Until more is known of the scale of the activities of the Ballad Partners before the Commonwealth, this must remain pure surmise, however. Whatever caught the inquisitive Samuel Pepys's attention did so so effectively that it is difficult to think we could find a better cross-section of the production of the small-book trade in the 1680s. Our impression of these wares, published by the specialists in the trade, advertised by them for sale by the network of country chapmen which covered the countryside, found in chapmen's inventories of the post-Commonwealth, and presumably bought by the barely-literate who were tempted by a new story, is likely to be correct.

I would like to thank Roger Schofield and Victor Neuburg, who encouraged me to pursue this enquiry, and the Trustees of the Marc Fitch Fund, who gave me a grant to xerox Samuel Pepys's collection of chapbooks in 1975, before popular culture had become a respectable object of enquiry for a social historian. Mr Robert Latham, the Pepys Librarian, has treated my demands with great patience. The Social Science Research Council has supported my enquiries about the chapmen who distributed the chapbooks. The earliest results of this work will be found in Chapter V. I am also much indebted to the Department of History at Keele, which made me an Honorary Lecturer in 1974, and has continued to provide me with warm hospitality.

I would like very much to thank the friends who have helped me in a variety of different ways with information or encouragement. Amongst them are David Cressy, Cedric Parry, Roger Pooley, Colin Richmond, Peter Tudor and Hassell Smith. Christopher Harrison spent much time improving my text. I would particularly like to mention Bernard Capp, whose *Astrology and the Popular Press: English Almanacs 1500–1800* (London and Boston, 1979) so fully covers another part of the trade, and who, with Victor Morgan and Victor Neuburg have provided me with so much encouragement and so many references. I would very much like to thank Victor Morgan for his reference to K. du Jardin's 'The Strolling Ballad Singers', which is reproduced in this book. John Morris, of the National Library of Scotland, has made his unpublished paper on Scottish chapmen in the eighteenth and nineteenth centuries available to me, and supplied me with my Scottish references. David Vincent's work on the reading matter of the nineteenth-century working-class auto-biographer gave me many useful leads. As always, my principal thanks are due to my husband, who makes too many relevant sugges-tions for them ever to appear in the footnotes.

KEELE, THE   MARGARET SPUFFORD
TRANSFIGURATION,
1979

REFERENCES

1 Spufford, M. (1974) *Contrasting Communities*; London.
2 Schofield, R. S. (1973) 'Illiteracy in Pre-Industrial England: the work of the Cambridge Group for the History of Population and Social Structure', in Johansson, E. (ed.) *Literacy and Society in a Historical Perspective*, UMEA Educational Reports, II, Sweden, 2.

I

The mental world of the peasant reader

❧

Complaint of the dying peasantry

> Our old songs are lost,
> Our sons are newspapermen
> At the singers' cost.
> There were no papers when
>
> Sir Patrick Spens put out to sea
> In all the country cottages
> With music and ceremony
> For five centuries.
>
> Till Scott and Hogg, the robbers, came
> And nailed the singing tragedies down
> In dumb letters under a name
> And led the bothy to the town.

EDWIN MUIR (1960) *Collected Poems*, 262

The attention of historians interested in pre-industrial communities and in non-élites within them has only recently slowly turned from the reconstruction of the economic framework of such communities to the much more nebulous and more difficult attempt to recreate the mental world and imagery which such people had at their disposal.[1] One of the very limited ways in which this can be done is to describe the fictional world to which the men, or women, who could read but could not necessarily write could be admitted in the late seventeenth century, if he, or she, had 2*d* to spend on the type of small book sold by chapmen up and down the country – which in the nineteenth century became known as a chapbook.

The importance of reading may have been still marginal at a social level below that of the yeoman in a world in which the regular social functions were predominantly oral. Yet increasingly the attender at church, at manor and hundredal court, and even at market, would find the written and the printed word was physically present, if not actually necessary. The sheer volume of cheap print available after the Restoration was very great. Blagden has shown that as many as 400,000 almanacs were coming out annually in the 1660s.[2] The implication is that one family in three could be buying a new almanac yearly. A single member of the group of specialist publishers of chapbooks at the end of the seventeenth century had in stock one chapbook for every fifteen families in the kingdom (see below, Chapter IV, p. 101). Sommerville, who has worked on religious print, suggests that although New Testaments and Bibles sold in smaller numbers they were kept longer and reached an equally wide market.[3]

The relative importance of these publications in the lives of the people in the countryside is impossible to estimate, but it need not have been negligible, as both contemporary and later examples demonstrate.

In about 1830, the seven-year-old James Bowd of Swavesey in Cambridgeshire caught scarlet fever. His father was one of that 'Class of people that are so lightly esteemed', a farm labourer. Despite their poverty, James's parents managed to send him to school, so that when, fifty-nine years later, he was no longer fit for field labour himself, he was able to write an account of his life in a penny notebook. The memory of the fever was still vivid to him as an old man; the doctor had ordered leeches to be applied, and the child loathed them, so that, he wrote:

My Father and Mother had to get me a new Halfpenney or Penney Book before those Leeches went on, nor do I think it was Money spent in waste, for when I got a little better I read those Books and I shall never forget the Impressions one of them left upon my mind the title of the Book was Blue Beard . . . my Father and Mother never tryed to keep the books from me as I was so fond of Reading. I remember One Day having a Bible to read I was looking in the book of Psalms and I read the Twenty-third psalm and when I had read it I said to my Mother Here is a nice psalm, the Lord is my Shepherd, I shall not want the words never wholly Left me from that day to this.[4]

So the Bible and the chapbooks between them provided the only imagery drawn from print James Bowd ever knew, as he battled through a life in which he experienced, despite the twenty-third psalm, acute want.

John Clare, son of a Northamptonshire labourer, provides the best evidence of all of the mental world of an, admittedly brilliant, child in a poor rural home, and the intellectual tools, and toys, that were available to him. He describes both his education and books in his autobiography and, in his *Shepherd's Calendar*, epitomizes, month by month, his village world. He was born in 1793.

> Both my parents were illiterate to the last degree, my mother knew not a single letter . . . my father could read a little in the Bible, or Testament, and was very fond of the superstitious tales that are hawked about the streets for a penny, such as Old Nixon's Prophesies, Mother Bunches Fairy Tales, and Mother Shipton's Legacy, etc., etc.; he was likewise fond of Ballads, and I have heard him make a boast of it over his horn of ale, with his merry companions, that he could sing or recite above a hundred; he had a tolerable good voice, and was often called upon to sing those convivials of bacchanalian merry-makings.[5]

John Clare himself later made one of the first two collections of ballads from oral sources.[6] He gives a very vivid account of his schooling. Although his parents both wanted him educated, necessity forced his father to put him to work at ten, although, until he was twelve he wrote 'three months or more at the worst of times was luckily spared for my improvement, first with an old woman in the village, and latterly with the master at a distance from it'.[7] His 'taste and passions for reading were furious', but apart from the Psalms and the poetry of the Book of Job, which delighted him, all his 'stock of learning, was' as he wrote,

> gleaned from the sixpenny Romances, of 'Cinderella', 'Little Red Riding Hood', 'Jack and the Beanstalk', 'Zig-Zag', 'Prince

Cherry', etc., etc., and great was the pleasure, pain or surprise, increased by allowing them authenticity, for I firmly believed every page I read and considered I possessed in them the chief learning and literature of the country.[8]

He saved every penny he came by to buy these things 'when hawkers offered them for sale at the door'.

His *Autobiography* gives an even fuller account of the chapbook literature available to him.

> I was fond of books before I began to write poetry these were such that came my way 6 py Pamphlets that are in the possession of every doorcalling hawker & found on every bookstall at fairs & market bills are as familiar with everyone as his own name shall I repeat some of them *Little Red Riding Hood, Valentine & Orson, Jack & the Giant, Long Tom the Carrier, The King & the Cobbler, Tawney Bear, The Seven Sleepers, Tom Hickathrift, Johnny Armstrong, Idle Laurence,* who carried that power spell about him that laid everybody to sleep – *Old Mother Bunch, Robin Hood's Garland, Old Mother Shipton & Old Nixon's Prophecys, History of Gothan* & many others shall I go on no these have memorys as common as Prayer books Poulters with the peasantry such were the books that delighted me.[9]

The other influences on him were his own perpetual absorption in the landscape around him, in minute detail, and the story-telling of the old women who worked with the children too young for regular field labour, at weeding and bird scaring. 'The old womens' memories never failed of tales to smooth out labour; for as every day came, new Giants, Hobgoblins and Fairies was ready to pass it away.'

All these elements fused in his *Shepherd's Calendar.* His delight in nature, and minute observation of change round the year informs the whole poem, but it is also full of social observation. Amongst this is the picture of an old farmer reading a well-thumbed *Old Moore's Almanac* in the tavern, and a description of the cottage evening in January. The central figure in this evening is the shepherd's wife, clearly Clare's own illiterate mother, who, as she sits and knits or sews by the fire, tells a group of stories, some of them from the oral tradition, like the diminutive fairies who steal through the keyhole with their glow-worm lanterns and

> crowd in cupboards as they please
> As thick as mites in rotten cheese
> To feast on what the cottar leaves.

Others, like Cinderella and Jack the Giant killer, are retellings of common chapbook tales. She tells her stories so successfully that the children are terrified to go to bed, and

> Hide their heads beneath the cloaths
> And try in vain to seek repose
> While yet to fancys sleepless eye
> Witches on sheep trays gallop bye
> And fairies like to rising sparks
> Swarm twittering round them in the dark.

So John Clare's childhood world, despite its poverty and its near-illiteracy, was enriched by images drawn from both folk-stories, and from the printed ballads and chapbooks that the hawkers brought to the door.

Clare's account of his mother's story telling, and of the old women whose tales smoothed the childrens' field labour, come late in the history of such tale telling. Henry Bourne, a curate in Newcastle-upon-Tyne, was the first to see in the habits of the common people a subject for enquiry.[10] He wrote in 1725:

Nothing is commoner in Country Places than for a whole Family in a Winter's Evening, to sit round the Fire, and tell Stories of Apparitions and Ghosts. . . . From this, and seldom any other Cause, it is, that Herds and Shepherd have all of them seen frequent Apparitions. . . . Some of them have seen Fairies, some Spirits . . . and some have seen even the Devil himself, with a cloven Foot. . . . Another Part of this Conversation generally turns upon Fairies. These, they tell you, have frequently been heard and seen, nay that there are still some living who were stolen away by them, and confined seven Years. According to the Description they give of them . . . they are in the Shape of Men, exceeding little: They are always clad in Green, and frequent the Woods and Fields; when they make Cakes (which is a Work they have been often heard at) they are very noisy; and when they have done, they are full of Mirth and Pastime.

Henry Bourne's censorious editor capped this in 1776 by adding a verse recently written by a butcher's son of Newcastle, who rose to be a doctor. It scarcely demonstrates his superior genius, but it does show Clare's mother was heiress of a long and well-known tradition:

> by Night
> the Village Matron, round the blazing Hearth,
> Suspends the Infant Audience with her Tales,
> Breathing Astonishment! Of witching Rhymes,
> And evil Spirits: Of the Death-Bed Call
> To him who robb'd the Widow, and devour'd
> The Orphan's Portion: Of unquiet Souls
> Ris'n from the Grave to ease the heavy Guilt
> Of Deeds in Life conceal'd: Of Shapes that walk
> At Dead of Night, and clank their Chains and wave
> The Torch of Hell around the Murd'rer's Bed. . . .
> Around the Beldame all erect they hang,
> Each trembling Heart with grateful Terrors quell'd![11]

The telling of tales has continued to be a rural pastime to this day. Early this century, a young boy of Willingham in Cambridgeshire got the job of waterboy supplying the threshing machine when it came round. Whenever the weather was bad, and work stopped, the men, some of whom were then in their seventies, sought cover and passed the time telling stories. Some of these were drawn from oral tradition, some were recent jokes, and some like the story of the princess who had three chances to guess the 'imp's name correctly', were very old folk-tales indeed. The listening boy collected, and remembered them, and in turn passed them on to his nephew, who still retells them as a pastime.[12]

John Clare's experience was not an isolated one. John Bunyan is the only one of the seventeenth-century humble spiritual autobiographers whose early reading had a demonstrable effect on his later writing. He is also a particularly good example for my purpose, because he did indeed come from a poor background. Bunyan was no yeoman's son. His father held a cottage and nine acres in Bedfordshire.[13] This was barely adequate for subsistence. He eked out a living by tinkering rather than by wage labour, and so is classifiable either as a very modest husbandman on his acreage, or as a poor craftsman on his trade. Despite their relative poverty, Bunyan wrote, 'notwithstanding the meanness . . . of my Parents, it pleased God to put it into their heart to put me to School, to learn both to read and write'. He was fully conscious of having had educational advantages which exceeded his parents' social and economic position.

In his maturity, Bunyan repented of his childhood reading matter as a sin, and wrote about it in some detail:

> give me a Ballad, a News-book, *George* on Horseback or *Bevis of Southampton*, give me some book that teaches curious Arts, that tells of old Fables; but for the Holy Scriptures, I cared not. And as it was with me then, so it is with my brethren now.[14]

The implication is plain that Bunyan's peer group, his 'brethren', at the time Bunyan wrote this in the 1660s, were commonly readers of the ballads and chapbooks that Bunyan himself avoided after his conversion.[15] The reading matter which Bunyan describes is chapmen's ware. He is likely to have got it from the chapmen, either at the door, or at market. Elstow, where he was brought up, is two miles from the county town of Bedford; Bedford was too small a provincial town to have a bookshop in the mid-seventeenth century.

Bunyan's reading seems to have left some mark on him.[16] *Bevis of Southampton* was a typical, breathless medieval chivalric romance, in which adventure follows adventure in quick succession. The hero's mother betrays his father to death, and marries his murderer. Her son first escapes, and keeps his uncle's sheep on a hill near his father's castle, and then is sold into slavery to the 'Paynims'. There he refuses to serve 'Apoline', their god, kills a gigantic wild boar, is made a general over 20,000 men, and wins the love of the princess. Alas, he is betrayed and thrown into a dungeon with two dragons, who quickly get the worst of it. He is still able to kill his gaoler, after seven years on bread and water, and then runs off with the princess and a great store of money and jewels. He is next attacked by two lions in a cave, meets an 'ugly Gyant thirty foot in length and a foot between his eyebrows', defeats him and makes him his page, and kills a dragon 40 ft long. He then has the heathen princess baptized and, after numerous further adventures, including a tumble into a holy well that cures all wounds, invades England, revenges his father's death, marries his paynim lady, and is made Lord Marshall. There is no attempt at characterization, and the whole piece of blood-and-thunder writing

seems aimed at pre-adolescent or adolescent males;[17] very successfully, if Bunyan's testimony is to be believed. Although his own
writing was very far removed from this, some of his imagery does
seem to have come from his early reading. The lions that Christian
meets on the way, the description of the monster Apollyon, and the
cave where the giants Pope and Pagan dwell, all owe something to it,
as perhaps does Giant Despair himself. It is worth remembering also
that Bunyan's own voluminous output was certainly aimed at the
rural readership in the villages around Bedford amongst whom he
had his ministry. He knew his readership was familiar with the
giants, lions, dragons and battles of the chapbooks, just as it was with
the cadences of the Authorized Version.

James Bowd, John Clare and John Bunyan give us individual
examples of the impact reading could have on an unlettered man. The
significance of the social change involved in the gradual extension of
literate skills down to at least some members of the humblest social
groups, and the implications of the use of these skills, is extremely
nebulous and difficult to assess. Professor Davie has recently drawn
attention to the literary implications of the problem. He quotes
Leslie Stephen writing on Isaac Watts's hymns in 1876:

> It is said that for many years 50,000 copies of Watts's *Psalms and
> Hymns* were annually printed. . . . Watts's influence must have
> been greater than many legislators, and, indeed many more dis-
> tinguished writers. But such an influence is too intangible in its
> nature to be easily measured.

Davie comments:

> We too, a century after him, have no way of dealing with such
> phenomena, no method by which to translate the quantitative facts
> of so many copies printed and sold year after year, into the
> qualitative consideration of how they conditioned the sensibility
> of the English-speaking peoples. But what we can, and should do,
> however, is to confess and to insist – as Leslie Stephen does not –
> just what a vast lacuna this reveals in our pretensions to chart
> cultural history, and diagnose cultural health, on the evidence of
> printed literature.[18]

One of the ways in which the sensibility of English rural society
had been permanently modified by the influence of one of the types

of cheap print has recently been demonstrated with great force by Professor Robert Thomson of Miami in his study of English folk-song survivals.[19] This gives a convincing statistical piece of evidence of the general importance of literacy, not only to exceptional men like Clare and Bunyan. Thomson shows that at least 80 per cent of folk-songs gathered in the major collections of Alfred Williams, Cecil Sharp, Vaughan Williams and Percy Grainger early this century were derived from printed broadsides. A suggestive series of maps shows the regions in which folk-song collectors worked, over-laid on the routes taken by the chapman working for the ballad and chapbook printers in the eighteenth and nineteenth centuries. There is a high degree of coincidence. This is conclusive evidence of the effects of eighteenth- and nineteenth-century literacy and its indel-ible impact on the popular imagination. The efforts of the ballad partners of the seventeenth century also left a permanent mark, even if this is naturally normally overlaid by later printing. Professor Thomson has also identified just over ninety songs gathered by folk-song collectors, which can only derive from broadsides printed before 1700. It is in fact impossible to study English folk-songs without also studying the development of the broadside ballad trade, as Professor Thomson has done.

It has been suggested that a great preponderance of the surviving ballads can be internally dated to between about 1550 and the first decades of the seventeenth century,[20] and that the decline in the creation of ballads after that was perhaps caused by the existence of printed texts eroding the oral tradition. If this is indeed so, it can be restated in another way. The appearance of a great number of popular songs of satisfying content and artistry at just this point in time, in the half-century or so after 1550, is a form of phenomenon a little like the phenomenon of the Great Rebuilding[21] and is very likely related to it. The same upsurge of spending power in the countryside which permitted the yeomanry to rebuild their houses, also permitted them to send their sons to school and to free them from the labour force. Children of less prosperous men could perhaps only be spared from school until six or seven, when they were able to become useful wage-earners, and so only learnt to read.[22] The appearance of popular literature just at this time is surely related to a rise in the availability of popular education and literacy and goes with an increase in school-ing. This coincides with the mechanical means, printing, to make reading material widely available, and also to record and perpetuate oral tradition. Printing may have led to the fossilization of ballad creation, but it also spread ballads that had previously been regional much more widely.

The Registers of the Stationers' Company, from their opening in 1557–8, show that the presses were already hard at work feeding a popular, as well as educated market. Ballad titles made up an important part of their output. The Puritans were quick to recognize the potential propaganda value of the medium, as well as concerned by the way it was being used for, in their eyes, frivolous purposes. John Rhodes first brought out *The Countrie Man's Comfort* in 1588. It was a book of instructional songs for all the occasions and seasons of the year, and he was very specific about the intended audience in the preface:

> If therefore it happens to light into hands that are wise and learned; know this that I doe not count it so fit a book for thee as for the Scholler of pettie Schooles the poor Countrieman and his familie, who wil aske these vain questions, somtimes saying: what shall we doe in the long winter nights: how shall we passe away the time on Sundayes, what wold you have us doe in the Christmas Holydayes: for such have I made this booke, wherein I shall no doubt please their merrie minds a little, for that they are naturally given to sing, if happily I may winne them to sing good things and forsake evill.[23]

John Rhodes's idea was very far from new in 1588. A search of the titles licensed for the Stationers' Company shows many deliberate attempts of a similar kind from the end of the 1550s to influence humble readers into godly beliefs. An entry licensing three ballads in 1561, for instance, gives their titles as 'Repente ye o ye England', 'When Ragynge Love' and 'Blessed ar they yat Dye in the Lorde'.[24] Unfortunately, however, calls to repentance in ballad form did not establish the hold on popular imagination their authors desired. 'When Ragynge Love' and its like seem, from the laments of Nicholas Bownde in 1595, to have sold better:

> In the shops of Artificers, and cottages of poore husbandmen . . . you shall sooner see one of these newe Ballades, which are made only to keepe them occupied . . . then any of the Psalms, and

may perceive them to bee cunninger in singing the one, then the
other. And indeed ... the singing of ballades is very lately
renewed ... so that in every Fair and Market almost you shall
have one or two singing and selling of ballades.[25]

In 1602 John Rhodes was complaining again, this time that Puritans were not the only manipulators to use the ballad to spread their
gospel abroad. He had come across some Catholic pamphlets and a
Catholic ballad. To the latter he wrote a rhymed rebuttal. Again he
showed his awareness of the width of the market and the scale of the
distributive network:

I am persuaded, there are many such Pamphlets, together with
other like Romish wares, that are sent abroad amongst the common people, both Protestants and Papists in London and in the
country, and that, by certaine women Brokers and Peddlers (as of
late in Staffordshire there was) who with baskets on their arms,
shall come and offer you other wares under a colour, and so sell
you these.[26]

It is no wonder that printing on this scale, which religious propa-
gandists on both sides were so anxious to turn to good account,
should have left many ballads in permanent recorded form.

Other evidence of the effects of popular literacy on popular imagination in a completely different area, which is as potent proof as
that of the impact of the printed ballads on folk-song, comes from
the folk-plays. Although Richard Johnson's *Seven Champions of
Christendom*, which first appeared in 1596, is no longer thought to
have had the formative effect that was supposed in 1933,[27] it is agreed
that the brash introductory speech put into the mouth of St George
all over the country, in many of the thousand or so plays which
survive, comes from Johnson. The spread of chapbook versions of
the play is supposed later to have had the same stultifying effects on
the plays as the spread of printed songs on the creation of ballads.

St George was not the only character to have printed words put
into his mouth. Baskerville[28] gives examples of three separate traditional wooing plays into which printed matter has been introduced.
In the Swinderby Play, a ballad has been grafted in; in a Somerset
play, passages from the seventeenth-century pastoral droll by Cox,
Diphilo and Granida, are inserted; in the Broughton Play, there are

passages of dialogue from *Wily Beguiled*, a comedy of 1606. Basker-ville concludes, 'from the latter part of the sixteenth century on, there is undoubted evidence that the folk plays borrowed from songs, jigs, and plays – probably as performed in feasts, wakes and fairs.'[29]

By 1700, then, the circulation of the printed ballads, chapbooks and plays had already made an indelible mark on oral tradition.

The changes involved may seem slight, but a study of the cultural changes involved in north-eastern Scotland showed that they were profound. There agricultural improvement and enclosure between 1750 and 1820 involved the gradual destruction of close-knit communities, and increasing social differentiation between the farmers and their in-servants and labourers. The second half of the eighteenth century also saw the advent of literacy, probably mainly taught as reading by rote-memorization. Improving farmers put this to good use in the new parish Agricultural Libraries, whilst a trade in broad-side ballads sprang up to cater for less strictly utilitarian purposes. The first extant ballads printed at Aberdeen are dated as late, by English standards, as 1775–6. The boom in cheap printing in Scotland lasted from 1775 for fifty years.

Widespread literacy, and cheap print to satisfy it, came so late to north-eastern Scotland, according to this reconstruction,[30] that the *corpus* of one ballad singer was recorded before it happened, and before the changes it brought about. From this *corpus* can be demon-strated the method of oral composition and, by comparison with later singers influenced by the chap literature, the changes that literacy did bring.

Anna Gordon was born in 1747. She had an inauspicious back-ground for a ballad composer, as she was the daughter of a professor of Greek and married in middle age to a minister. However, Anna learnt her ballads entirely by hearing them sung as a child, before she was ten or twelve, mainly by her aunt, who had

> spent her days from the time of her marriage, amongst flocks and herds at Allan-a-quoich, her husband's seat. . . . She had a ten-acious memory, which retained all the songs she had heard the nurses and old women singing in that neighbourhood.

Anna Gordon therefore had access to a tradition of rural ballad-making, going back to a time in the early eighteenth or late seventeenth century, when her aunt learnt her ballads in Allan-a-quoich. But because Anna belonged to a literate group her ballad-making was recorded. In later life, the ballads of Anna Gordon, or Mrs Brown as she became, were transcribed by different people on three separate occasions from her singing or recitation. The same ballad was on one of these occasions re-recorded after a seventeen-year interval. Comparison of the various texts of Mrs Brown's ballads taken from these different recordings shows that she had learnt from her aunt a series of stories, which she recreated afresh on each occasion she sang them. She had no concept of fidelity to one text or to one set of words; she remade her ballads afresh, changing characters, words and even rhymes and sound, yet retaining fidelity to the story. The ballad-singer in a non-literate society, if we may believe that Mrs Brown indeed had learnt and faithfully reproduced the tradition of the old women of Allan-a-quoich at the end of the seventeenth century, was bound by no effort to remember or to memorize a set of rote-learnt words, but had very considerable creative power.

The effect of literacy and the distribution of printed song sheets on this tradition was disastrous. As Buchan puts it:

> the end result of the spread of printed songs in a newly literate society is that people, with an awed respect for the authority of the printed word, come to believe that the printed text is *the* text; they lose their acceptance of the textual multiformity of the oral ballad story. Once they believe in the fixed text, then it is only a short step towards their memorizing the one 'right' text to the song.

People lost their ability to recreate traditional stories dramatically and also lost the grasp of ballad structure and composition that Mrs Brown had had, ending up like the literate servant girl Bell Robertson, whose ballads were collected in the nineteenth century. She recited songs that she had learnt by heart from other singers, or the printed page. She reproduced what she had learnt faithfully whether it made sense or not, and her text was incomplete. Much of her language was sub-literary, derived from the authors of the chap literature. According to this author, the advent of literacy was in fact extremely damaging to the old oral culture. It changed traditional modes of thought and slackened people's adherence to traditional beliefs and customs, and it reduced the importance of the oral community's entertainment, proverbs, riddling sessions and tale telling.

The combination of agricultural revolution and the social differentiation it brought, together with the advent of schooling and literacy, led also to a class differentiation in the way in which people chose to spend their leisure time in the rural areas of north-eastern Scotland. Ballad singing and story telling now became the perquisite of those whose work demanded fewest literary skills, and so it descended the social scale to the ploughman and the travelling folk. It had previously been one of the occupations which involved the whole non-literate, non-socially differentiated communities of the 'ferm touns' from lord to hired hand.[31] If Buchan's description of the development of literacy, the expansion of the cheap printing trade to meet the new market, and the effects of this in north-eastern Scotland forms a model that may be fittingly translated elsewhere, it is an extremely suggestive one when applied to sixteenth- and seventeenth-century England. A great social change may have taken place between the time when Miles Coverdale grumbled in the 1530s that he wished 'women at the rockes, and spynnynge at the wheles . . . should be better occupied than with "hey nonny nonny – hey trolly lolly", and such-like fantasies',[32] and the time when Dorothy Osborne in 1653 walked 'out into a common that lies hard by the house where a great many young wenches keep sheep and cows and sit in the shade singing of ballads'.[33] A recent writer on ballads is of the opinion that it is 'highly probable' that the milkmaid who sang 'Come Live with me and be my Love' to Isaac Walton 'learnt the ditty from a broadside'.[34] In the satirical chapbook *Mistress Money* (1674), the personified Mistress Money makes her last will and testament. This includes the direction 'to all maids that are in Love, I give pence apiece, to buy the next new ballet of Love, so that they may sing it over their milking pails'.[35] Dorothy Osborne's wenches on Chicksand common may well have been singing learnt words; Miles Coverdale's spinning women almost certainly were not. For the same chronological interval may also be expressed as the time between the period in the 1520s when the Oxford bookseller John Dorne noted in his day-book[36] that he was selling up to 190 'ballats' a day at a halfpenny each, and the agreement in 1689 between the members of the Stationers' Company known as the 'Ballad Partners' to split up the profits of the lucrative trade between them (for the wealth of the associates of the Ballad Partners see below, pp. 85–9).

If such a change indeed took place, it will not be possible to prove it. England became partially literate too early. No interested auditor noted down the words of a sixteenth-century English Mrs Brown as she sang or recited; no late seventeenth-century antiquarian gentleman collected up the repertoire of one of Dorothy Osborne's wenches to compare with the five volumes of broadside printed ballads, diligently assembled by Mr Samuel Pepys. We cannot know whether such a change did take place in that period, from creation of popular song and popular plays to memorized words from printed texts. This change had certainly happened in songs by the early nineteenth century. The Copper family of Rottingdean in Sussex have been singers at least since the farm carter John Copper, who was born in 1817. His sons indirectly brought about the formation of the English Folk Song Society in 1897. But they, according to the grandson of one of them, who continues the family singing tradition, learnt their songs by rote, exactly as the Scottish girl Bell Robertson did.

> Grand-dad, according to my father, instead of 'you gentlemen of high renown' used to sing 'you Gentlemen of hiring hounds'. In 'You Seamen Bold' he used to sing, instead of 'those very words did he regret', . . . 'those very words did he dezigrate'.[37]

It is well worth bearing in mind, however, that between 1500 and 1700 provincial England was being transformed from a late medieval peasant society – which was well aware of the value of the written instrument, the deed, the court-roll, the rental, but in which reading and writing were special skills exercised by experts on behalf of the community – to one in which writing, and particularly reading, were used over much wider areas of human activity including pleasure and self-education, by more members of the community including some of the labouring poor. This transition can and does involve far-reaching changes, which the historian usually leaves to the literary specialist on the one hand, or the anthropologist on the other.

NOTES AND REFERENCES

1 See, for instance, Burke, P. (1978) *Popular Culture in Early Modern Europe*, London.
2 Blagden, C. (1958) 'The Distribution of Almanacs in the Second Half of the Seventeenth Century', *Studies in Bibliography* 11, Table I and *passim*.

3 Sommerville, C. J. (1974) 'On the Distribution of Religious and Occult Literature in Seventeenth-Century England', *The Library*, 5th series, 39, 221–5; and (1977) *Popular Religion in Restoration England*, University of Florida, Monographs in the Social Sciences 59.

4 Bowd, W. J. (ed.) (1955) 'The Life of a Farmworker', *The Countryman* 51 (2) (Summer).

5 Blunden, E. (ed.) (1931) *Sketches in the Life of John Clare*, London, 46.

6 Grainger, M. (1964) *John Clare: Collector of Ballads*, Peterborough Museum Society, Occasional Papers 3.

7 Blunden, op. cit., 48.

8 ibid., 50–2.

9 John Clare, *Autobiography* in Tibble, J. W. and A. (eds) (1951) London, 19. Seven of these titles would have been equally familiar to seventeenth-century readers.

10 Bourne, H. (ed.) (1725) *Antiquitates Vulgares*, reissued by Brand, J. (1776) as *Observations on Popular Antiquities including the whole of Mr Bourne's Antiquitates Vulgares*, Newcastle-upon-Tyne. These quotations are from the 1810 edition, 113, 118.

11 Bourne, op. cit., 127.

12 Information from Mr Dennis Jeeps of Willingham.

13 Sharrock, R. (1968) *John Bunyan* (first edn 1954), London 911–12.

14 Bunyan, J. (1666?) *Sighs from Hell* (second edn), London, 147–8. The italics are his own.

15 It is an interesting implication since Bunyan's education was abnormally good for his economic and social background, and he had learnt to write as well as to read. It might imply that his 'brethren' who had not learnt both skills, did still read the chap literature.

16 When Mrs Leavis wrote of the literary inadequacy and emotional poverty of twentieth-century mass fiction in 1939, she was unaware of the existence of the voluminous chap literature of the seventeenth and eighteenth centuries, the content of which would have provided her with an apt comparison with modern bestsellers. She wrote of Bunyan's prose as if only the Authorized Version was available to form his style, and of the cultural contact of working-class men up to the 1850s as if only the Bible, *Pilgrim's Progress*, *Paradise Lost* and *Robinson Crusoe*, with works

by Addison, Swift and Goldsmith and so on, were on the market. 'No energy was wasted, the edge of their taste was not blunted on bad writing and cheap thinking' (Leavis, Q. D. (1939) *Fiction and the Reading Public*, London, 97–102, 106–15).

17 As indeed it was, except that they were aristocratic bored youths of the twelfth century. See Duby, G. (1968) 'Northwestern France: The "Youth" in Twelfth Century Aristocratic Society', in Cheyette, F. L. (ed.) *Lordship and Community in Medieval Europe*, New York, 198–209, particularly 205.

18 Davie, D. (1978) *A Gathered Church: the literature of the English dissenting interest, 1710–1930*, London.

19 Thomson, R. S. (1974) 'The Development of the Broadside Ballad Trade and its Influence on the Transmission of English Folksongs', University of Cambridge Ph D.

20 Grigson, G. (1975) *The Penguin Book of Ballads*, Harmondsworth, 13.

21 Hoskins, W. G. (1953) 'The Rebuilding of Rural England, 1570–1640', *Past and Present* 4, 44–59. But the dating is reconsidered in Machin, R. (1977) 'The Great Rebuilding: A Reassessment', *Past and Present* 77, 33–56.

22 Spufford, M. (1979) 'First Steps in Literacy: The Reading and Writing Experiences of the Humblest Seventeenth Century Spiritual Autobiographers', *Social History* 4 (3), 407–35.

23 Rhodes, J. (1588, reprinted 1637) *The Countrie Man's Comfort, or Religious Recreatione, Fitte for All Well Disposed Persons*, London.

24 Arber, E. (1875) *A Transcript of the Register of the Company of Stationers of London; 1554–1640*, I, London, 154.

25 Bownde, N. (1595) *The Doctrine of the Sabbath*, London, 242. I am grateful to Keith Wrightson for the reference both to this and to John Rhodes's book.

26 Rhodes, J. (1602) *An Answere to a Romish Rime lately printed . . .*, Preface to the reader, London.

27 Chambers, E. K. (1933) *The English Folk Play*, Oxford. See below, pp. 227–31, 253. Helm, A. (1965) 'In Comes I, St George', *Folklore* 76 (Summer), 121–4. Brody, A. (1969) *The English Mummers and their Plays*, London, 10, 48–9.

28 Baskerville, C. R., *The Elizabethan Jig*, Chicago, 250–1; commented on by Brody, op. cit., 112–13.

29 Baskerville, op. cit., 251.

30 This picture is almost certainly mistaken. R. Houston, 'Aspects of Society in Scotland and North-East England, c. 1550–1750: Social structure, literacy, geographical mobility', Cambridge PhD in progress, demonstrates levels of literacy which are approximately comparable with that shown in the English Protestation Returns in the seventeenth century. Great progress was made in the north-east between 1690 and 1720.

31 This whole survey of literacy in north-eastern Scotland is taken from Buchan, D. (1972) *Ballad and the Folk*, London, 2, 62–4, 70, 72, 76, 155, 172–3, 177, 185, 190–3, 199, 215, 219, 236 and 251.

32 Quoted by Thomson, thesis cit., 3.

33 Parry, E. A. (nd) *Letters from Dorothy Osborne to Sir William Temple* (1652–4), London, 84–5.

34 Friedman, A. (1961) *The Ballad Revival*, Chicago, 53. I am indebted to Dr Peter Burke for this reference.

35 *PM*, II (24), 572.

36 Maden, F. (ed,) (1885) 'The Daily Ledger of John Dorne, 1520', in Fletcher, C. R. L. (ed.) *Oxford Historical Society, Collectanea I*, V, Oxford, 71–177. Also published separately (1885).

37 Personal communication from Bob Copper, in whose book (1975) *A Song for Every Season*, St Albans, these two songs will be found, 272, 210, and the family singing history, 8–9, 12.

II

Elementary education and the acquisition of reading skills

❧

If English society was indeed moving, between 1500 and 1700, from an oral society ruled by an educated élite to a semi-literate society in which some members, even of the humblest social groups, the women and the agricultural labourers, could read, this change was brought about by the availability of elementary education. Since Brian Simon's pioneering article on elementary schools in Leicestershire,[1] a massive amount of work has been done on the numbers and quality of schoolmasters working in different dioceses over the period. Despite the possible drawbacks of the episcopal records, which provide the evidence for the existence of these men,[2] surveys of the licences, subscriptions and testimonials for schoolmasters that survive in diocesan archives do at least give information on the minimum amount of elementary education available. Wherever, so far, this has been studied, the results are not unimpressive.

David Cressy's work on the dioceses of London and Norwich[3] covered the counties of Hertfordshire, Essex, Norfolk and Suffolk. It showed a sharp rise in the number of schoolmasters found at visitations in rural Essex and Hertfordshire from 1580 to 1592, followed by a decline in the 1620s, and a 'virtual disappearance', which might of course only reflect the weakness of the Church in enforcing its licensing prodecure, after the Restoration. The picture in Norfolk and Suffolk was not dissimilar; there was a boom in the number of schoolmasters teaching in the 1590s, followed by a slump in the early seventeenth century, some recovery by the 1630s, but a severe decline after the Restoration.

In Cambridgeshire, approximately one-fifth of the villages, mainly the larger ones and the minor market towns, had a schoolmaster licensed continuously from 1570 to 1620. Maps of masters teaching show that except in the poor western boulder clay area and the chalk down areas of the county, some sort of teacher was almost always within walking distance for a determined child in the late sixteenth and early seventeenth centuries. In one village, Willingham, parents were sufficiently determined to set up and endow their own school, which had a measurable effect, since it produced a group of farmers who were capable of writing wills for the whole community. Again, there was a diminution in the number of masters recorded in the episcopal records after the Restoration, which may simply reflect a loss of ecclesiastical control.⁴ Cambridgeshire, where one-third of the masters in unendowed schools licensed only to 'teach younge children to read, write and caste accompte' were graduates, was not well-provided with teachers simply because of the work of the university town at the centre of the county. Maps of the schools functioning in Kent show that, again with the exception of the poorest areas in Romney Marsh and on the downs of Canterbury, that county was also reasonably well provided. Between 1601 and 1640, half the settlements had a teacher at some time or another, and one-eighth of them had a school functioning continuously, against only one-sixteenth of them in the forty years before, from 1561 to 1600.⁵

Work on the availability of teachers in north-western England shows a very different chronological picture. In the diocese of Coventry and Lichfield, covering Staffordshire and Derbyshire, north Shropshire and north-eastern Warwickshire, schools had already been established in all the main centres of population by 1640. A large number of new endowments were made between 1660 and 1699. The majority of these were intended for the teaching of reading and writing, and specifically mentioned the poor.⁶ Even more interestingly, there was a general development of educational facilities between 1660 and 1700, when masters appeared in no less than 119 places where there had not been a reference to one between 1600 and 1640.⁷ The sort of interest taken was epitomized in a letter of recommendation of a teacher from the minister of Bakewell in Derbyshire in 1697, who wrote in support of a teacher for Middleton, only a mile away from Youlgrave, where there was already a schoolmaster, that it was inconvenient for little children to go there to learn to read and write 'and that as in former times they have been taught by schoolmasters and schoolmistresses at home, so it is as necessary that they be still taught there'.[8]

One hundred and thirty-two places in Cheshire had masters teaching at some point between 1547 and 1700.[9] There again, there was an increase in the number of teachers appearing after 1651. Analysis of the number of places for which schoolmasters were licensed in Cheshire in fifty-year periods showed a continuous increase, from fifty-three before 1600, to seventy-nine in 1601–50, to as many as 105 between 1651 and 1700. Again, a map shows that schools, or rather schoolmasters, were scattered at reasonable distances all over the country, with the exception of noticably poor areas. The child who lived in Delamere Forest or on the heath area south-west of Nantwich would not find it easy to learn to read or write.[10]

Wherever education has been looked at in the country so far, a surprising number of masters have been found teaching outside the grammar schools between 1575 and 1700. Teaching may have been patchy and sporadic, but it was there. Even if the teachers were available, however, the children were not, unless they were of a certain social status.

There is only one standard literary skill capable of measurement that can be used as an index of literary skill for the whole population, and that is the ability to sign one's name. This skill[11] has been conclusively shown to be tied to one's social status in Tudor and Stuart East Anglia,[12] for the simple reason that some degree of prosperity was necessary to spare a child from the labour force for education as soon as it was capable of work. So literacy was economically determined. Between 1580 and 1700, 11 per cent of women, 15 per cent of labourers, and 21 per cent of husbandmen could sign their names, against 56 per cent of tradesmen and craftsmen, and 65 per cent of yeomen. Grammar school and, even more, university education, was heavily socially restricted. From amongst the peasantry, only sons of yeomen had much chance of appearing in grammar school or college registers. There was, however, 'general and substantial progress in reducing illiteracy' amongst all social groups except labourers in the late sixteenth century, followed by some stagnation or decline both in the 1630s and the 1640s, and in the late seventeenth century.[13] It is possible, though, that these improvements and decreases in literacy levels in East Anglia may have been quite differently timed in other parts of the country, since increasing numbers of teachers were found at periods after the Restoration in the dioceses of Coventry, Lichfield and Chester. Examination of literacy rates elsewhere might, therefore, give a completely different picture.

The Protestation Returns of 1642, which should have been signed or marked by all adult males, give, where they survive, the only seventeenth-century evidence providing both a cross-section from all over the country of the results achieved by those teachers who appear in the episcopal records, and also comparisons between different parts of the country of the percentages of those unable to sign. They have been extensively quarried by historians, and are fully discussed elsewhere.[14] Briefly, they reveal that, from parish to parish in the countryside, a proportion of men varying widely from between 53 per cent and 79 per cent were unable to sign their names. The average was around 70 per cent. In accordance with international convention, these figures are always expressed in negative terms, and 'illiteracy' rates rather than 'literacy' rates are cited. Despite the somewhat gloomy interpretation Schofield and Cressy have put on their analyses of the 1642 returns, it appears equally possible to reverse the image, and point out that, where the negative statement can be made that the least advanced parishes in England had no less than 79 per cent of illiterate adult males, so equally can the positive statement that, even in the most backward parishes in England, one-fifth of men could write their names. There was an absolute minimum reading public of 20 per cent of men in the least literate areas in 1642. Nineteenth-century evidence suggests that those who could sign their names could also read fluently. It also shows that as many as three-quarters of the women making marks could read, since writing was frequently omitted from the school curricula for girls from the sixteenth to the nineteenth centuries.[15]

The existence of a 30 per cent male readership, combined with a female readership of unknown size, since girls were not generally taught to write, must have been the incentive to publishers of *ephemera*, ballads, almanacs and chapbooks, the sales of which were all booming in the 1660s. Literacy rates may indeed have been stagnating in East Anglia, but in compensation, are likely to have been rising in the west and north Midlands. In any case, the political and religious ferment of the Civil War in itself led to a heightened

level of debate in the countryside, and to interest in print. The wealth
of political tracts and newsbooks are covered elsewhere,[16] as is the
growth of the trade in almanacs.[17] The Quakers, a sect that drew its
members mainly from the yeomanry and the craftsmen, deliberately
used print as a means of spreading their gospel, and reached some
very humble people that way.[18] The proliferation of *ephemera* probably owes as much to their heightened awareness of, and involvement in, events, as to any further rise in literacy rates.

In the political situation of the 1830s, which was also one of
heightened awareness, there was a tremendous explosion in cheap
print. Twenty years earlier Cobbett had increased the circulation
of his *Political Register* from between 1000 and 2000 to between
40,000 and 50,000 within months of reducing its price to 2*d*. By 1836,
around 200,000 papers a week were sold at 1*d* to 3*d*. Non-political
literature was affected too: between 1840 and 1850, the Religious
Tract Society issued over twenty-three million publications.[19] This
boom in cheap publication aimed at the poor was not caused by a
dramatic increase in literacy amongst the poor: in 1839, 33 per cent
of men and 50 per cent of women were unable to sign their names at
marriage, and the rate of improvement between 1840 and 1850 was
slow.[20] Political interest and awareness and the deliberate policy of
publishers led to this proliferation of cheap print in the nineteenth
century, once literacy had crossed a threshold figure, which, from
the seventeenth-century experience, may have been 30 per cent or
below.

In the seventeenth century, the opportunity to receive any schooling was socially restricted. Once a child could earn wages which
made a difference to the family economy, it would be removed from
school unless these wages could be dispensed with. The experience of
the seventeenth-century autobiographers gives practical information
on the length of time it took children to learn to read and to write,
and the ages at which they did so.[21] The poorest of them also give
irreplaceable information on the ages at which children could
become effective wage-earners, and so on the age and level of skill at
which a poor child would be removed from school, if he ever went
there in the first place.

The seventeenth-century educationalists suggested that, in the
country schools, children normally began at seven or eight.[22] Six
was early. This fits well, on the whole, with the experience of the

autobiographers who learned to read with a variety of people, mostly women, before starting with the 'formal' part of their education at seven, if they got that far.

A bright child was able to learn to read in a few months in the seventeenth century, although so much depended on intelligence, the sort of teacher available, and the size of group he was in that it is difficult to generalize. Oliver Sansom, born in 1636 in Beedon in Berkshire, wrote:

> when I was about six years of age, I was put to school to a woman, to learn to read, who finding me not unapt to learn, forwarded me so well, that in about four months time, I could read a chapter in the Bible pretty readily.

Latin and writing began at seven.[23] John Evelyn, the diarist, began his schooling earlier, at four, when he joined the village group to begin the 'rudiments' in the local church porch. But he was not 'put to learn my Latin rudiments, and to write' until he was eight.[24] James Fretwell, eldest son of a Yorkshire timber-merchant, born in 1699, began lessons earlier still.

> As soon as I was capable of learning [my mother] sent me to an old school-dame, who lived at the very next door. . . . But I suppose I did not continue here but a few days, for growing weary of my book, and my dame not correcting me as my mother desired, she took me under her as pedagogy untill I could read in my Bible, and thus she did afterwards by all my brothers and sisters. . . . And as my capacity was able, she caused me to observe what I read, so I soon began to take some notice of several historical passages in the Old Testament.

He was admitted to the small grammar school of Kirk Sandall,

> my dear mother being desirous that I should have a little more learning than she was capable of giving me . . . where [the master] placed me amongst some little ones, such as myself . . . when he called me up to hear what I could say for myself, he finding me better than he expected, removed me higher, asking my mother if she had brought me an Accidence, which I think she had; so she had the pleasure of seeing me removed out of the horn-book class, which my master at first sight thought most suitable for me.

The master's assumption was not surprising. James was then aged four years and seven months.[25] He was obviously precocious. Other precocious children's achievements were also recorded because they were unusual. Oliver Heyward married the daughter of a Puritan minister who had learnt both to read and to write fluently before the normal age in the 1640s. 'She could read the hardest chapter in the Bible when she was but four years of age' and was taught to write by the local schoolmaster 'in learning whereof she was more than ordinarily capable, being able at six yeares of age to write down passages of the sermon in the chappel'.[26] Anne Gwin of Falmouth, daughter of a fisherman and fish merchant, born in 1692, likewise 'took to learning very Young, and soon became a good Reader, viz. when she was but about Three yeares and a Half old, she wrote tolerably well before five'.[27] The biographers of these girls recognized their unusual forwardness; it seems safer to use Oliver Sansom as a specific example of the time it took more normal children to learn to read.

The autobiographers give the impression that, unless their schooling had already been broken off, they were reading fluently by seven at the latest, even if, like young Thomas Boston, who 'had delight in reading' the Bible by that age, and took it to bed at night with him, 'nothing inclined me to it but . . . curiosity, as about the history of Balaam's ass'.[28]

Writing began with Latin, if a grammar school education was in prospect, whether the boy began this stage of his education at seven like Oliver Sansom, at eight like John Evelyn, or at four like the forward little James Fretwell. It is even more difficult to find evidence on the time it took to master the second skill than the first. Yet one piece of very precise evidence does survive. Alderman Samuel Newton of Cambridge kept a diary from 1664 to 1717.[29] It contains very little personal information, amongst the accounts of corporation junketings and funerals of prominent persons. But on 12 February 1667, Alderman Newton wrote: 'On Tewsday was the first time John Newton my sonne went to the Grammar Free Schoole in Cambridge.' In October the same year, between a note on the assembly of Parliament and a family baptism, appears an entry in a child's hand:

I John Newton being in Coates this nineteenth day of October

Anno Domini 1667 and not then full eight yeares old, wrote this by me

John Newton

There is no paternal comment on this entry, but Alderman Newton must have shared his son's satisfaction in the new achievement to allow the entry to be made. Obviously, to the seven-year-old John, the new skill of writing, which had taken six months to acquire, was a matter of as much pride as his emergence into manhood in his newly acquired breeches.

If it took the autobiographers, who may have been exceptionally gifted, four to six months to learn to read, and they began to acquire the skill at various ages from four to six, it seems reasonable to double this learning period to allow a margin of safety for less intelligent or forward children.[30] A working hypothesis would then be that children who had the opportunity of going to school would have learnt to read by seven. Similarly, since the autobiographers normally began the writing part of their curriculum at seven, and it took John Newton six months to write a good hand, it seems reasonable to double this period also, and suggest that the ability to write was normally acquired by eight.

If these hypotheses are accepted, it follows from the evidence collected by Dr Cressy on occupational differences in ability to sign – showing that only 15 per cent of labourers and 21 per cent of husbandmen, against 65 per cent of yeomen (see above, p. 21) – that these percentages roughly represent the proportion of these social groups which had the opportunity for schooling between seven and eight. Nothing could show more clearly that the economic status of the parents was the determinant of schooling,[31] along, of course, with the existence of some local teaching. The children of labourers and, to a lesser extent, of husbandmen,[32] were needed to join the labour force as soon as they were strong enough to contribute meaningfully to the family economy.[33]

It is difficult to conceive that they could have made a real contribution before six. The case of Thomas Tryon, whose father urgently needed his son's earnings, but still sent him to school from five until he was nearly six (see below, pp. 27–9), bears this out. So also does the evidence from workhouse regulations of the sixteenth and seventeenth centuries governing the ages at which children could be set to work. These seem particularly likely to be reliable, since a municipal workhouse was very unlikely not to try to profit from children's labour if it were possible to do so. Westminster workhouse, in 1560, sent its children above six, but not yet twelve, 'to wind Quills for weavers'.[34]

The Aldergate workhouse, in 1677, admitted children of from three to ten, and its founder wrote 'as to young children, there is nothing they can more easily learn than to spin linen, their fingers, though never so little, being big enough to pull the flax and make a fine thread'. At the time in 1678 and 1681 when he wrote, he had 'some children not above seven or eight years old, who are able to earn two pence a day'.[35] In 1699, the Bishopsgate workhouse was established for all poor parish children over the age of seven. They were to be employed from seven in the morning until six at night, with an hour off for dinner and play, and two hours' instruction in reading and writing.[36] This workhouse, which was, incidentally, a humane one by contemporary standards, was obviously run on the assumption that its children could all work these hours. It is highly significant, therefore, that it did not admit children under seven. It looks very much as if seven was thought to be the age at which a child could cope with a full working day and start to earn a wage which began to be significant.[37] It was also the age at which Tudor parents had a statutory duty to see that their sons practised regularly at the butts,[38] that is, were strong enough to begin to be thought significant in the adult world of the militia.

From this evidence on the likely age at which wage earning began, there is a considerable likelihood that boys below the level of yeomen quite frequently learnt to read, since reading was taught at an age when they could earn little, whereas writing was commonly taught at an age after the meaningful earning lives of such boys had begun. An account of 'literacy' based on the only measurable skill, the ability to sign, takes no account of the implications of the fact that reading was a much more socially diffused skill than writing.

The case of Thomas Tryon, and his social group, demonstrates this perfectly.

Thomas Tryon,[39] of the autobiographers who identified their backgrounds, came from the poorest home, and he certainly had the most prolonged struggle to get himself an education. He was born in 1634 at Bibury in Oxfordshire, and was the son of a village tiler and plasterer,⁴⁰ 'an honest sober Man of good Reputation,; but having many Children, was forced to bring them all to work betimes'. The size of the family did much to dictate educational opportunity, for obvious reasons.⁴¹ Again and again, only children or those from small families amongst the autobiographers appear at an advantage. Despite his numerous siblings, young Thomas was briefly sent to school. 'About Five Year old, I was put to School, but being addicted to play, after the Example of my young School-fellows, I scarcely learnt to distinguish my Letters, before I was taken away to Work for my Living.' This seems to have been before he was six although his account is ambiguous. At six young Thomas Tryon was either not strongly motivated, as he obviously thought himself from his mention of the importance of play, or he was not well taught. Yet it is worth remembering that he was removed from school to work at about the age Oliver Sansom began to learn. His failure to learn to read was going to take great determination to repair.

His contribution to the family economy began immediately and he obviously took tremendous pride in his ability to contribute. 'The first Work my Father put me to, was Spinning and Carding, wherein I was so Industrious and grew so expert that at Eight Years of Age I could Spin Four Pound a day which came to Two Shillings a week.'⁴² He continued to spin until he was twelve or thirteen but by the time he was ten 'began to be weary of the Wheel' and started to help the local shepherds with their flocks on Sundays, to earn 1*d* or 2*d* on his own account. When his father wished to apprentice him to his own trade he obeyed very reluctantly, for by this time he was determined to become a shepherd.

> My Father was unwilling to gratifie me herein . . . but by continually importuning him, at last I prevailed, and he bought a small number of Sheep; to the keeping and management whereof, I betook myself with much satisfaction and delight, as well as care.

But now, at last, at the age when his most fortunate contemporaries were about to go to University,⁴³ the desire for literacy gripped Thomas. It is worth quoting his account of the way he managed to satisfy it in full (see below, p. 125, for the availability of primers):

> All this while, tho' now about Thirteen Years Old, I could not Read; then thinking of the vast usefulness of Reading, I bought me

a Primer, and got now one, then another, to teach me to Spell, and so learn'd to Read imperfectly, my Teachers themselves not being ready Readers: But in a little time having learn't to Read competently well, I was desirous to learn to Write, but was at great loss for a Master, none of my Fellow-Shepherds being able to teach me. At last, I bethought myself of a lame young Man who taught some poor People's Children to Read and Write; and having by this time got some two Sheep of my own, I applied myself to him, and agreed with him to give him one of my Sheep to teach me to make the Letters, and joyn them together.

Here is a perfect example of a semi-literate group, which had acquired some stumbling ability to read. Thomas Tryon's fellow-shepherds were not 'ready readers' but, as a group, they could sound out letters, enough to get him reading.[44] Writing, on the other hand, was quite beyond them. The chapbooks provide supporting literary evidence that schooling to the level of reading was a commonplace. Thomas Hickathrift, son of a day-labourer, was 'put to good learning'. Tom Ladle, illegitimate child of a sewing-maid married to a ploughman, went off to school. This was presented in a matter-of-fact way as a very ordinary thing to do. *Tom Ladle* was certainly not written to appeal to a select or refined audience.[45] Honest John, the serving man to a maltster, could make up verses to his girl, to her great surprise. To her enquiry,[46] 'I did not think indeed you had been so good a Schollar, pray how long did you go to School?', he replied, with irony meant to demonstrate his dullness to the reader,

> Not long, for I had more mind to go to plow and look after my Father's Horses than to learn my book, yet I was pretty apt, for *by the time I was fourteen I could read the Psalter pretty well.*[47]

Even the wretched *Wanton Tom*, fatherless son of a poverty-stricken London whore, was 'put to School' after his mother's remarriage.[48] The compliment books, poking fun at countrymen writing love-letters, quote one distrastrously ill-expressed epistle by a farmer to his city mistress. She heaps scorns upon him by saying 'The Parish-Clerk or Town-schoolmaster was not at home, or else you was loath to bestow twopence on a scribe' (both quoted in full below, pp. 52–3). Yet he could, as befitted a farmer, write. Another 'literary' lover of the chapbooks, 'Dick the Plowman', equally as befitted his station, could not. He had written to the girl he was courting, Joan the Dairymaid,

> ise a Poet born;
> And to be help'd by learning, ise do scorn,
> Jone, in good faith ise did these lines indite;
> Though ise must fess ise never learned to write
> Yet for a pot of Ale I had them Writ.[49]

More realistic insight into the world of the labourer and the in-servant in husbandry is given by the memoirs of Josiah Langdale, who was born in 1673 in the East Riding of Yorkshire.[50] He came from a family prosperous enough to send him to grammar school until he was eight, but his fortunes changed dramatically on the death of his father, before he was nine. Then his mother found his labour essential to the family economy. Like Tryon, he took great pride and pleasure in his skills, which in his case were specifically rural, not industrial.

> I then was taken from School, and being a strong Boy of my Years, put to lead Harrows and learn to plow . . . Also, in the Summer Time, I kept Cattel (we having in our Country both Horses and Oxen in Tethers) and moved them when there was Occasion with much Care, for I loved to see them in good Liking. In those Days, both when I followed the Plow and kept Cattel in the Field, I was religiously inclined . . . I had not time for much Schooling, being closely kept to what I could do in our way of Husbandry, yet I made a little Progress in Latin but soon forgot it; I endeavoured however, to keep my English, and could read the Bible, and delighted therein. . . . I now being about Thirteen Years of Age and growing Strong, did my Mother good service; having attain'd to the Knowledge of ordering my Plow, and being expert in this Employment could go with Four horses and plow alone, which we always did except in Seed time; I very much delighted in holding the Plow, it being an Employment suitable to my Mind, and no Company to disturb my Contemplation, therefore I loved it the more, and found by Experience that to have my mind inward and to contemplate the Ways and Works of God was a great Benefit and Comfort to me.

Josiah's fortunes changed again, when his mother remarried after

seven years of widowhood, and no longer needed him. At that point
the fifteen-year-old became an in-servant in husbandry. His spiritual
search continued, and was fed by an influential close friend in his
second year as a servant. His account of this friend shows just how
limited seventeenth-century literacy could be.

> After I was come to my new Master, he had a young strong Man
> that was his Thresher, but he was blind, and had been so for about
> Twenty Years, who had lost his Sight when about Ten Years of
> Age; He was never Taught further than the Psalter as I have heard
> him often say; yet this Man taught our Master's Children, and
> afterwards became a famous Schoolmaster. . . . He was a Man of
> great Memory, and of good Understanding.

If reading could be taught by the blind, the role of memorization and
rote-learning must have been very great indeed.

Josiah's description of his conversations and recreations with this
friend gives some insight into the world of this literate pair of
labourers in the 1680s, and the astonishingly cool and appraising
round of sectarian sermon-tasting they indulged in, and their worries
about the necessity of the sacraments, which held them back from
Quakerism for some time. Their opinions were based on Bible
reading.

> We would walk out together on First-Day mornings in the Sum-
> mertime several Miles a-foot, to hear such Priests as were the most
> famed for Preaching; and as we walked together we should have
> such Talk as was profitable. One Time as we were coming home
> from hearing one of the most famous and learned of these Priests in
> our County, Well, said he, Josiah, I am weary with hearing these
> Priests, they are an idle Generation, they cannot be Ministers of
> Jesus Christ; This Sermon that we heard to Day I heard this man
> preach some years ago; as soon as he took his Text I thought how
> he would manage it, and accordingly as I thought he would go on
> so he did – I do not know, said he, what People to join in Society
> with – I have looked in my Mind over the Church of England,
> Presbyterians, Baptists and the Quakers, and do say the Quakers
> excel all people in Conversation . . . but, said he they do not use
> Baptism and the Lords Supper . . . So, as I followed my Business,
> which was mostly Plowing, serious thoughts began again to flow

afresh in upon me. . . . We Two would often go on First Day
Mornings into the Field, taking a Bible with us, and there we
would sit down together, and after I have read a while, we have sat
silent, waiting with Desires in our Hearts after the Lord.

The blind thresher and the literate ploughman had possibly
become in-servants for the same reasons that their education had
been disrupted, in one case the accident or disease that had caused
blindness, in the other the demographic accident of parental loss. But
there must have been a steady trickle of semi-literate people into
agricultural labour for just these reasons, and although this literate
pair in Yorkshire were probably unusual, they were certainly not
unique. Richard Baxter's first 'stirrings of conscience' in about 1630
in rural Shropshire were prompted by 'a poor day-labourer' in the
town who normally did 'the reading of the psalms and chapters' in
church, and who lent Baxter's father 'an old, torn book . . . called
Bunny's Resolution' which influenced young Richard.[51] These examples of literate labourers may be taken to represent the 15 per cent
of labourers who could sign their names between 1580 and 1700.[52]
We may firmly deduce from the evidence of the order in which
reading and writing was taught, and the experience of the autobiographers given above, that those who could sign their names could all
read. The existence of this literate group amongst agricultural labourers is one of the reasons which leads me to stress the magnitude of the
change in English society between 1500 and 1700. It proves my
contention that illiteracy was everywhere face to face with literacy,
and the oral with the printed word. Dr Schofield suggested some time
ago that 'there were probably groups in the population, such as
agricultural labourers in certain parts of the country, which were
entirely cut off from any contact with the literate culture'.[53] Dr
Cressy recently concurred. Although he concedes that the presence
of even one reader amongst a group of rural labourers could act as a
significant bridge to the literate world, he feels that 'normally these
ordinary people were indifferent to the political and religious con-
troversies which exercised their betters'.[54] Langdale's account of
lively debate scarcely bears him out. I think the combination of the
existence of a measurable proportion of labourers able to sign over a
period of time, combined with the amount of cheap print in circulation, combined again with the brief impressions I am able to gather

from Langdale, Baxter and Thomas Tryon's group of reading shepherds, justifies my contrary view.

Dr Cressy also casts some very justifiable doubts on whether book-ownership, particularly ownership of the Bible, can be taken as evidence of any habit of reading, or whether the Bible did not itself satisfy a whole range of magical or quasi-magical needs, without any perusal of the contents. He is undoubtedly right that the Bible did fulfil some of the protective and comforting functions once assumed by a rosary. However, it would be equally wrong to assume that the Bible only fulfilled these protective functions, when there is a good deal of evidence that it was actually read. The best account of such communal reading at Puritan conferences in the late 1580s, is well known, but will bear requoting.

> From the very beginning a great number of Puritans gathered here. Some came from the outlying parts of the town, some from the villages round about, eager and vast crowds of them flocking to perform their practices – sermons, communions and fasts. . . . Each of them had his own Bible, and sedulously turned the pages and looked up the texts cited by the preachers, discussing the passages among themselves to see whether they had quoted them to the point, and accurately, and in harmony with their tenets. Also they would start arguing among themselves about the meaning of passages from the Scriptures – men, women, boys, girls, rustics, labourers and idiots – and more often than not, it was said, it ended in violence and fisticuffs.[55]

Since it was written by a Jesuit, it is open to a charge of exaggeration. However, there is other evidence which shows that it was normal for a congregation to bring its Bibles with it. The Quaker, John Burnyeat, was 'moved' to disrupt a service in Brigham, near Loweswater, and to testify against the priest there, in about 1657. It became abruptly apparent that the Bibles of the devout, undoubtedly brought for pious consultation in church, could prove useful in another, unorthodox, capacity too, and one not yet listed by Dr Cressy. For according to Burnyeat, 'his hearers fell on him, and beat him with their bibles and staves, out of the house [church] and graveyard'.[56]

In 1676, when the Calvinist Francis Holcroft and the Quaker Samuel Cater met in Thriplow in Cambridgeshire for a public disputation on whether grace was available to all, or only to the elect, Cater proclaimed his belief that grace was freely available and proclaimed: 'I'll prove by the Scripture that it does, People, look in your Bibles, and look into Titus, 2.11, and you may read it as I say.'[57]

Congregations did not regularly carry only Bibles with them. Prayer books were sometimes used in the same fashion, much to the indignation of Thomas Daynes, the vicar of Flixton in Suffolk from 1588 to 1590, who was deprived for his Puritan views. He refused to use the prayer book, began his services with a prayer, read a psalm, and then expounded the Scriptures. He said that 'they which wolde have service sayde according to the boke of common prayer are papists and atheists'. But, much to his annoyance, his congregation insisted on 'looking in their bookes'.[58]

The best testimony that such occasions happened all over the country, not only in Suffolk, Cambridgeshire and the Lake District, was the fact that they were sufficiently commonplace to be lampooned in the chapbooks. A village idiot who was illiterate dressed up as a minister and went to a village where he was unknown, where he persuaded the sexton to toll the bell since he was going to preach that afternoon. When the people had come in, he rose up

> and having a Common-prayer-book in his hand, he opens it and turning over the leaves, he speaks thus to them: Beloved, saith he, my Text is in the four and fortieth Chapter of St John, and the hundredth verse: then shutting the book again, he begins to preach, as he call'd it, speaking such gibberish and nonsense as did amaze the people: some turned over the leaves of their books backward and forward to find the Text . . . some thought he had spoken Latin or Greek.[59]

If this kind of parody was acceptable as funny to a mass audience, congregations were accustomed to searching, or watching others search, for the text of a sermon in their own Bibles.

The only group more illiterate in seventeenth-century society than the labourers were, of course, the women. The evidence of many school curricula, like that of Orwell school, in which boys were taught to read, write and cast accounts, whereas girls were taught to read and sew, knit and spin,[60] shows that girls were not usually taught the skill that is capable of measurement at all. Actual cases demonstrate the same point. William Stout noted that 'our parents were very careful to get us learning to read as we came of age and capacity first at a dame school, then after at the free school at Boulton' where he and his brother went when they were seven, and which a writing master attended in the winters. 'Our sister' on the other hand, 'was early taught to read, knit and spin and also needlework.'[61] There is therefore absolutely no way of knowing how many women below the level of the gentry in England learnt to read. There are some very suggestive individual examples, though insight into the lives of relatively poor women is even rarer than into the lives of day-labourers.

The mother of Oliver Heywood, wife of a Lancashire fustian-weaver, and a devout Puritan, seems only to have been able to read. As a young girl, after her conversion in 1614, she 'took her Bible with her, and spent the whole day in reading and praying'. She got her sons to take notes of sermons for her, and as an old woman wakeful at night, it was 'her constant course in the night when she lay waking to roll them in her mind, and rivet them there'. She paid for poor children to learn to read also.[62] She was of course relatively well-to-do.

The widow Sneesby, who joined the Cambridgeshire General Baptists in the early 1650s, was certainly not well-to-do. She earned her living in her widowhood, by day-labour. However, she was converted to Quaker teaching by reading 'many of the books' of a Quaker teacher. The General Baptists advised her instead 'to con-tinue reading' the Scriptures but, despite this, she was imprisoned as a Quaker in 1660. Another woman, who was perhaps even poorer, deeply impressed John Evelyn in 1685. He described her as

> a Maiden of primitive life: The daughter of a poore labouring man, who sustain'd her parents by her labour . . . lives on fouer pence a day which she getts by spinning: she says she abounds, can give almes to others, living in strange humility and contentednesse . . . she is continualy working, or praying *or reading*, gives a good account of her knowledge in Religion; Visites the sick. . . . In summ, appeares a Saint of an extraordinary sort, in so religious a life as is seldom met with in Villages now a daies.[63]

It is impossible to know how common these women, able and willing to read, were. Schooldames teaching the first step, reading, come up with suspicious frequency in the autobiographers' accounts of their

education, although they appear with suspicious infrequency in episcopal records. The most striking case of a group of women teaching
reading I have yet come across was at work in the small Staffordshire
market town of Eccleshall in the 1690s, when its inquisitive lord, the
Bishop, surveyed it.[64] Although Eccleshall itself had had only about
615 families in the 1690s, the Bishop noted no less than five women as
schoolteachers. Reading was implied, since he also noted a 'writing
master' who came twice a year. Four of these were not the type of
women who have so far been thought of as, in any sense, lettered.
'Stephen Dimock's wife' was the wife of a day-labourer living in a
cottage in the waste. Thomas Alsop's wife, 'the best knitter in my
parish', was also the wife of a day-labourer. 'Barnet's wife' was
married to a shoemaker, and 'Curly' Wollam's wife was married to a
labourer who thrashed and thatched part time, wove the rest of the
time, and earned the Bishop's approbation as a 'very honest man,
laborious and Religious, sings Psalms in Church'. It seems impossible that all these schooldames merely acted as childminders, from
an incidental remark of the Bishop's made about a labourer and his
wife who lived in the town. 'Neither of them can read' he noted, as if
this fact was both worthy of remark, and extraordinary.[65] It was the
only comment of this kind for the whole parish. These women
teaching letters perhaps indicate to us the possible extent of a network of schooldames teaching the alphabet, and creating a reading
public in late seventeenth-century England, the true size of which we
shall never be able to assess.[66]

Oxford and Cambridge had nothing to do with the 'literate'
worlds of the Yorkshire labourers Langdale and Hewson, the
Gloucestershire shepherds who taught Tryon to read, the Bedfordshire small craftsman, John Bunyan, whose tastes in reading changed,
and the urban artisan with the rural education, Tryon, widow
Sneesby, Evelyn's saintly spinster, and the wives of Stephen Dimock,
Thomas Alsop, Barnet and 'Curly' Wollam. Much more important,
only Langdale amongst them owed anything at all to a grammar
school. The picture they jointly convey is one of a society in which a
boy even from a relatively poor family might have a year or two's
education to the age of six or eight. His almost invisible sister,
historically speaking, sometimes was taught to read. If a boy was at
school until seven, he could read, if he was at school until eight, or at
the latest nine, he could write. Either way he would be able to make

sense of whatever cheap print the pedlars brought within his reach. Either way his mental environment had undergone an enormous and very important change.

NOTES AND REFERENCES

1 Simon, B. (1954) 'Leicestershire schools 1625–40', *British Journal of Educational Studies* 3(1), 42–58; and (1968) *Education in Leicestershire 1540–1940*, Leicester.

2 O'Day, R. (1973) 'Church Records and the History of Education in Early Modern England, 1555–1642: a Problem in Methodology', *History of Education* 2, 120ff.

3 Cressy, D. A. (1972) 'Education and Literacy in London and East Anglia, 1580–1700', University of Cambridge PhD, 99–100, 111–13, 129–35.

4 Spufford, M. (1970) 'The Schooling of the Peasantry in Cambridgeshire 1575–1700' in Thirsk, J. (ed.) *Land, Church and People*, Reading, British Agricultural History Society, 123–30, particularly 123 n. 1; and (1974) *Contrasting Communities*, London, map 11, p. 185, compared with maps 4 and 5, pp. 15 and 17, and pp. 192–7.

5 Clark, P. (1977) *English Provincial Society from the Reformation to the Revolution: Religion, Politics and Society in Kent, 1500–1640*, Hassocks, 199–203.

6 Smith, A. (1975) 'Endowed Schools in the diocese of Lichfield and Coventry, 1660–1699', *History of Education* 4 (2), 5–8.

7 Smith, A. (1976) 'Private Schools and Schoolmasters in the Diocese of Lichfield and Coventry', *History of Education* 5 (2), 117–26.

8 Quoted Smith, op. cit., 120.

9 Rogers, C. (1975) 'Development of the Teaching Profession in England, 1547–1700', University of Manchester PhD. Dr Rogers lists schoolmasters appearing in the records for Lancashire and Cheshire in his Appendix, pp. 245ff. I am extremely grateful to Dr Rogers for allowing me to use this material, and to Mrs Elizabeth Key who mapped it for me and analysed it by period, and who also found, unhappily, no correlation whatever between the work of schoolmasters in the diocese and the apparent literacy of twenty-one Cheshire parishes in the Protestation Returns of

1642, demonstrated by Roger Schofield in his (1973) 'Some Dimensions of Illiteracy in England, 1600–1800', unpublished draft, 11–14 and map 3.

10 This sort of survey of the availability of teachers in different dioceses is of course very superficial indeed. What is really needed is a pooling of results, made available in map form, showing the geographical distances between licensed teachers, since geographical distance is one of the crucial determinants of education to an aspiring child. The other need is for a comparison, diocese by diocese, of the number of schoolteachers appearing in the records within twenty-five year periods, and a comparison of the number of schoolteachers with the size of the villages concerned. The second crucial determinant is the number of teachers per household taxed.

11 The whole question of the use of the signatures to provide a measure of diffusion of literary skills over time, and of the crucial relationship of writing ability to reading ability, is discussed in Schofield, R. S. (1968) 'The Measurement of Literacy in Pre-Industrial England', in Goody, J. R. (ed.) *Literacy in Traditional Societies,* Cambridge, 318–25; and (1973) 'Some Dimensions of Illiteracy in England, 1600–1800', unpublished draft. A part of the latter has appeared as (1973) 'Dimensions of Illiteracy, 1750–1850', *Explorations in Economic History* 10 (4), 437–54. I am very grateful for Dr Schofield's permission to use the unpublished, definitive discussion of the relationship between signing and reading ability.

12 Cressy, D. (1976) 'Educational Opportunity in Tudor and Stuart England', *History of Education Quarterly* (Fall), 314; and (1977) 'Literacy in Seventeenth Century England: More Evidence', *Journal of Interdisciplinary History* 8 (1) (Summer), 146–8; also (1977) *Historical Journal* 20, 4–8.

13 ibid., 10–11; Cressy, op. cit., *Journal of Interdisciplinary History,* 146–7. Dr Cressy does not have a large enough sample of labourers to divide by decades and therefore cannot speak for this social group.

14 First by Stone, L. (1969) 'Literacy and Education in England, 1640–90', *Past and Present* 42, 99–102. The figures were reworked by Roger Schofield, and discussed, mapped and tabulated in his (1973) art. cit., unpublished, pp. 11–13, map 3 and table 5,

on which I rely here. They have recently been reworked again in Cressy, D. (1980) *Literacy and the Social Order,* Cambridge.

15 The relationship between the two skills is discussed by Schofield, R. (1973) op. cit., unpublished, 3–5, who came to the conclusion, on the basis of nineteenth-century surveys examining both skills, that up to one-half of those making marks instead of signing were in fact able to read. The possibility of total diversity in the numbers of those with the two skills may be seen very clearly in Sweden, in the late eighteenth and early nineteenth centuries, where over 80 per cent of the population was able to read when less than 30 per cent could write. Johansson, E. (1977) *The History of Literacy in Sweden*, Umeå, Educational Reports 12, particularly 55–60.

16 Thomas, P. W. (ed.) (1971) *The English Revolution: III News-books*, London, facsimile reprints. George Thomason collected some 22,000 tracts and pamphlets between 1640 and 1661: *Catalogue of the Pamphlets, Books, Newspapers, and Manuscripts . . . collected by George Thomason, 1640–1661* (1908), London, British Museum.

17 Capp, B. (1979) *Astrology and the Popular Press 1500–1800*, London and Boston.

18 Spufford (1974) op. cit., 215–17.

19 Vincent, D. M. (1981) *Bread,Knowledge and Freedom*, London, Chapter 5; (ed.) (1977) *Testaments of Radicalism: Memoirs of Working Class Politicians 1790–1885*, London, 11.

20 Schofield, art. cit., unpublished, 5–6, graph 1.

21 More fully discussed in my (1979) 'First Steps in Literacy: the Reading and Writing Experiences of the humblest seventeenth century autobiographers', *Social History* 4 (3).

22 Cressy, D. (1975) *Education in Tudor and Stuart England*, London, 70–2.

23 Sansom, O. (1710) *An Account of the many remarkable passages of the life of Oliver Sansom . . .*, London.

24 Evelyn, J. (ed. E. S. de Beer) (1959) *Diary*, Oxford, entries for 1624 and 1628, 5–6.

25 Fretwell, J. (1877) *Yorkshire Diaries*, Surtees Society, Durham, 183–4.

26 Horsfall-Turner, J. (ed.) (1881) *The Rev. Oliver Heyward, BA,*

1630–1702: His Autobiography, Diaries, Anecdotes and Event Books, I, Brighouse, 58.

27 Gwin T. (1715) *A memorial of Anne Gwin*, London; and the (1837) *Journal of Thomas Gwin of Falmouth*, Falmouth.

28 Low, G. D. (ed.) (1908) *A General Account of my Life by Thomas Boston, A M Minister at Simprin, 1699–1707 and at Ettrick, 1707–32*, Edinburgh.

29 Foster, J. E. (ed.) (1890) *The Diary of Samuel Newton, Alderman of Cambridge (1662–1717)*, Cambridge Antiquarian Society, Octavo Publications 23, 17 and 23. The original is in Downing College Library, and the entry by John Newton appears on p. 74 of the ms.

30 This coincides well with the expectations of the early nineteenth-century monitorial schools, in which a child was expected to learn to read in eleven months (Schofield (1968) art. cit., 316).

31 *Pace* Peter Clark, who suggests that

> The husbandman who depended entirely on familial labour was probably . . . unable to afford the loss of labour which his child's school attendance entailed . . . is stronger in the context of higher education than in the case of primary instruction. It does not take into account those many *longeurs* in the agri-cultural year . . . when parents were probably quite happy to send a noisy son out to school for a month or so. (Clark (1977) op. cit., 191)

The acquisition of the ability to sign was certainly normally acquired young, probably between seven and eight, and Dr Cressy's evidence shows quite conclusively that economic status deter-mined education to this level.

32 See above, p. 7, for John Bunyan, who knew perfectly well that his ability to write was unusual in the economic circumstances of his home, and had to be accounted for.

33 Christopher Wise in his *New Discovery of the Old Art of Teaching School* (1660) wrote: 'many parents will not spare their children to learn if they can but find them any employment about their domestic or rural affairs whereby they may save a penny', although he also implied that such families spared their children to learn to read and write. Quoted in Cressy (1975) op. cit., 45.

34 Clark, A. (1919) *Working Life of Women in the Seventeenth*

Century, London, 131. In the 1640s, unskilled agricultural labourers were earning 12*d* a day (Thirsk, J. (ed.) (1967) *Agrarian History of England and Wales*, IV, 1560–1640, Cambridge, 864). This rate was the same as that for building labourers, which remained constant at 12*d* a day until just after 1690 (Phelps Brown, E. H. and Hopkins, S. V. (1962) 'Seven Centuries of Building Wages', in Carns-Wilson, E. M. (ed.) *Essays in Economic History*, II, London, 172–3 and 177). These children were therefore earning a sixth of a man's wage. Exceptionally skilled children, like Thomas Tryon, could earn a third of a man's wage at eight.

35 Pinchbeck, I. and Hewitt, M. (1969) *Children in English Society*, I, London, 161.

36 ibid., 154–6.

37 ibid., 10.

38 Obviously, rural children could only be regularly employed in areas where textile industries provided the kind of outwork performed by these city orphans. In many areas, their opportunities for work were likely to be more seasonal, and more along the lines described by Henry Best. His 'spreaders of muck and molehills' were for the most part women, boys and girls, and they were paid 3*d* a day for the 'bigger and abler sort' and 2*d* a day for the 'lesser sort' (Best, H. (ed. C. B. Robinson) (1857) *Rural Economy in Yorkshire in 1641*, Surtees Society 33, Durham, 59). He does not give the age of his 'lesser sort', unfortunately.

39 *Some Memoirs of the Life of Mr. Tho: Tryon, late of London, merchant: written by himself . . .* (1705), London. I have discussed Thomas Tryon's career, including his list of publications, further in my 1979 article, op. cit., 416–17. He took a great interest in the teaching of reading to children, no doubt influenced by his own experiences. It is likely that he was the 'TT', together with 'GF' and 'GC', who produced *The Compleat School Master or Child's Instructor* (1700). I am grateful to Victor Neuburg for drawing this connection to my attention.

40 Tilers and plasterers were building craftsmen, and as such were more prosperous than agricultural labourers, but the purchasing power of their wages was very low in the early seventeenth century (Thirsk, op. cit., 865). In London in 1586 their day-wages without food had been fixed at 13*d* a day, along with masons,

coupers and glaziers, under the Statute of Artificers. This compared with 9*d* a day for 'common labourers', Tawney, R. H. and Power, E. (eds) (1924) *Tudor Economic Documents*, I, London, 369–70.

41 The brutal reality was most simply stated later by John Clare in his autobiography. He was born the son of a Northamptonshire day-labourer in 1793.

> As my parents had the good fate to have but a small family, I being the eldest of 4, two of whom dyed in their Infancy, my mother's hopeful ambition ran high of being able to make me a good scholar . . . but God help her, her hopeful and tender kindness was often cross'd with difficulty, for there was often enough to do to keep cart upon wheels, as the saying is, without incuring an extra expence of pulling me to school. . . . I believe I was not older than 10 when my father took me to seek the rewards of industry. . . . (but) As to my schooling, I think never a year pass'd me till I was 11 or 12, but 3 months or more at the worst of times was luckily spend for my improvement. (Blunden, E. (ed.) (1931) *Sketches in the life of John Clare*, London)

42 This is approximately double the earnings of eight-year-olds quoted as an example of industrious good management (see above, p. 27).

43 The autobiographers whose parents were prosperous enough to enable them to go to university, quite frequently went as early as fourteen. This conflicts with David Cressy's findings that the mean age for entry to university was sixteen (thesis cit.) and bears out the suggestion that the autobiographers were probably an exceptionally gifted group.

44 Jenkins, G. H. (1978) *Literature, Religion and Society in Wales, 1660–1730*, Cardiff, 303–4, discusses a number of shepherds who learnt to read.

45 *PM*, I (58), 1249–69. See below, p. 184, n. 91.

46 *PM*, I (10), 227.

47 My italics. He should, of course, have been able to read it by seven (above, pp. 23–7).

48 *PM*, I (13), 285.

49 'Love's Masterpiece', *PM*, II (18), 436.

50 Langdale, J. (nd) 'Some Account of the Birth, Education and Religious Exercises and Visitations of God to that faithful Servant and Minister of Jesus Christ, Josiah Langdale' (died 1723), Friends House Library, MS Box 10/10, 1–3.

51 Keeble, N. H. (ed.) (1974) *Autobiography of Richard Baxter*, London, 7.

52 Cressy (1976) art. cit., 314; (1977) art. cit., 146–8.

53 Schofield (1968) art. cit., 313. Jenkins, op. cit., 299, has some examples of book-owning labourers.

54 Cressy (1977) art. cit., 8–9.

55 Weston, W. (trans. and ed. P. Caraman) (1955) *The Autobiography of an Elizabethan*, London, 164–5.

56 Whiting, J. (1715) *Persecution Exposed in Some Memoirs*, London, 418.

57 For a fuller account, see Spufford (1974) op. cit., 209.

58 Evans, N. (1978) 'The Community of South Elmham, Suffolk, 1550–1640', University of East Anglia MPhil, 171. I am grateful to Mrs Evans for permission to quote from her thesis.

59 'The Birth, Life and Death of John Frank', *PM*, II (20), 475.

60 Spufford (1974) op. cit., 203, n. 32.

61 Marshall, J. D. (ed.) (1967) *The Autobiography of William Stout of Lancaster, 1665–1752*, Manchester.

62 Horsfall-Turner (1882) op. cit., I, 42, 48, 51, 53.

63 My italics. Evelyn, J. (ed. E. S. de Beer) (1959) *Diary*, III, Oxford, entry for 1685, 831, quoted in Clark (1919) op. cit., 115.

64 'Transcripts of the Survey of the Township of Eccleshall, 1697, with the Parish of Eccleshall, 1693–8', made from the original shorthand by N. W. Tildesley (1969) Lichfield Joint Record Office, 'List of householders and heads of families' (1693).

65 ibid., 28.

66 Dr Claire Cross has recently drawn attention to the apparent key importance of relatively humble women Lollards in the early sixteenth century. 'It may be', she writes,

> that considerably more women than the churchmen suspected acquired the ability to read in order to peruse Lollard books. Certainly a reverence for books characterize women in a majority of communities, and in several Lollard women took a major part in organizing book distribution. As mothers and

grandmothers they had unique authority over impressionable children, and far more women than have been recorded may have been responsible for helping educate succeeding generations in heresy. (Cross, C. (1978) 'Great reasoners in scripture; women Lollards 1380–1530', in Baker, D. (ed.) *Medieval Women, Studies in Church History*, Oxford, Subsidia I, 378)

III
Direct and indirect evidence for readership of the chapbooks

We can state the existence of the schoolteachers in the dioceses which have so far been surveyed, give the firm figures of differing ability to sign amongst different social groups in East Anglia, and say from the number of signatories to the Protestation Returns of 1642 that there was at the very least a reading public of 30 per cent of men in the second half of the seventeenth century. We can postulate further that, since the age at which paying work for a child began was the same at which the teaching of writing began, but a year later than that at which the teaching of reading began, reading was a much commoner skill than writing. We can even suggest that some women shared it. The market for cheap print was there.

We can start from the other end of the argument, and produce firm evidence of the fortunes made by the specialist ballad and chapbook publishers catering specifically for the cheap end of the market (see below, Chapter IV). We can add evidence on the volume of these publications. We can point out that all the advertising of the specialist publishers was aimed at the distributors, the country chapmen. We can then continue to provide evidence of the size of the distributive network. Pedlars, hawkers and petty chapmen were taxed in England in 1697–8, and there were then over 2550 who failed to avoid tax (see below, Chapter V). The distributive network appears to have been extremely well developed. What we cannot do, however, is to close the argument convincingly by showing the humble reader actually in possession of ballads and chapbooks. John Bunyan is the only specific example of the humble reader being influenced by this cheap

print who can be produced. The only figure who is more elusive in
the whole trade than the chapman, is the man who bought from him.
The very suggestive woodcut of a country yokel buying from a
chapman[1] that appears as frontispiece to one of Samuel Pepys's
collection of small merry books selling at 2*d* in the 1680s is one of the
very few pieces of direct evidence. Proof of the readership, however
suggestive such a woodcut may be, is a very real problem.

Yeomen, as we know, were 65 per cent literate in East Anglia. The
type of yeoman who could not only read fluently, and could sign his
name, but was moved to write his memoirs, or a journal, with a
record of his opinions, was usually the kind of yeoman who was
engaged in building up his estate by marriage and purchase. He was
heavily involved in local government, and gradually transforming
himself and his family into minor gentry. He did not read chapbooks,
or at least he did not bother to say that he did. Robert Furze of
Devonshire, writing in the 1590s[2] so that his descendants should
comprehend the family achievements, had been sixteen years con-
stable of his hundred, and had been proudly taxed on £10 in lands in
the 1590s, 'far excidying anye of [my] predissesors'. He charged his
heirs 'Give yourselves to the redying and hearing of the holy scriptures and such like good doctrine, be learned in the laws of the realm,
and have to read the old cronicles and such like auncient histories'.

William Honneywell, a near contemporary, also of Devon, was a
yeoman who lent his books on *The Passions of the Mind* and the
Mysteries of Mount Calvary to friends. He records a discussion on
religion with his friends, and their wives, over the dinner table; his
books were obviously read.[3]

Adam Eyre, of Yorkshire, fifty years later, seems to have followed
Furze's precepts. He read Raleigh's *History of the World*, the Bible,
the *Book of Martyrs*, Paracelsus, sermons and the works of Presby-
terian and millenary writers.[4] The highly respected Quaker yeoman,
John Whiting, in Ilchester Jail in the 1680s, regularly had parcels of
Quaker books delivered by the carrier: 'I had a parcel of friends
books, etc, come down from London, as I used to have; and the
carrier left them, as he used to do for me, at Newberry-inn.'[5]

So the keepers of journals and diaries were either too well-
educated to read the chapbooks, or, at least, to record doing so as a
serious matter; a spiritual autobiographer's interests lay in another
direction, and the only two who admitted to reading cheap print,

Baxter and Bunyan, did so as a sin. It may be that Bunyan, the rural artisan's son, gives us a real indication of the social level at which the chapbooks circulated, and that it was below that of the yeomanry. In this case, the division of which Peter Burke writes, between popular culture and the culture of the élite, had already taken place.[6]

Certainly it had taken place a hundred years later in Scotland, as a ballad specialist has already indicated (see above, pp. 12–14). The same division was present between farmers who read full-scale books, and the cottars who read chapbooks. George Robertson, writing his *Rural Recollections* of agriculture in the Lothians in 1829, described minutely the state of affairs in the area as he first remembered it, before 1765. He describes the domestic interiors of the husbandmen, or farmers, in great detail and covers their reading too:

> In their religious sentiments, as they were nearly all the descendants of the more ancient covenantors, so they were actuated by similar principles, and with veneration for their practices. Hence their books were all of that cast; such as the works of Sir David Lindsay, of Buchanan, of Knox, of Rutherford, of Bunyan and of Boston; and of Wodrow too: but as his was a more bulky and expensive work, it was in fewer hands, but was lent about from one to another. They also had a taste for ancient histories connected with their country; such as Abercrombie's *Lives*, and Blind Harry's *Wallace*; and stories about Bruce, and Bannockburn; and of Chevy-Chase, and the Douglas; and of Roslin-Muir, and Pentland Hills ... and Duc William, and the Pretender. But no book was so familiar to them as the Scriptures; they could almost tell the place of any particular passage, where situated in their own family Bible, without referring to either book, chapter, or verse; and where any similar one was situated.

The much poorer cottars were also of a convenanting descent, and

> had books of a similar tendency with those of their masters, but on a lesser scale, being usually pamphlets, or religious tracts ... purchased from travelling chapmen at a cheap rate, which they made their grown-up children read to them alternatively on Sabbath afternoons, with the singing of their questions, from the *Mother's Catechism* or other question books. With their Bibles too they were well acquainted.

The social inference is clear. In eighteenth-century Scotland, the two cultures had drawn apart. It is perfectly feasible that there may already have been that sort of stratification in readership in seventeenth-century England.

It cannot be proved by the most obvious means, however, for chapbooks were not listed in probate inventories, which would give a proper picture of their social distribution. The reason for this omission is simple: they were not worth listing. The chapbooks in Charles Tias's shop were priced at 2½d to 6d in 1664; by the 1680s most of them sold at 2d and 3d. From the 1640s to 1690s the average agricultural and building wage rates were 12d a day.[7] These chapbooks really were priced within the reach of the agricultural labourer if he could read, and if he desired to. I have not yet personally found a single chapbook listed in a probate inventory apart from those waiting to be sold. I am not alone in this. The contents of just under 1500 inventories covering both urban and rural Norfolk and Suffolk in the sixteenth and seventeenth centuries were discussed and analysed in March 1978 at a one day conference at the University of East Anglia on book ownership and readership. Amongst these 1500 inventories were only five references to the kind of 'little books' priced at under 6d that I have been discussing here. All these were for sale (see below, p. 125). The scarcity of these references implies, not that the books were not there, but that they were not worth listing. My impression is that items like chapbooks worth 2d new would not be down in an inventory anyway, that items worth under 1s had a very poor chance of being listed.[8] Recorders and flageolets were never listed in inventories either, yet it is perfectly clear that the music of the pipe and drum was a commonplace, and one to which the Puritans strenuously objected, in most late sixteenth-century villages. David Vaisey has well said that no-one has ever suggested that the sheepdog did not exist in seventeenth-century England, simply because none have yet been found recorded in an inventory.[9]

Although part of the problem is undoubtedly caused by the reluctance of appraisers to bother to enter items worth twopence or less in an inventory, the evidence may also have gone unremarked because the chapbooks, with the rest of the cheap print, had a secondary function of supplying the very real social need for lavatory paper. We know this was so amongst the gentry, if Sir William Cornwallis is in any way typical. He kept 'pamphlets and lying-stories and two-

penny poets' in his privy, to be read there, and then used.[10] Although
there is no evidence from further down the social scale, the need must
have been just as great.[11] If we admit as a witness the scurrilous song
collected by Anthony Wood which begins 'Bum-Fodder or Wast-
Paper proper to wipe the Nation's Rump with, or your own',[12] we
know that paper was pressed into general service in this way. This
remained the doom of cheap print as late as the 1920s. There is a
description of a print-starved daughter of a poor miner in the Forest
of Dean whose only reading matter, very frustratingly, was the torn-
up pages of newspapers and comics in the privy, all of which had the
first and last words of the lines missing.[13] As early as the 1590s,
Thomas Nashe in a satirical dedicatory epistle was pointing out some
ultimate uses for his work that do not immediately leap to the mind
of the modern reader, accustomed to a superfluity of wrapping-
paper. The hero

> hath bequeathed for wast paper here among you certaine pages of
> his misfortunes. . . . If there bee some better than other, he craves
> you would honor them in theyr death so much as to drie and kindle
> Tobacco with them: for a need he permits you to wrap velvet
> pantofles in them also. . . . But as you have good fellowship . . .
> rather turn them to stop mustard-pottes, than the Grocers should
> have one patch of them to wrap mace in.[14]

The thought of twists of printed paper wrapped conically round
spices and so circulating is a particularly intriguing one. Did print, in
this way, become familiar by sight to some 'readers' who would
never have bought a ballad or a chapbook?

Certainly paper was at a premium in the countryside, and did not
last long there. Richard Brathwait, who wrote a blast against 'coranto
writers and their lies' in the 1630s,[15] concurred with Nashe on one of
the uses for paper. He said it was as well that most of these lasted little
more than a week after reaching the country, for they were also
useful for lighting pipes. Yet another use for paper, this time undoubtedly the 'histories', was alluded to in 1749 by Henry Fielding.[16]
He wrote of 'those idle romances which are filled with monsters . . .
and which have therefore been recommended by an eminent critic to
the sole use of the pastry-cook'. The eminent critic was Dean Swift,
who wrote of the way pastry-cooks used unwanted books for lining
their pie-dishes. It does not sound, between the list of uses compiled

by Nash in the late sixteenth century, and those given by Brathwait, Swift and Fielding in the seventeenth and eighteenth centuries, as if cheap paper had much chance of survival. If this is indeed what happened to the chapbooks, it is no wonder it is so difficult to prove their readership.

INDIRECT EVIDENCE FOR READERSHIP

Because there is so little direct evidence of the readership of the chapbooks, we are forced back on the indirect evidence of the contents of the chapbooks themselves. Two of the main groups of the chapbooks had originally had very different audiences. They were the burlesques and bawdy stories written in the sixteenth and seventeenth centuries with 'heroes' drawn specifically from both the urban and the rural poor. These were invariably printed as octavos or duodecimos priced at 2*d* in the 1680s. The second group was the cut-down chivalric romances of the middle ages, which were more commonly printed as quartos, and as a rule cost at least 1*d* more. These two groups retained, in the 1680s, considerable differences in complexity of style and price range. Yet the intended audience had by then probably fused. Peter Burke writes: 'the English gentry abandoned the romance of chivalry to the lower classes. From the mid-seventeenth century on, *Guy of Warwick* and *Bevis of Hampton* were reprinted only in chapbook form.'[17] This is true. Pepys, the London tailor's son, educated at a Huntingdonshire grammar school with brothers at St Paul's, tellingly called the chivalric chapbooks he collected the *Vulgaria*. One of the quartos, *The Shifts of Reynardine, Son of Reynard the Fox*,[18] a lineal descendant of Caxton's *Reynard*, a version of which was still reprinting,[19] had the most insulting epistle to the unfortunate reader that could well be devised.

> I here offer the present Work . . . not garnished with Eloquence, but rurally habited, to the view of all: well knowing that a Clown is as well pleased with a Cock's Feather in his Cap, as a Young Gentleman with a costly Plume . . . because such books as these are more frequently read by persons of mean Understanding, than by Men of sound Judgement; I have good Reason to expect either less Censure, or more Praise than I deserve.

The publishers themselves seem to have made little distinction, except in selling price, by now, between the quartos and the 'small' books. One of the little compliment books began, as a *raison d'être*, 'The histories of Guy and Bevis are grown very old, therefore new conceits may be more pleasing'.[20]

The social diffusion of the romances of chivalry, printed as quartos, had begun much earlier. It had probably already happened long before Cox, the mason of Coventry, collected thirteen chivalric romances in the 1570s.[21] The Jacobean dramatists regularly satirized the ignorant apprentices and the merchants' wives to whom the neo-chivalric tales appealed (see below, pp. 233–4). We know from the young John Bunyan's reading of *Guy* and *Bevis* that the chivalric tales had a readership below the yeoman level in the countryside (see above, pp. 7–8, 46–7). Yet there is nothing in these chivalric and neo-chivalric chapbooks themselves to indicate their audience.

The small books selling at 2d often tell their own tales about their readers, however. These were aimed to appeal to a very wide cross-secion of the urban and rural lower sections of society, from merchants to apprentices in towns, and from country-farmers to day-labourers in the countryside. Some of them were specifically aimed at one of these groups in the community; others, amongst which the courtship and the letter-writing manuals predominated, apparently tried to appeal to a complete cross-section of society, from gentlemen to country bumpkins.

The sympathies of townsmen must have been particularly engaged by those chapbooks that took as their principal objects of mockery the clodhopping countryman come to town. These began relatively early; *The Sackfull of News*, first registered with the Stationers' Company in 1557–8, contained a group of jokes of which the countryman was the butt.[22] This was in the collection of Cox of Coventry. It was reprinted by Hazlitt in *Old English Jest Books*, but he supressed two of the stories as too gross for publication.[23] One man went to St Paul's, and since he had never heard an organ, or singing, thought he had gone to heaven. Another man from Essex, who had nails in his shoes, was teased by the apprentices of Cheapside and persuaded to take them off, lest he should break the stones of the streets. Yet a third countryman visiting London 'where he had never been before' saw the sailing ships from London Bridge, and returned home to try to fix sails to his plough. *The Mad-Men of Gotham* were, of course, the archetypal countrymen.[24] The pull of growing London extended even to the 'gentry' however, Sir Humphrey Frollicksome had never seen London and had a great desire to go there.²⁵

The mockery of citizens extended to the countryman in love. One of the compliment books contained a splendid pastiche of a farmer's letter to a city gentlewoman couched in phraseology far from felicitous.

> Good Mistress, since I was at your fathers house, and saw you sit mimping so prettily at Dinner, I have had a great disturbance in my brest, or belly, I know not well which; but, to be plain, I think I am beastly deap in love with you; for if I should be hanged, I cannot put you out of my mind: therefore, pretty Pigsnies, I would have you to consider on't against I come to Town with my next Quarters Rent: For if I am not mistaken, I heard my Londlord say, he would willingly bestow you upon a good, honest, plain, downright, fair and square-dealing man; And in faith, if thou'lt believe me, such a one am I: Therefore, not doubting to fit thy fathers expectation to a Cows Thumb, I say, no more at present. . . . And so I shall rest
>
> Yours to command,
>   *honest Nedd Trotter*

Her reply mocks his suit, and his phraseology too.

> Sir, When I received your Letter, at the hands of your man, I could not, for a while, imagine to what end you should send a Letter to me, who never had the least business with you in my life; but having perused the Contents, I verily supposed you to be a little crazed, or your braines disturbed by the effects of Midsummer Moon, or that you had been toping too many Canns, or black Potts, at Mother Louses; for truly I could not, neither can I yet imagine that any man in his senses, should render himself so nonsensically ridiculous, first, in writing to me about love, with whom he had never any converse, and, secondly, in such a strain as might have made the Philosopher laugh as loud to read it, as he did when he beheld the Ass mumbling Thistles. Certainly the Parish-Clerk, or Town-schoolmaster was not at home, or else you was loath to bestow two-pence on a scribe; yet not to detain you longer in suspence, know your suit, if you move it any further will prove

vain; therefore I would desire you to desist, before you render yourself more ridiculous: And so, as far as civil respect and good manners obliges me, I remain your friend.

MC.[26]

Some heroines were specifically designed for Londoners. The horrendous figure of Mother Bunch, the ale wife, supposedly the teller of the jokes in *Pasquil's Jests*[27] is one of the few to be drawn with any literary skill. She was

the onely dainty, well favored, well proportioned, sweet complexioned, and most delightfull Hostess of England; she was squared into inches, being in height twenty thousand, and a half, wanting a fingers bredth . . . in bredth eleven thousand, and two inches and a nayles bredth just; she spent most of her time in telling of tales, and when she laughed, she was heard from Algate, to the Monuments at Westminster, and all Southwark stook in amazement, the Lyons in the Tower, and the Bulls and Beares of Parish-Garden roar'd (with terror of her laughter) lowder then the great roaring Megge, she was once wrung with wind in her belly, and with one blast of her taile, she blew down Charing-Cross, with Pauls aspiring steeple. She danced a Galliard on tower hill, and all the great Ordnance leapt for joy, and London shook as it had been an Earthquake. . . . From this noble Mother Bunch proceeded all our great greasie Tapsters, and fat swelling Ale wives, whose faces are blown as bigge as the froth of their bottle Ale, and their complexion imitating the outside of a Cooks greasie dripping-pan, and you could hardly go round about her in a Summer after-noon. Mother Bunch lived one hundred, seventy and five yeares, two dayes and a quarter, and half a minute, and died in the prime of her charity, for had she lived but two months longer, she had knit Pauls a night-cap, and bought London bridge a payre of Pantoffles to keep his feet out of the cold swelling water.[28]

The first part of one of the, surprisingly few, chapbooks in Pepys's collection centred on the criminal underworld[29] describes in doggerel a purely farcical fight between Londoners incarcerated in Wood-Street Counter. The mock hero, a goldsmith, responds to the insults of a soldier who calls the City of London a cuckoo's nest. The fight begins with his proclamation

> For though I am a Man of Trade,
> And free of London City made,
> Yet can I use Gun, Bill, and Blade
>
> >   In Battle:
>
> He threw the Jugg, and therewithall
> Did give the Captain such a mall,
> As made him thump against the Wall
>
> >   his Crupper:
>
> With that the Captain took a Dish,
> That stood brim full of butter'd Fish,
> As good as any Heart could wish
>
> >   To Supper;
>
> And as he threw his Foot did slide,
> Which turn'd his Arm and Dish aside,
> And all be-butter-fishified.

The second part of this chapbook, the *Counter Rat* describes the prisoners brought in one night by the Watch. The Epistle to the Reader explains:

> No, these are no Rats with four Legs, but only two; and though they have Nests in a thousand places of London, yet for the most part they run but into two Rat-Traps, that is to say, the Counters of Wood-street and the Poultrey, and for that cause are called Counter-Rats.

Other chapbooks were slanted for an audience, not of Londoners in general, but of specific groups of craftsmen. From 1597 onwards, the ex-weaver Deloney's novels were written to appeal to urban and rural clothiers, weavers and shoemakers.[30] They included, however, passages designed to attract the sympathies of the poor, including the sons of cobblers, blacksmiths, tailors, ploughmen, carters and gardeners, and even whores, who are all encouraged to feel that they, too, could make good in the clothing trade.

These novels and their burlesque descendants included as heroes men practising crafts in other towns as well as London, like the drunken *Poor Robin, the Merry Saddler of Walden*[31] who was incapable of distinguishing his wife's face from her arse.

Apprentices, another group with their own culture, also had their own chapbooks. *Aurelius, the Valiant London Prentice*,[32] was cast in the chivalric mode of the middle ages, and indeed was fired by 'reading the famous adventures of knights-errant how successful they were in overcoming Gyants and Monsters and rescuing beauteous Ladies from death and misery'. His own adventures, after the mishap of falling in love with the daughter of his master, who was a 'Turkey-merchant on London Bridge', closely imitated those of *Guy* and *Bevis*. He went to Constantinople as his master's factor, and wearing a suit of borrowed armour, overcame and killed a Turkish prince in a great tournament. He was sentenced to be thrown to the lions for this outrage, but killed them with his bare hands instead. He was then rewarded with the hand of a Turkish princess, who had 'great Riches'; and, after her baptism, they returned 'to England with great joy, where they lived many years after, loving and happy'. Other chapbooks catered for more specifically sexual adolescent fantasies. In *John and His Mistress*,[33] the handsome apprentice who is the hero simply seduces his master's wife; *Tom Stitch the Tailor*[34] caters on a much grander scale for such fantasies. Tom is himself the son of a London woman with 'the French disease'. He cuckolds his own master and blackmails his mistress, who visits London brothels, as a mere beginning in the minor key to his adventures. As a grand finale, he gets no less than sixteen servant girls to all of whom he had promised marriage, with child in fifteen weeks, and leaves them all, along with a rich widow, waiting at the same place to go through the ceremony with him. Here, in the career of 'Wanton Tom', is one side of apprentice culture. Other, very different sides, of course existed. The intense involvement of apprentices in godly and spiritual meetings in post-Restoration London is evident from the writings of some of the spiritual autobiographers.[35]

By no means all the mockery at the chapbooks was directed from town to country. There is much evidence in them of regional feeling. Presumably the mockery here was intended to apply, not merely between town and country, but between the regions themselves. *The Sackfull of News* again contains laughter at the expense of the Essex man brought up in Norfolk, who unhappily took the bellowing of a cow for his mother's voice, as well as the boy from the North, who had never seen a salad made with oil and vinegar. The same publication ridiculed Dutchmen, Italians and Frenchmen. Local speech was satirized, as in the letter from a Somerset man printed in one of the compliment books.

> Zir,
>
> I received a piece of Paper from you, which I think volks cal a Letter; but when I pull it open, I am zure I could not read won word in it: I gave it to a neighbour, that is to zay, one of our Town, that is to zay, one that lives in three doors of our door; and he being a little better Scholard than my zelf, he made a shift to pick out the words, but the devil a bit of zense can I vind in it: you talk of bliging and vavers; in my Conscience you are not like me one joy: you also talk of garitude and merits, I'll zwear I cannot make nay thing of your Lingua: my Neighbour tells me it's Latin; I wonder you would write Latin to me, you know I cannot stand under it, I am your old Friend.[36]
>
> *Dick Downright*

The most constant butt amongst the regional figures of fun was, however, the Welshman (see below, pp. 182–4). The 'Welsh' jokes of the sixteenth and seventeenth centuries, like the 'Irish' jokes of the nineteenth and twentieth centuries, seem to have been a reaction to waves of poverty-stricken immigrants. The cumulative evidence of the jokes in the chapbooks against figures of fun speaking one form or another of local dialect seems to bear witness that they were catering for an audience full of xenophobic feeling, in whose eyes all strangers were suspect, or at least objects of mockery, at a time when such strangers could easily be picked out because of the strength of their local accents. They were also, in the chapbooks, as in reality, likely to be travelling towards London as long-distance immigrants.[37]

Just as some chapbooks were clearly composed for town, or craft audiences, so others were equally clearly composed with the country reader in mind. Even in the jest-books, countrymen did not always come off worst, as the tale of the country tanner and the butcher's dog shows.

> A Country Tanner that was running hastily through Eastcheap, and having a long pike-staff on his shoulder, one of the Butchers Dogs caught him by the brach. The fellow got loose, and ran his pike into the Dogs throat, and killed him. The Butcher seeing that his Dog was kill'd tooke hold of the Tanner, and carried him

before the Deputy, who asked him, What reason he had to kill the Dog: For mine owne defence (quoth the Tanner.) Why, quoth the Deputy, hadst thou no other defence but present death? Sir quoth the Tanner, London fashions are not like the Countries, for here the stones are fast in the streets, and the Dogs are loose, but in the Countrey, the dogs are fast tied, and the stones are lose to throw at them: and what should a man do in this extremity, but use his staffe for his own defence? Marry (quoth the Deputy) if a man will needs use his staffe, he might use his blunt end, and not the sharp pike. True Master Deputy, quoth the Tanner, but you must consider, if the Dog had used his blunt end, and run his taile at me then had there been good reason for me to do the like.[38]

The Horation tale of *The Country Mouse and the City Mouse*[39] carried the moral, hard-learnt by the country-mouse, that it is best to be poor, but contented. It was also a vehicle for a marvellous description of the rich food and furnishing of a London merchant's house.

> The Tables in this dining-room were spread,
> With Turkey carpets all embroidered,
> The Stools, the Cushions, and every Chair,
> Cloath of Silver and rich Tissue were.

As Buchan wrote of the ballads, they are based on the implicit assumption that the folk like singing about the gold and silver of their betters, rather than their own pigsties.[40] *The Country Mouse and the City Mouse* is also interesting in its stress on city diet, particularly the amount of sugar contained in it. The impression is given that sugar in a country diet may be in very short supply, and a matter of much craving. The country mouse is amazed at the city mouse's access to beef, woodcock, turkey and pheasants, but overwhelmed by the sweet conserves and sugar plums, marchpane and marmalade which is quite unknown in his own diet of bacon, 'chippings', acorns and crab-apples. All the same he

> Told the City mouse he would repair,
> Unto the countery where without all care,
> He could live freely, telling him he thought
> Pleasure far too dear, that with such fear is bought,
> Although my Country fare is not so dainty,
> Contentment is better worth unto me then plenty.

Cawwood the Rook has the same moral as *The Country Mouse*. It is a political satire in which the 'hero' is an avian imitation of *Reynard the Fox* and his progeny. He unwisely abets the wicked regent of the kingdom of birds in the royal Eagle's absence. His ultimate doom, since his principal wants to be rid of his accomplished expert in crafty

Cupid's Sports and Paſtimes.

ſhewing, how Cupid *did here on earth,*
Play many Tricks, full of wit and mirth.

His purpoſe being all the while,
To make his Mother *Venus* ſmile;
And put her out of Melancholly,
VVith hiſ ſtories of wit and folly.

By *Henry Sparrow.*

Printed for *W, Thackeray,* at the ſign of the *Angel* in Duck-Lane. 1684.

dealing, was pronounced thus: 'I do here banish thee out of the Country, and send thee to live for ever in the City . . . as the Acquaintance of the City Rooks.'[41]

Both *Cawwood* and *The Country Mouse and the City Mouse* were, of course, double-edged, and could have appealed to town as well as country. This was true of a whole range of heroes drawn from country models alone. *Simon and Cisley*, two Lancashire lovers,[42] are son and daughter of farmers, who conduct their wooing in the tavern at market after selling off their fathers' sacks of oats and hemp. Some of the country characters in the compliment books (see below, pp. 163–6) are shrewdly and accurately observed, like the dutiful daughter in the *Country Garland* of 1687[43] who had 'full forty' pounds for her portion, and married a grazier. *Neptune's Garland*[44] contained a real shepherd, no pastoral Corydon, who almost lost his girl because his sheep were lean and few, and her dower larger than his expectations warranted.

Tom Thumb, the diminutive neo-chivalric Arthurian knight, was a son of a ploughman and milkmaid. The story is supposed to reflect the oral tale-telling of women and children in the countryside, and in view both of the way Richard Johnson, its 'author', picked up known stories from the oral tradition to embellish and publish (see below, pp. 227–31) and also of John Clare's later evidence, it very likely does so. The author claims that Tom Thumb's

> Fame lives here in England still
> Among the country sort
> Of whom their Wives and Children small
> Tell tales of pleasant sport.[45]

The story was written in 1621. *Thomas Hickathrift*[46] was the son of a day-labourer in the Fens, who worked as carter to a brewer. *Tom Ladle*[47] was the illegitimate son of a sewing maid, who married a ploughman.

The world of the in-servant was not forgotten in this 'literature'. It, like almost everything else in the chapbooks, is the object of satire. Yet the aspirations of the servants who formed the bottom of the social pyramid are reflected and catered for. Even if the reflection is sometimes distorted by laughter, it seems likely that these 'small merry books' were intended to be read by the servants themselves. *Long Meg*,[48] the Lancashire lass who first made her appearance in

1582, made her career as a servant in a London inn. Dialogues between lovers intending to marry referred to this social level. *Andrew and his Sweetheart Joan*[49] conduct their wooing after ten o'clock at night, since Joan's master is deaf, and she can let Andrew in without fear of interruption. Joan has 40s, half of which she will give to Andrew for a new coat and shoes and half of which will pay for the merrymaking at the wedding. Her only other goods are

> My Grandmother's Gridiron to broyl Sprats, and likewise . . . her Earthen-Pipkin that boyle a good Sheeps-head six days . . . then I have three wooden spoons, two Oaken trenchers and a dainty vessele to wash our hands in, or use by our bedside at night.

She does however hope for a bequest of £10 when her old master dies. Andrew's wooing is as heavily burlesqued as Joan's pitiful dower of household goods. 'I love thee more than a Bear does Honey, and I hope you'l affect me as much as a Sow does a bunch of Carrots.'

Honest John and Loving Kate[50] are a much more realistic pair of lovers, though even the evidence for the way a couple in this social situation plan to marry and set up together has to be handled with caution.[51] John was launched in the world with a lump sum of £10 from his father, and is hired by the year to a maltster; Kate was left £10 by her father at his death, and has saved £5 since she went into service. Their modest ambition is to set up an alehouse, and they plan their wedding and their future lives together sitting drinking in a tavern on a holyday, while the rain falls outside. It is difficult to imagine that an audience drawn from a much more prosperous level of society in the countryside could have felt its sympathies involved, and identified with the careful impecunious planning of this pair of servants, who yet dream, as the ultimate peak of grandeur, of eventually hiring a servant themselves, at £2 a year.

Samuel Pepys did not like practical manuals on gardening, husbandry or horsemanship (see below, p. 133). Apart from the cookery books he collected, the sole exception to this rule was the *Countryman's Counsellor, or Everyman his own Lawyer.*[52] This very useful little book was indeed aimed specifically at the countryman, not the country gentleman, as a brief perusal of its contents shows.[53] It contains such matters as the form of a bond for £20, and detailed directions for the payment of interest on such a bond; a receipt for a quarter's rent, for £5; a form of indenture for an apprentice, who is the son of a clothier, to learn the butcher's trade; a bill of sale for household goods worth £8, which may be redeemed if the vendor can afford it; the form of a will, and the form of a letter of attorney from a seaman, to recover a £20 debt. It also, thoughtfully, includes directions about how to obtain justice if one is not worth £5. There was nothing here for the gentry, but a great deal for the small craftsmen, husbandmen and less substantial yeomen.

The rest of Pepys's practical guides were to cookery and, despite his own interest, these were mainly aimed at women readers, as the frequent recipes for washes 'to beautify the face' show. A pair of them not only carried the word 'Gentlewoman'[54] in the title, but also seemed from the ingredients to have been aimed at gentle or mercantile households. It seems likely that the servants of such households formed the intended market. Both of them used quantities of cream, egg yolks and egg whites, and one of them covered the cooking of venison and veal, as well as mutton and pork; woodcock, pheasant, heron and bustard, as well as chicken and rabbit; and oysters and salmon, as well as pike and eels. Quantities of spices, cloves, mace, nutmeg, ginger and cinnamon, as well as anchovies, white wine, wine vinegar and claret were also used, along with lemon and orange juice. The other pair, *The Compleat Cookmaid* and *The Compleat Cook, or Accomplished Servant-Maid's Necessary Companion*[55] were somewhat less lavish, and the first was proclaimed to be 'principally for the Country Cookmaid'. The last of the group was a book of medicinal and herbal remedies. The title, *The Queen's Royal Closet Newly Opened*,[56] appealed to snobbery in the title, but many of the remedies for common diseases, aches, burns, pains in the back, and even consumption and rickets, were quite easy to obtain – rosemary, boar's grease, nightshade, radishes and bettony – although there were some *exotica* there, too, most notably a human skull.

Another type of manual, also to Pepys's own taste, and again designed specifically for the countryside, and for female readers at that, was *Mother Bunch's Closet*.[57] This taught simple spells to discover one's future husband, to be practised on St Agnes Eve and Midsummer Eve. A mixture of bawdy and practical common sense for the avoidance of trouble was never far absent. Girls were to fast on St Agnes Day, let no-one kiss them, put on a shift and sleep on their right sides, with their right hands under their heads, and then they would dream of their true husbands. But if the dream should too closely simulate reality, 'if he offered to salute thee, do not deny him, but show as much favour to him as thou can: but if he offer to be uncivil with thee, make sure to hold thy Leggs together'.

This raises the whole question of feminine readership.[58] It is patently wrong for us to suppose, cut off as we are by the great Victorian watershed of propriety, which in any case applied to middle- and upper-class women only, that the extreme bawdiness of the 'merry books' necessarily implied a mainly male readership. Thomas Hardy, son of a Dorset bricklayer, married to a girl who had been brought up at parish expense, had several agricultural labourers for uncles. His early close relationships were with girl cousins who were servants. He was cut to the quick by a reviewer's criticism of his first novel's 'remarkably coarse expressions' in 1871. A recent biographer has written of Hardy's conscious attempt from the mid-1870s to conceal his origins and relations from his middle-class wife and from society at large. His next book *Under the Greenwood Tree* contained 'not an unsuitable word in the whole of the writing', even though a ballad learnt from Hardy's own uncles about 'three sons of whores' was bellowed by an unacceptable suitor. Not until 1896 did Hardy dare to defend himself against the first criticism made of him in a new preface to *Under the Greenwood Tree*, in which he wrote of that 'ancient and broad humour which our own grandfathers, and possibly grandmothers, took delight in, and is in these days unquotable'.[59]

The chapbooks specialized in just that broad humour which, Hardy knew perfectly well, both sexes in his own rural labouring environment had delighted in when he was young. It probably survived, through Hardy's time, to be found amongst women's field gangs in the First World War, and, in a somewhat changed style, on factory floors today. Yet it is still practically unquotable, even by a woman writing now. There is no straight historical evidence for the degree of bawdy tolerated and enjoyed by seventeenth-century women in a similar environment to Hardy's. There is evidence that even the most cultivated of early seventeenth-century ladies enjoyed dirty jokes.[60] It seems unlikely that their counterparts lower in the social scale were more prudish. Indeed, from the nature of the ripostes made by women often quoted in ecclesiastical court cases, it seems not unlikely but impossible. However, there may well have been distinctions between the type of bawdy stories intended to be enjoyed by males and those intended to be enjoyed by females. Shakespeare suggests as much in his description of the ware carried by Autolycus, that prince of literary pedlars.

> He hath songs for man or woman, of all sizes; no milliner can so fit his customers with gloves: he has the prettiest love-songs for maids; so without bawdry, which is strange; with such delicate burthens of dildos and fadings, 'jump her and thump her'; and where some stretch-mouthed rascal would, as it were, mean mischief and break a foul gap into the matter, he makes the maid to answer, 'Whoop, do me no harm, good man'.[61]

Certainly, the whole tenor of the merry books conveys that seventeenth-century women enjoyed their own sexuality and were expected to enjoy it.[62] This female enjoyment of the senses had certainly been thought to be a basic attribute of the sex in the sixteenth century: that acute and practical agriculturalist, Sir Anthony Fitz-Herbert, listed in his *Boke of Husbandry* amongst the ten main properties of a woman, following the nine properties of an ass, and preceding the section on diseases of horses, that she would be found 'to be well sturryinge under a man'.[63] Women were depicted in the chapbooks, after the many first shynesses of virginity, as taking positive pleasure in lovemaking. 'Mother Bunch's' innuendoes to her audiences were plain. For

> those that languish in single sheets till fifteen . . . I will tell . . . how you shall know and see the persons that shall ease you of the simple thing, so much talked of, called a *Maidenhead*, by him that must be your Husband.

She herself recounts her own dreams on St Agnes Eve to an interested girl. Her third husband

> was of the Gentle-Craft and he came to me with his Awl in his hand, and would need prick me, aye, and did prick me, but it did not hurt me, for when I awakened out of my dream I was never the worse, but I thought the time very long until he came again, and so will all Maidens do, who have a desire to be marryed.

A girl in one of the *Country Garlands*[64] speaks to her mother with similar longings:

> You little do think while I sleep in my bed
> How many strange fancies do run in my head;
> I dream that my love upon my breast he leans,
> Dear Mother, you know I am now in my teens
> Therefore, I am just in my prime.

These longings of both Mother Bunch's and the adolescent girl's may perhaps be dismissed as the wish-fulfilment of the male authors of the chapbooks, but it is interesting that Sarah Jinner, the first woman astrologer, who issued an almanac from 1658 onwards, prescribed an anti-aphrodisiac for women. She may have been thinking of limiting family-size but, in that case, an abatement of feminine desire seems to her to have been a reasonable method, that would have some effect[65] (see below, pp. 158–60, for other examples of feminine satisfaction).

All through the chapbooks, particularly in the compliment books, with the exclusion of the group railing at insatiable women, the convention is that all virgins, that is, maids being courted, were shy and relatively easily frightened, although they eagerly looked forward to a consummation normally, if they were wise, found within marriage. Married women left alone, and widows, on the other hand, suffered from deprivation of the sexual pleasures that they thoroughly enjoyed. This convention seems completely at odds with another, equally strongly expressed in the chapbooks. In most of the burlesques, the type of sexuality that so much predominates is conveyed in terms of immediate, unskilled and very brief male satisfaction, which would be highly unlikely to bring about the pleasure expressed by the first convention. It would be unwise to suggest that either of these conventions is anything more than a sub-literary cliché, rather than any real reflection of social mores. Since the two conventions are so internally contradictory psychologically, it does seem possible that although both conventions reflect the interest of men and women in stories with a sexual emphasis, an attempt was made to cater for the different sexes in the degree and the type of bawdy employed.[66] In this case, the art of compliment chapbooks would be written more with women in mind, and the marital stories and the burlesques for men.

Some chapbooks were, then, written with a town readership in mind, others with a rural readership. Some were known to appeal more to women, others even more certainly were written to appeal to men. Some also were aimed at specific groups within the community, from weavers to in-servants.

Yet another section of the chapbooks made a deliberate appeal to the men who could perhaps be called the purveyors and intermediaries of popular culture. The importance of the alehouse as a meeting place[67] and a vital centre for the exchange of information and gossip is referred to in the dedicatory epistle to another of the crime chapbooks.[68]

> News and greene bushes at Taverns new set up, every man hath his penny to spend at a pinte in the one, and every man his eare open to receive the sound of the other. It is the language at first meetings used in all Countries; What news? In Court, 'tis the mornings salutation, and noones Table-talke; by night it is stale. In Citty 'tis more common than What doe you lack? And in the Countrey, whistling at Plough is not of greater antiquity. Walke the middle of Pauls, and Gentlemens teeth walke not faster at Ordinaires, then there is a whole day together, about enquiry after News.

This enquiry after news in taverns is parodied in one of the chapbook jokes.[69] A gentleman in an alehouse relates excitedly that 'forty thousand men rose yesterday in London'. He is of course met with a

The alehouse

clamour 'Why?' 'Why,' he replies, 'only to go to Bed when night come again.'

The alehouse keeper is a key figure in the process of disseminating news and stories and therefore in the world of cheap print. Mother Bunch is the most magnificent teller of tall stories amongst the alehouse keepers. All the stories in *Pasquil's Jest Book* are supposed to be hers. The whole group was famed for its tales, though, and it was the remarkable gift of Cox, the mason of Coventry, to be able 'to talk as much without book as ony Inholder betwixt Brainford and Bagshot'.[70] Inn-keepers were not infrequently named in the wills of the chapmen who both carried and sold the chapbooks,[71] some of whom were likely to have regularly stayed at the same inn, and presumably, as itinerants, were in a better position to strike up a relationship with the host than with most other people. Since inns formed the distributive centres from which chapmen worked, it is perhaps no accident that the publishers of ballad and chapbooks sometimes owned them, as John Wright owned the Prince of Orange's Head at Bermondsey on the river.

There is little evidence yet on the extent to which inns and alehouses formed the foci at which new stories and jokes, fresh in from the pedlar making an overnight stop, were read aloud. Inns formed the meeting places of the godly.[72] Inns and alehouses were also the accustomed meeting place of courting-couples, according to the chapbooks. *Honest John and Loving Kate* spent their day off together in an alehouse planning their future. A less innocent pair of lovers, who could not get their parents' approval to their marriage, met to sleep together in a Canterbury inn. The sack posset she got to greet him was smelt by the travelling bear in the stables below, who came up and drank it and then shambled into bed. The amorous youth, when he eventually arrived, found himself 'clasping the bear to his bosom'.[73]

It is only sensible to suppose that alehouses also acted as centres where ballads and chapbooks and corantos were handed round, or read aloud. As yet I have only one exact piece of evidence of this happening, however, and that is of a man in an alehouse in the village of Orwell in 1553, making rude gestures about the reintroduction of the Mass, and promising to let someone see a ballad called 'Maistres Masse'.[74]

The subsidiary figures of the distributional world of inns and the carrying trade figure in the chapbooks too. *Long Meg* who works at an inn protects 'Packmen and Carriers' (see below, pp. 245–6). The pedlar himself is a figure of one of the songs in *The Country Garland*.⁷⁵ The satirical piece *The Death and Burial of Mistress Money*,⁷⁶ which purports to show the dependence of the whole society on the personified lady, and so ends with a ballad mourning her departure, has verses specifically devoted to the mourning of different social groups. Nearly a third of these verses are to do with people concerned with inns and fairs, which seems a very high proportion from the whole of society. There are verses on tapsters, fiddlers, chapmen and ostlers, as well of course as the statement,

> The Countrey Inns will mourn,
> For they shall have little trading
> Since money is dead and buried,
> Their custom will be fading.

Inn-keepers were not the only people who could be supposed to increase the drawing-power of their houses by new songs to old known tunes for the clientele to roar aloud, and by a replenished fund of tall new stories and bad jokes that the ballads and the chapbooks between them could provide. A particularly interesting dedicatory epistle addressed to 'Bakers, Smiths, and Millers' stands at the beginning of the *Canterbury Tales*.⁷⁷ The *Tales*, we are told, are

> Composed for the Entertainment of All Ingenious Young Men and Maids at their merry Meetings, upon Christmas, Easter, Witsuntide, or any other time; especially upon long Winter Evenings, to keep good Wits imply'd. Intermixt with pleasant Stories, witty Jests and delightful Songs very proper for either City, Town or Country.

The dedicatory epistle tells the craftsmen to whom it is addressed, all of whom have clients who may be obliged to wait while the job is done:

> You are here presented with a choice Banquet of delightful Tales, pleasant Stories, witty Jests and merry Songs to divert the young Men and Maids when they come to the Bake house, Forge, or Mill, and by these you may increase your Trade, and call Customers to you.

Print is here again shown to lead not to the introversion of the literate, and their remoteness from the non-literate, but, on the contrary, to feed into the oral tradition. The importance of tale-telling as a pastime, particularly during the winter, is emphasized, just as it was by John Clare at a later date (see above, pp. 4–5). It is also shown to be one of the elements of leisure at the three main feasts of the year. But perhaps most interesting of all is the implication that the tradesmen and craftsmen may build up trade by increasing the importance of forge, mill or bake-house, as a secondary social centre to the alehouse, where a good story may be enjoyed in the course of the leisurely business of the working day. Reading did not necessarily lead to isolation, either for the Puritan, who regularly used it at his, or her, conferences; or for the conformist, who obstreperously read his Prayer Book while his Puritan incumbent prayed *extempore* (see above, p. 34); or even for the 'unreformed' audience of the merry books.

The courtship and the letter-writing manuals cast their net wide socially. Many of them apparently aimed at an audience which was mixed both socially and sexually.[78] On the other hand, the intention of most of the chapbooks in both of these groups is so satirical that their evidence must be handled with great care. The only one of the 'art of love' books that appears to be simply an etiquette book, without satirical intent at all, is the *Court of Curiosities*,[79] which gives straightforward advice to those who are genuinely uncertain of their manners and seeking good company. The reader is told how to enter a room, how to bow or curtsey, or how to carve, as well as how to address a virgin, or, on the other hand, a widow. Some of the phrases used are those mocked by the other art of courtship books. The audience here appears to be those genuinely rising in society, and concerned to avoid social disaster. Almost all the rest are books of mockery.

Love's Masterpiece, or the Grove of Pleasure and Delight[80] declares its intent both on the title page, and in the conclusion. It is published for 'the Recreation of all Gentlemen, Ladies and others' and proclaims at the back Cupid's over-ruling of all social distinctions:

> Gallants, and Ladies, Rusticks, and each sort,
> That to this Grove for pleasure do resort,
> See various changes, all fit for delight. . . .

> For in this little piece is plainly shown
> The various humours both of Court and Town.
> The Rustick-Scenes and . . . sphere are plac'd,
> With all Varieties this Grove is grac'd.

A deliberate antithesis between language, social level and mood is often created. This booklet contains at least two deliberate contrasts. One page contains, firstly, a letter of a lover to his mistress, in verse, which runs:

> Madam, behold and pitty him, who lies
> The wretched victim of Love's sacrifice,
> Wounded by you; he bleeds, death is his doom,
> Unless within your heart you'l give him room.
> All else is vain; no other Medicine can
> Restore a poor, desparing, dying Man.
> In one so fair let Cruelty not dwell:
> Nor me, where heaven I seek, e'r find my hell.
> Nature such beauties never bid again
> To torture mankind, whilst they sigh in vain.
> Then smile on me thou center of my joys,
> And give me hope e'r fate my hope destroys.

This is immediately followed by 'Clodpate's Letter to Margery the Cook-maid':

Vaith Margery, He was vain to gife sixpence for a pair of Gloves, to send thee with this Letter, least thou sud'st a thout He ha forgotten thee; never bear it mine Pigsnise, He not forget thee these forty year, and more, He worrant thee: But being in woundie haste, He con write no more at this time, but woll tell thee the rest to morrow, when He come and see thee; and till then remain

Your nown Sweet-heart, J. Clodpate.

Another contains a would-be 'literary' invocation to Cupid, lapsing somewhat on the author's rhyming for the last couplet:

> Haste Cupid, haste away,
> The lovely Nymph is gone astray;
> Fetch her, fetch her back again,
> Or let her feel they fiercest flame:
> Let Feavours dwell within her brest,

> Who has rob'd me of my rest:
> Let her suffer, let her fry,
> Since for her, alas! I die.
>   Let her suffer, &c.

This is at once juxtaposed with a bawdy catch:

> Johney took Jone by the Arm,
> And lead her unto the Hay-cock;
> And yet he did her no harm,
> Although he felt under her Smock,
>   Although he did touze her,
>   Although he did rouze her,
> Untill she backwards did fall,
>   She did not complain,
>   Nor his kindness refrain,
> But pray'd him to put it in all.

In these chapbooks, the rural lovers Hodge and Sarah, Clodpate and Margery, Dick the ploughman and Joan the dairymaid[81] are no more objects of laughter that the Bashful Lover and his Mistress, the Old Man writing to a young Gentlewoman, the Verses in Praise of his Mistress, and the Gentleman writing to his Mistress:[82]

Considering with my self, excellent Lady, the many vertues nature hath in a superabundant measure adorn'd you with: and weighing the sufficiency of any service I can do you; my trembling hand is sacrce able to hold the pen, and my stammering tongue dares hardly express what my . . . heart desireth to manifest to you; yet love who holds in his Dominion my inflamed heart, desireth me to lay open to your self, the secrets of my Love tormented breast. Excuse then, I humbly beseech you, these lines that I invisibly present to your fair hands, a more humble suit then can be exprest; I beseech you extend a gracious hand to stay a fainting Soul from dying, that without you is nothing, whose worth and remembrance gives me life; for I desire not to be where your Being is not it is that only betters my joy, and makes me sensible of content, no content being equal to the enjoying such a companion of so great worth. To conclude, I shall expect the Sentence of my Life and Death in your answer, and remain so perfectly yours, that I can say nothing near it; when I say, I am your most faithful, most affectionate, and most obedient Servant,

J.D.

The audience is difficult to deduce. Were Hodge and Sarah supposed to laugh at themselves, and at the windy, high-flown epistles of their betters? Or were country yeomen, and city officials like Pepys, supposed to laugh both at the infelicities of the one, and the pomposities of the other? One thing at least emerges clearly; late seventeenth-century England was not only addicted to slapstick, but also to social satire. The French chapbooks seem to be entirely free of this theme, which is so marked in the English twopenny books (but see below, pp. 148–9, n. 4). It seems that English society was less subservient, more aware of the possibilities of upward social movement, and more liable to ridicule its 'betters' than the French.

The earlier letter-writing manuals, like Nicholas Breton's two collections called the *Post with a Mad Packet of Letters* of 1603 and 1637,[83] were more satirical than the later. Pepys had three other collections of letters. Two of them were mainly intended to amuse[84] but the last was specifically to instruct.[85] It explained how to lay out a letter, how to open and close and how to address persons of different rank, and discussed paper and ink, right down to the sealing and superscription of the finished epistle. The tremendously mixed contents demonstrate the wide audience the publishers hoped the book would have. A merchant writes to his factor in the West Indies, requesting him to expend the profits of the next cargo on tobacco, and receives a reply; a country shopkeeper complains to a London grocer of the quality of his last consignment of goods, but none the less orders four hundredweights of the best new raisins, and more besides; a London citizen writes to a friend in the country, requesting him to find a reliable apprentice at a premium of £40.

But there are also letters for gentlemen. A gentleman writes to a country schoolmaster desiring him to educate his ten-year-old son; another writes to his son at university, yet another receives, and acknowledges, a petition; there are the usual groups of lovesick letters to gentlewomen and kind and unkind answers, mingled with less well-phrased countrymen's letters to their loves. There are also models of family letters: mothers to daughters, daughters to mothers, fathers to sons, and reproachful elder brothers to profligate younger ones. The woodcut cover emphasizes the potential appeal of the book; it shows postboys careering along the roads between London, Bristol, Norwich and York. The addresses of the fictitious writers likewise cover the whole kingdom.

From the contents of the chapbooks themselves and the very wide audiences to which they were obviously meant to appeal, it seems fair to deduce a readership from merchants down to apprentices in towns, from yeomen to in-servants in the countryside. Whether the 'gentlemen' to whose style of correspondence mocking reference was so frequently made actually read the little books is an open question. Pepys's description of even the quartos as *Vulgaria* seems apt enough. Yet it seems highly unlikely that Sir William Cornwallis was alone in his habits of light reading (see above, p. 48).

Even if the culture of the rich and the poor, the fully-educated and the just literate, was increasingly drawing apart, it is probably not true that the English élite became non-participant to the extent of being ignorant of the chapbook culture, and therefore of the old chivalric stories.[86] The 'mediators' between the two cultures were the schoolboys.

Schoolboys do not immediately leap to mind as a market worth publishing for, but the chapbook publishers thought otherwise. A book of conjuring tricks, which includes directions not only on how to 'fetch a shilling out of a hankerchief', write invisibly and make representations of a curry-comb, a 'cover for an Italian coach' and a rose for a shoe-buckle with paper, but also directions on how to smoke rabbits out of a warren, snare wild duck, hatch eggs in a home-made incubator, and make a disagreeable maid-servant fart uncontrollably, was written specifically with both urban and country boys in mind.[87] The author writes in his introduction, 'The design of this was for the recreation of Youth, especially Schoolboys, whose wits are generally sharpened on such Whetstones'. As it happens there is more direct evidence on the reading of schoolboys, although it remains pitifully little, than any other social group.

Francis Kirkman, who was so enraptured by his boyhood reading that he not only frustrated his father's plans for him to become a bookseller, but also wrote additional parts for the *Palmerin* cycle in the late seventeenth century, wrote of his schoolboy taste in fiction very clearly indeed in 1673.

Once I happened upon a Six Pence, and having lately read that

famous Book, of the *Fryar and the Boy*, and being hugely pleased
with that, as also the excellent History of the *Seven wise Masters
of Rome*, and having heard great Commendation of *Fortunatus*, I
laid out all my mony for that, and thought I had a great
bargain . . . now having read this Book, and being desirous of
reading more of that nature; one of my School-fellows lent me
Doctor Faustus, which also pleased me, especially when he
travelled in the Air, saw all the World, and did what he listed. . . .
The next Book I met with was *Fryar Bacon*, whose pleasant
Stories much delighted me: But when I came to Knight Errantry,
and reading *Montelion Knight of the Oracle*, and *Ornatus* and
Artesia, and the Famous *Parisimus*; I was contented beyond measure, and (believing all I read to be true) wished my self Squire to
one of these Knights: I proceeded on to *Palmerin of England*, and
Amadis de Gaul; and borrowing one Book of one person, when I
read it my self, I lent it to another, who lent me one of their Books;
and thus robbing Peter to pay Paul, borrowing and lending from
one to another, I in time had read most of these Histories. All the
time I had from School, as Thursdays in the afternoon, and Satur-
days, I spent in reading these Books; so that I being wholy affected
to them, and reading how that *Amadis* and other Knights not
knowing their Parents, did in time prove to be Sons of Kings and
great Personages; I had such a fond and idle Opinion, that I might
in time prove to be some great Person, or at leastwise be Squire to
some Knight.[88]

He thus indicated not only that he, a London merchant's son, read a
corpus of popular tales that was collected in its entirety by Pepys
in the *Vulgaria* in the next decade, but also that a lively system of
exchange and barter of sixpenny quartos existed among his
schoolfellows.[89] It sounds as if a very high proportion of the boys
would have read the stories in the *Vulgaria*. The preface to Thomas
Howard's imitation, the *Wise Mistresses*, made a general claim for the
utility of the 'Histories' to schoolchildren.

History ought to be praised, not Contemned; for it doth encourage Youth through the pleasantness of the Story, whereby he doth
sooner attain to his English Tongue, and is still more desirous to
read further. For many thousands at School, in their innocency,
are more naturally given to learn first Historical Fables, by which

they sooner come to read perfect, than to begin, first in Hard
Books appertaining to Divine knowledge.[90]

The confessions of the spiritual autobiographers seem to bear this
claim out, and show that not only St Paul's boys, like Kirkman, who
had easy access to the chapbook publishers, read the chivalric novels.
Other boys, less physically easily circumstanced, could get them too.
Richard Baxter, a yeoman's son from a small Shropshire village,
bewailed his early sins, committed about the age of ten, which
included, as well as excessive eating of stolen apples and pears, the
confession 'I was extremely bewitched with a love of romances,
fables and old tales which corrupted my affections, and lost my
time'.[91] Baxter does not say where these came from, but he does say
that a pedlar bringing both 'ballads and some good books' came to his
father's door. Vavasour Powell came from even further west, from
between Kingston and Llanfair Waterdine on the Welsh border.
Despite his 'training up in learning', he repented of his lack of esteem
for the holy scriptures. 'Either Hystorical or Poetical Books,
Romances and the like were all my delight.'[92] He seems to have had
no trouble in getting them. The chapbooks spread to schoolboys yet
further west, and crossed the Irish Sea. The preface of Pepys's
threepenny abbreviated version of the medieval story with oriental
origins, *The Seven Wise Masters*,[93] made the unusual claim, 'of all
Histories of this nature, this exceeds, being held in such esteem in
Ireland, that it is of the chiefest use in all the English Schools for
introducing Children to the understanding of good Letters'. The
claim would appear wildly improbable, despite the fact that Irish
chapmen were often specifically appealed to in the advertising of the
publisher-booksellers, if it were not for the astonishing evidence
provided by Hely Dutton writing of County Clare in 1808. He lists
with disgust the Histories of the *Seven Champions of Christendom,
Montelion, Parisimus, Fair Rosamund, Jane Shore* and *Doctor
Faustus* along with some more recently written additions as the
reading books most generally found, as cottage classics, with a few
spelling books. Soon afterwards, a writer on County Wicklow concurred on the list. If the *Histories* were there in the nineteenth
century, they may well, in view of the advertising, have been there in
the seventeenth century also.[94]

Another schoolboy, slightly later, who read the *Histories* was young Samuel Johnson. The conscience-ridden Doctor Johnson in later life blamed his fits of idleness on the habits he had acquired of reading the romances in his father's shop, in about 1720. He informed the Bishop of Dromore that 'when he was a boy he was inordinately fond of reading romances of chivalry'. Michael Johnson was a bookseller of Lichfield, who ran bookstalls on market days at Birmingham, Ashby-de-la-Zouch and Uttoxeter, and so augmented the work of the chapmen. His sensitive son, who hated serving at Uttoxeter market, not only read the romances in his boyhood, but re-read them in his later life. He quoted from *Don Bellianis*[95] when he read *Paradise Lost*, and is said to have had *Palmerin of England*[96] with him on a jaunt in 1776.[97] He was not alone. Boswell also had a very considerable fondness for his childhood reading, for once quite uninfluenced by his mentor. He made a pilgrimage in 1763 to the Dicey printing office in Bow Church yard. He wrote:

> There are ushered into the world of literature *Jack and the Giants*, *The Seven Wise Men of Gotham*, and other story books which in my dawning years amused me as much as *Rasselas* does now. I saw the whole scheme with a kind of romantic feeling to find myself really where all my old darlings were printed. I bought two dozen of the story-books and had them bound up with the title *Curious Productions*.[98]

Burke confessed in the House of Commons that a favourite study of his had been the 'old romances *Palmerin of England* and *Don Bellianis of Greece*, upon which he had wasted much valuable time'.[99] Even in the nineteenth century, upper- or middle-class schoolboys remained aware of the chapbook literature. William Morris, product of a prosperous middle-class background, who was educated at a small private school before he went to Marlborough, wrote an unfinished novel in 1872, which contained a passage describing the hero's fear of the supernatural: 'He rose up from his chair in terror for he really began to think she was a ghost: all . . . the naif and gross ghost stories read long ago in queer little penny garlands with woodcuts.'[100] If Johnson and Boswell, Burke and Morris all read the chapbooks as schoolboys, as well as Bunyan, Clare and Bowd of Swavesey, the gap between the culture of the élite and popular culture was not complete. The medieval romances became the childhood reading of the upper classes.

NOTES AND REFERENCES

1 See cover, *PM*, I (22), 484.

2 Carpenter, H. J. (1894) 'Furze of Moreshead. A Family Record of the Sixteenth Century', *Report and Transactions of the Devonshire Association* 36, 169–84.

3 I am very grateful to Dr Bernard Capp for this reference. Snell, F. J. (1907) 'A Devonshire Yeoman's Diary: William Honeywell of Ashton 1596–1614', in Apperson, G. L. (ed.) *Gleanings after Time*, London.

4 'A dyurnall, or catalogue of all my accions and expences from the 1st of January 1646' by Adam Eyre in Morehouse, H. J. (ed.) (1877) Surtees Society 65, Durham.

5 Whiting, J. (1715) *Persecution Exposed in some Memoirs*, London. Jenkins shows that yeomen figured largely amongst non-gentle subscribers to Welsh devotional books (Jenkins, G. H. (1978) *Literature, Religion and Society in Wales, 1660–1730*, Cardiff, 284–8).

6 Burke, P. (1978) *Popular Culture in Early Modern Europe*, London, 276–8.

7 Thirsk, J. (ed.) (1967) *Agrarian History of England and Wales*, IV, Cambridge, 864.

8 Peter Clark disagrees with this view and says 'items worth a few pence' are listed in inventories in Kent before 1640. His conclusion is that either the chapbooks and the almanacs were not bought, or they fell apart, too quickly to keep. Clark, P. (1976) 'The ownership of books in England', in Stone, L. (ed.) *Schooling and Society*, Baltimore, Md., 95–111.

9 Vaisey, D. (1975) 'Provincial retailers in the seventeenth century: the evidence of probate inventories', unpublished paper given in Oxford. Mr Vaisey was speaking with particular reference to the dangers of using inventories as negative rather than positive evidence, especially for the non-ownership of books. I am particularly grateful to him for his generosity in lending me this paper.

10 Allen, D. C. (ed.) (1946) *Essays by Sir Wm. Cornwallis*, Baltimore, 50.

11 The earliest reference in the Oxford English Dictionary to lavatory paper is as late as 1884.

12 'Rats Rhimed to Death', Wood, 326 (1660), 40.

13 Foley, W. (1974) *A Child in the Forest*, London, 51–2.

14 Introduction to 'The Unfortunate Traveller, or Life of Jack Wilson', Wood, C 31 (3) (1594).

15 Brathwait, R. (1631) 'Whimzies, or a New Cast of Characters' quoted in Frank, J. (1961) *The Beginnings of the English Newspaper, 1620–1660*, Cambridge, Mass., 276.

16 Fielding, H. (1749) *Tom Jones*, 1966 edn, Harmondsworth, 151 and 879, n. to Bk. IV, Ch. 1.

17 Burke, op. cit., 278.

18 *Vulgaria*, IV (9). This had over 160 pages, and is therefore too long to be included here, or considered as 'cheap'. Therefore the insulting preamble is even more interesting.

19 *Vulgaria*, IV (8). Baker, E. A. (1924) *History of the English Novel*, I, London, 261, 281, 287, traces Reynard's antecedents to the twelfth century.

20 'Cupid's Sports and Pastimes', *PM*, I (43), 931.

21 Furnivall, F. J. (1871) *Captain Cox, His Ballads and his Books; or, Robert Langham's Letter*, London; and see below pp. 143–145.

22 *PM*, I (6), 122–4.

23 Furnivall, op. cit., lxvi.

24 *PM*, II (21), 489–512.

25 *PM*, II (25), 602–3.

26 *PM*, II (18), 434–5.

27 *Vulgaria*, IV (5).

28 All taken from the Epistle to the Reader. Mother Bunch can be paralleled by other ale wives who are equally specifically country figures, however. Captain Cox had *Elynor Rumming*, a story written by Skelton about a Surrey ale wife in the time of Henry VIII who presided over a drinking bout by country women at her inn. Furnivall, op. cit., lxxv–lxxvi.

29 *Vulgaria*, IV (19). See below, p. 139 and Table III, pp. 136–7 for the other crime chapbooks.

30 For the different culture of these groups, see Burke, op. cit., 36–42. For a description of Deloney's novels, see below, pp. 238–44.

31 *PM*, I (19), 425–47.

32 *PM*, I (14), 305–27.

33 *PM*, I (35), 745–60.

34 *PM*, I (13), 281–4.

35 See, for instance, Crook, J. (1706) *A Short History of the Life . . .*, London, in which he shows that a considerable group of apprentices all went to Puritan lectures and occasions; and Orme, W. (ed.) (1823) *Remarkable Passages in the Life of William Kiffin*, London. The latter wrote:

> about this time [1632] I began to be acquainted with several young men who diligently attended on the means of grace . . . being apprentices, as well as myself, they had no opportunity of converse, but on the Lords days. It was our constant practice to attend the morning lectures, which began at six o'clock, both at Cornhill and Christchurch.

They also agreed to meet together an hour before service, to pray together and to communicate the experiences they had received from the Lord to each other.

36 'True Lover's New Academy', *PM*, II (28), 677–8.

37 For a summary of the evidence on immigration to London see Spufford, P. (1974) 'Population Mobility in Pre-Industrial England: the Magnet of the Metropolis', *Genealogists' Magazine* 17 (9), 475–8. For the growth of London, Wrigley, E. A. (1967) 'A Simple Model of London's Importance in Changing English Society and Economy 1650–1750', *Past and Present* 27, 44–70.

38 *Vulgaria*, IV (5), 4.

39 *PM*, I (8) (twelfth edn 1683), 161–85.

40 Buchan, D. (1972) *The Ballad and the Folk*, London, 76–81.

41 'Pleasant History of Cawwood the Rook, or, the Assembly of Birds . . .', *Vulgaria*, IV (10) (1683), 22.

42 *PM*, I (57), 1,225–47.

43 *PM*, II (41), 986.

44 *PM*, II (49), 990.

45 *PM*, II (22), 534. See below, pp. 233 and 247.

46 *PM*, I (3). See below, pp. 247–9.

47 *PM*, I (58), 1249–69.

48 *PM*, II (26). See below, pp. 245–6.

49 *PM*, I (5), 97–112.

50 *PM*, I (10), 209–32.

51 Satire is only self-evident in one place (see above, p. 29).

52 *PM*, II (33), 783–806.

53 *Pace* Roger Thompson, who assumed the model injunctions, bills of sale and powers of attorney would 'only be of much use to the solid yeomanry and lesser squires, grudging fees to country attorneys', (1976) *Samuel Pepys' Penny Merriments*, London, 18.

54 'Gentlewoman's Delight in Cookery', *PM*, II (32), 759–82; 'Gentlewoman's Cabinet Unlocked', *PM*, (5), 81–104.

55 *PM*, II (11), 201–21, and *PM*, I (39), 833–56.

56 *PM*, I (12), 257–80.

57 *PM*, II (13), 249–73. The author was, however, one TR, 'your loving friend, poor Tom'.

58 Women are supposed to have enjoyed the romanticized love of the chivalric and neo-chivalric cycles. See below, Chapter IX, pp. 233–4.

59 Gittings, R. (1978) *Young Thomas Hardy*, Harmondsworth, 214, 272–3, 289–99, 219–20.

60 The outstanding example is the Renaissance princess, Marguerite of Navarre, whose ability to tell a crude tale when her plot demands it seems to startle even her modern editor. Saulnier, V. L. (ed.) (1963) Marguerite de Navarre, *Théâtre Profane*, xvi–xvii; and also Krailsheimer, A. J. (ed.) (1971) *The Continental Renaissance, 1500–1600*, Harmondsworth, 311–13. Well-born English country ladies sometimes had very salty tongues. Sir Nicholas Le Strange collected jokes in the first half of the seventeenth century. He included a variety of anecdotes, some extremely bawdy, gathered from his mother, Dame Alice, wife of the Sheriff of Norfolk who was twice MP. Not the least interesting feature of them is that such jokes could be passed from mother to son; Lippincott, H. P. (ed.) (1974) Sir Nicholas Le Strange, *Merry Passages and Jeasts: A Manuscript Jestbook*, Salzburg Studies in English Literature: Elizabethan and Renaissance Studies 29. I am very grateful to Christopher Smith and Victor Morgan of UEA for drawing my attention to these two ladies. The story of Lady Elizabeth Hatton's wedding riposte to Sir Edward Coke will bear recapitulation in this context. 'Laying his hand on her belly (when he came to bed) and, finding a Child to stirre, What, sayd He, Flesh in the Pott. Yea, quoth

she, or els I would not have married a Coke.' Dick, O. L. (ed.) (1962) *Aubrey's Brief Lives*, Harmondsworth, 162. The author of that *bon mot* made it from a social background in which her ears and tongue were accustomed to such verbal play.

61 *The Winter's Tale* (c. 1610) Act IV, Scene iii, lines 190–200. Partridge discusses bawdy dialogues between women alone. He comes to the conclusion that some of it is as erotic as that between men, but less brutal, and less direct, even in the longest wittiest passage in *Much Ado About Nothing* Act III; Partridge, E. (1968) *Shakespeare's Bawdy*, London, 31–3.

62 I base this judgement on the chapbooks in general, excluding the group of misogynist, anti-female chapbooks, which deliberately portray women as sexually insatiable.

63 FitzHerbert, Sir A. (1768) *Certain Ancient Tracts Concerning The Management Of Landed Property Reprinted*, II, London, 58.

64 *PM*, II (41), 984.

65 Capp, B. (1979) *Astrology and the Popular Press*, London and Boston, 87, 122.

66 Perhaps it is revealing that Roger Thompson dismisses the courtship chapbooks, which form one of the largest groups of the 'merry books', as a 'mélange of constipated and fulsome foppery . . . [with] a considerable portion . . . in the realm of fantasy or wish-fulfilment'. He does this in order to concentrate on the marital and sexual stories. It never seems to occur to him that these are also fantasies, but of the type more indulged in by the male than the female. Thompson, R. (1976) *Journal of Popular Culture*, 9 (3), 655, compare 658 *et seq.*

67 Clark, P. (1978) 'The Ale-house and the Alternative Society', in Pennington, D. and Thomas, K. (eds) *Puritans and Revolutionaries: Essays Presented to Christopher Hill*, Oxford, 47–72. Burke, op. cit., 109–10.

68 'Theeves Falling Out, True Men come by their Goods, or, the Bell-man Wanted a Clapper', *Vulgaria*, III (22), described as by Robert Greene, and probably based on his *Disputation between a Hee Conny-Catcher and a Shee-Conny-catcher* (1592). Pepys's edition was the earliest chapbook in his collection, printed for Henry and Moses Bell in 1637.

69 'Canterbury Tales', *PM*, II (12), 225–48.

70 That is, on the main south-west road out of London. Furnivall, op. cit.

71 For instance, John Rae, innkeeper, of St Andrews, Holborn, was the residuary legatee for a chapman who described him as 'my very good friend', Guildhall Library, Archdeaconry Court of London, Wills, 3 April 1715.

72 Spufford, M. (1974) *Contrasting Communities*, London, 231–3 (Royston), 246–7 (Colchester).

73 'Canterbury Tales', *PM*, II (12), 231.

74 Spufford, op. cit., 245.

75 *PM*, II (41), 979–81.

76 *PM*, II (24), 584.

77 *PM*, II (12), 225–48. All the heroes or victims of these tales lived in or near Canterbury or in Kent, and this is the only pretext for the title.

78 Although some, like the 'New Academy of Complements', *PM*, I (31), 681–8, are all 'choice Flowers of elegant and most Courtly Expressions for Young Gentlemen and Young Ladies', whereas others, like the 'Garland of Love and Mirth', *PM*, II (45), 1062–75, have an extremely non-genteel cast.

79 *PM*, II (30), 711–34.

80 *PM*, II (18), 417–40.

81 All from 'Love's Masterpiece', *PM*, II (18), 419, 423, 436.

82 ibid., 421, 426; 'The True Lover's New Academy', *PM*, II (28), 627, 670; 'Love's School', *PM*, II (15), 333–4.

83 Reprinted and possessed by Pepys in a form too long for consideration here, as a 'Poaste with a Packet of Letters', *Vulgaria*, IV (17). Considered by Baker, E. A. (1929) *History of the English Novel*, II, London, as one of the earliest character-writers, but dismissed as 'more curious than amusing', pp. 151–2.

84 'New Conceited Letters, Newly Laid Open', *Vulgaria*, IV (18), and 'A Speedy Post with a Packet of Letters', *Vulgaria*, IV (16).

85 'A Flying Post with a Packet of Choice new Letters', *Vulgaria*, IV (15).

86 See Burke, op. cit., 24–9, for the discussion of the participation of the élite in popular culture in the seventeenth century.

87 'Sports and Pastimes, or, Sport for the City and Pastime for the Country . . .', *Vulgaria*, IV (6), 4, 10–11, 12, 13, 17, 38–9.

88 Quoted in Wright, L. B. (1934) *Middle Class Culture in Eliza-bethan England*, Chapel Hill, N.C., 86–7.

89 The system still exists: I know of one school in which 'trash mags' form an unofficial currency.

90 *PM*, III (6), 634

91 Keeble, N. H. (ed.) (1974) *Autobiography of Richard Baxter*, London, 5.

92 *The life and death of Mr Vavasour Powell, that faithful minister and confessor of Jesus Christ . . .* (1671), 2. Powell and Baxter are both writing of experiences in the first half of the seventeenth century.

93 'Wisdom's Cabinet Opened: or the Famous history of the Seven Wise Masters of Rome', *Vulgaria*, III (6), priced at 3*d* on the trade-list, *PM*, I (4), 96.

94 Dutton, H. (1808) *Statistical Survey of the County of Clare with observations on the means of improvement*, 2 parts, Dublin; and Wakefield, E. (1812) *An Account of Ireland, statistical and pol-itical*, 2 volumes, London, quoted by Dowling, P. J. (1968) *The Hedge-Schools of Ireland*, Cork, 64–5. Mr Dowling takes these remarks to apply to reading books in the hedge-schools, but it is not absolutely clear from the quotations he gives that they do, in fact, do so.

95 *Vulgaria*, I (2).

96 *Vulgaria*, I (1).

97 Hill, G. B. (ed.) (1887) *Boswell's Life of Johnson*, I, Oxford, 34, n. 5, and 49.

98 Quoted by Neuburg, V. (1972) *Chapbooks: a bibliography* (second edn), London, 7. These are in the Houghton Library, Harvard College.

99 Hill, op. cit.

100 Lindsay, J. (1975) *William Morris*, London, 14. I am grateful to my son Francis for this reference.

IV

The fortunes and the volume of stock of the chapbook publishers

❦

THE WEALTH OF THE CHAPBOOK AND BALLAD PUBLISHERS

Since there is no direct evidence for the readership of the chapbooks, and the multifarious suggestions contained in them implying the audiences that would identify in sympathy with them are necessarily somewhat imprecise, a further approach suggests itself. The true scale and importance of the trade in chapbooks would be indicated by evidence on the fortunes of their specialist publishers. Indeed, the most convincing argument for the profitability of chapbooks and ballads in the second half of the seventeenth century is the common-sense one of the proliferation of specialist booksellers in the trade. The question of how lucrative or, on the contrary, how marginal a living these men made compared with other London shopkeepers and merchants immediately presents itself. If they made fortunes, the profitability of the trade is demonstrated. If the scale of their production of chapbooks can be documented, minimum figures for the quantity in circulation are at once supplied. Evidence of the wealth of the publishers, and the volume of their production is therefore crucial to any understanding of the true influence and degree of social penetration of the chapbooks.

The publication of both ballads and chapbooks in the late seventeenth century, up to the expiry of the Printing Act in 1695, was largely in the hands of a group of London men known as the Ballad Partners. Amongst these were Wright, Clarke, Passinger and Thackeray. Cyprian Blagden first worked out the succession of imprints published by this group of men, and made considerable use of their wills to do so.¹ A second group, frequently ex-apprentices of the first, were also vigorously engaged in the trade. They were Brooksby, Deacon, Blare and Back, with Conyers and Dennisson.

When Blagden searched so successfully for the wills of the Ballad Partners in the Archdeaconry Court of London and the Prerogative Court of Canterbury, he was not aware that his search could be taken one step further, and that the comparative wealth and perhaps even value of stock in hand of the Partners could be established, if the probate inventories that once accompanied the original wills could be found. Indeed, until very recently this next step could not be taken, since the inventories of the Prerogative Court of Canterbury are only now in the process of becoming available. The chances of finding an inventory for a specific individual amongst those which have survived time, floods and ill-treatment are extremely low. However, it seemed worth trying. In addition, the records of the Court of Orphans, which had powers of compulsory supervision until 1693 over any under-age orphan of freemen of the City of London, were examined.² The accounts of an estate that did come into the Court of Orphans are particularly rewarding; they set out in detail an inventory not only of the dead freeman's movable goods, as a probate inventory does, but they also list his other real estate, with a full list of debts owing to, and owed by, him, and a gross and net value of the estate. The only part of such an account that can be compared with a probate inventory is the total value of movable goods, including, of course, the stock in the shop.

Considering the odds against finding inventories or accounts for any of the particular men specializing in the ballad and chapbook trade in the last half of the seventeenth century, the search was surprisingly rewarding. Maddeningly, not a single inventory for any of the Ballad Partners themselves was found.³ However, evidence for the generation before the flourishing of the main partnership does survive, in the shape of the probate inventory for Charles Tias, who had young Thomas Passinger as his apprentice. Thomas Passinger was due to be freed in 1665, but Tias died in 1664, and Passinger married his widow, Sarah, and so acquired his stock. He continued to trade at the 'Three Bibles' on London Bridge, as Tias had done. He and young William Thackeray, who had acquired Grove's stock, then worked together, before becoming full Ballad Partners.⁴, ⁵

Evidence of Charles Tias's activities, therefore, bears very usefully on Passinger and on Thackeray.

Evidence for the main group of competitors contemporary with the Ballad Partners is provided by the probate inventory of Jonah Deacon, and by the orphans' accounts for Josiah Blare. Jonah Deacon had been apprenticed to Mary Wright, was freed in 1671 and died in 1699. Blare was ten years younger than Deacon in the trade; he was apprenticed to Thomas Passinger, and was only freed in 1682 to set up at the Looking Glass on London Bridge in the following year. He died in 1706.

The generation of chapbook and ballad specialists following both Ballad Partners and their competitors, when the trade was dominated by Charles Bates, Charles Brown and Thomas Norris, is represented by the orphans' accounts for the children of Charles Bates, who had been Deacon's apprentice, was freed in 1690, and died in 1716. Finally, the orphan's accounts for the only daughter of Edward Midwinter, who himself had married Norris's daughter Elizabeth, and was one of the pre-eminent figures in the trade in the next generation until his death in 1737 or 1738, form a lively epilogue to the whole.

The results obtained by comparing the wealth of the five men concerned are illuminating, not only in themselves, but in the glaring light they throw on the inadequacies of probate inventories, which have been so heavily used by economic historians, including myself, as guides to wealth (see Table I, p. 86).

When Tias died in 1664, his appraisers valued his movable goods at £418. Almost all of this total was made up of stock in the shop and house on London Bridge itself, and in his warehouse. Tias was owed another £310 by his debtors. Even by the standards of the City of London, Tias was not among the poor. Only 38 per cent of freemen were worth over £500 at their deaths between 1666 and 1677.[6] This suggests that Tias was a very comfortable tradesman by London standards, although he had probably not accumulated the sort of wealth that distinguished middling merchants from prosperous tradesmen.

The appraisers who valued Jonah Deacon's goods for probate at the end of the century priced them at less than those of Tias; his stock in the shop was worth £150, and the value of his other movables, including the sign of the Angel that hung outside (see illustration,

TABLE 1 The wealth of the chapbook and ballad publishers

Name	Date	Source	Value of stock only	Total movables including ready money	Debts owed to him		Debts owed by him	Net estate
					Good	Bad		
Charles Tias or Tynes	1664	PCC probate inventory	£368	£418	£310		?	?
Jonah Deacon	1699	PCC probate inventory	£150	£221	£30	£200	?	?
Josiah Blare	1707	Orphans' account	£191	£341	£84	£28.10	£296	£3274
Charles Bates	1716	Orphans' account	£316	£400	£98	£50	£263	£236
Edward Midwinter	1738 (exhibited)	Orphans' account	£665*	£1156*	£1399*	£1027	£954	£1353

* Includes £448 for stock sold at auction from list of debts paid after death, debited from good debt column.

At the afore-mentioned place, any Country Chapmen or others, may be Furnished with all sorts of Small Books and Ballads.

Deacon's sign of the Angel

p. 87), only brought his estate up to £220. Again, he was owed a considerable sum in debts. Judging from this inventory alone, the group of competitors to the Ballad Printers, Brooksby, Deacon, Blare and Back, were by no means outstandingly successful. The orphans' account for Josiah Blare's two children drawn up in 1707 shows just how misleading this judgement is. It also demonstrates exactly how misleading an inventory can be.

Blare died at a roughly comparable point in his career to Deacon, twenty-five years after the end of his apprenticeship, instead of twenty-eight. He had a little more stock in the shop, but was not working on a dissimilar scale, for it was worth just under £200 instead of £150. His movable goods included £100 in cash and one tell-tale item, eighty-three ounces of silver plate priced at 5s an ounce, worth £20 15s. All the same, this would have only given him a total estate, in terms of a probate inventory, of £341, plus another £84 of good debts

ADVERTISEMENT.

JOfiah Blare, Book-feller, *at the fign of the* Looking- Glafs *on* London-Bridge; *Furnifheth Country Chap-men or others, with all forts of Hiftory Books,* Small Books, *or* Ballads.

Blare's colophon and advertisement

owed him. It was neither a remarkable sum, nor one totally unlike Deacon's in scale. The orphan's accounts show, however, that the tenant of the Looking Glass, who was just starting in business on his own when Pepys collected five of his small books, had been making money on a scale which put him decisively amongst the richest fifth of the inhabitants of London, and into the league of the merchants. He had been saving hand over fist, and had invested the money in East India Company bonds, tallies on the Malt Tax, the Coal Tax, the Land Tax and an Exchequer annuity, worth in all £3110, which were bringing in a minimum income of at least £107 9s 4d in interest annually for his widow. Blare's estate confirms the inference of prosperity that may reasonably be drawn from the will of John Wright of the Ballad Partners, made in 1684.[7] This provides for the immediate sale of messuages and lands, some 'lately purchased', in the occupation of at least four tenants in Berkshire, as well as seven tenements in Old Fish Street, Bermondsey and the Prince of Orange's Head near St Saviour's stairs, Bermondsey, and four more freehold farms in Essex which were to be sold after the death of his wife. Out of these sales his five sons were to be maintained until their majority, and cash sums were to be paid out totalling no less than £3347. Nothing could demonstrate more clearly the profits of the chapbook trade in the last twenty years of the seventeenth century than the savings of these two men.[8]

On the other hand, chapbook specialists were not necessarily prosperous. It is fortunate that the accounts for the five daughters of Charles Bates, who were left minors when their father died in 1716, survive for a trade generation later, to correct any false impression that there was any necessary relationship between the value of a man's stock and movable goods at his death, and his capital. Bates, like his own former master Deacon, was twenty-eight years out of his apprenticeship when his goods were valued. His stock in trade in the shop was worth over £100 more than either Deacon's or Blare's. His 'books, paper and quills in the Shop', and 'Books in Quires in the Dining Room and Garrett', with those in the cellars, were worth £316. Judging from his stock, he was working on a larger scale than the generation before him.[9] But the size of Bates's operations had not led to mercantile prosperity in his case, as it had in Blare's. Again, this could not have been deduced from an inventory of his movable goods alone, particularly since his widow boasted an unusually well-furnished chamber, with an early walnut chest of drawers, an eight-day clock, a large looking-glass, sixteen old pictures in frames, and a walnut table and another recent nicety, a tea-table. Bates may have lived well, but he had no savings at all; his own debts of £263 heavily out-weighed the £98 owed to him, and, after all charges had been deducted, the net estate to be divided amongst his daughters was only £236 3s 3d. Each girl duly received the sad sum, by Blare's standards, of £15 14s 10½d. It seems unlikely that Mrs Bates can have continued to drink tea.

However, Blare was not alone in his prosperity, even though Edward Midwinter, in the 1730s, was only finally worth one-third of the sum. A printer trained by Midwinter, Thomas Gent, wrote a vivid account of the household in which he spent part of his apprenticeship, from 1710 to 1714. The first Mrs Midwinter earned his great respect, not only because she beat the apprentices and so reminded him of his own revered mother, but because of the power she exercised in the business. When one of the authors working for Midwinter was imprisoned in the Gatehouse, 'it being too long a walk [to fetch his copies] and Mrs Midwinter being fully satisfied of my genius at the pen obliged me . . . to turn author for them too'. Gent often worked, he said, from five in the morning until twelve at night, frequently without food from breakfast until five or six at night in the effort to satisfy the hawkers, who later in his career, he noted, were 'ready to pull my press in pieces for the goods'. Gent was an observer of the courtship of the widowed Midwinter and Elizabeth Norris, the only daughter of Thomas Norris. Norris was 'a very rich bookseller' on London Bridge who also had a 'country seat' at Holloway. Gent watched Midwinter's lifestyle change, and did not altogether approve of what he saw. Midwinter's presents to his intended bride 'were extraordinary . . . proportionable to his expectations'. Gent had a strong feeling that Midwinter was developing habits of extravagance which exceeded the scale of his business.[10] To some extent the Midwinter orphan's accounts bear him out, not least in the style of living of his daughter.

Unfortunately, the inventory of movables was taken later than usual, after both the household goods and the stock had been sold at auction. Midwinter had had a large sum of over £300 in cash at the house at his death. The household goods significantly included plate. The 'Books and Plays' and Midwinter's interest in a *Life of Christ*, in which he was heavily involved at the time of his death, brought in £448 10s at auction.[11] The detailed accounts of the estate show that unlike the shrewd Josiah Blare, Edward Midwinter had invested in loans and mortgages to private individuals, rather than in public funds.[12] This was possibly unwise, since over £1000 was written off in bad debts, on top of the good debts owed to him which included his savings in the form of loans. They also include another blurred reflection, of the type already familiar from Bates's accounts, of Midwinter's extensive dealings with the chapmen and hawkers of which Gent wrote. Over forty individuals owed him money 'on note' in relatively small sums.

Even if Midwinter had spent excessively and saved unwisely, as Gent and his estate accounts between them suggest, he and his family had certainly become accustomed to living in a style befitting considerable expectations. The prosperity of the eighteenth-century chapbook trade is attested to indirectly, but convincingly, in the brief notes of Midwinter's daughter's expenses in the year since his death. A half year's board for 'Miss and her Maid' cost £27 10s without her spending money, and amongst other miscellaneous expenses she had incurred, 'coach hire', 'calico' and, best of all, 'gilding for bird cages' featured. Little Miss Midwinter, Thomas Norris's grand-daughter, with her maid, her Indian cottons, her coach hire and her gilded bird cages, provides an elegant and convincing period to a somewhat arid description of the profits of the chapbook trade in which the most solid and weighty evidence is the account of Josiah Blare's savings, accumulated between 1683 and 1706.

THE STOCK OF TWO CHAPBOOK AND BALLAD PUBLISHERS

Understandably, appraisers were sometimes reluctant to make up detailed inventories of the stock-in-trade of a bookseller-publisher who specialized in the cheap end of the market. The men who valued Jonah Deacon's movables for probate in 1699 wrote simply, 'books bound bookes in Quires ballads and paper unprinted' which they valued all together at £149 19s.[13] The inventory made for Charles Bates for the Court of Orphans was only a little more informative,[14] and Edward Midwinter's stock had all been sold at auction.[15] None of these, therefore, add to our knowledge of the workings of the chapbook and ballad trade in the seventeenth century. Josiah Blare's appraisers for the Court of Orphans were inadvertently a great deal more helpful to historians, and gave the total numbers of books ready to go out in his shop,[16] although they gave no further details. Charles Tias's appraisers in 1664, on the other hand, made a list of his stock which at least began by being exhaustive.[17] It therefore sheds a good deal of new light on the world of the chapbook and ballad publishers.

Thomas Back and John Love, the appraisers, began by examining the stock in the warehouse in Tooley Street, immediately south of the Thames. Tias had there reserve stock of at least twenty chapbooks. They counted the number of copies of each title in the warehouse, recorded a value for each copy, and then gave a total value for each title.[18] Thus the first item in the inventory which survives, almost in full, runs,

348 Amadeus de Gaule at 6*d* per Booke £8 14s.[19]

The information on nine of these twenty chapbooks is still approximately legible, that on four of them has gone beyond recovery, and on the remaining seven, including 221 at 5*d*, is partial and open to informed guesswork.

After this very thorough piece of recording, the appraisers moved to Tias's shop and house on London Bridge. There he had books, reams of books and reams of ballads in the shop and also stored in the lower chamber on the street, the hall, the chamber within the hall, the garret and even over the stairs. At this point, perhaps understandably, they stopped recording titles, with a few exceptions. Amongst these were dictionaries and various Bibles, Testaments, Common Prayer Books and 'Primers, Hornbooks and Table books'. The inventory from this point is expressed in terms of number of books and their sizes and prices, number of reams of books sometimes described as 'small books',[20] which were presumably octavos or duodecimos, with a value per ream, numbers of reams of ballads, and reams of pictures, as well as reams of coloured paper, writing paper, and unprinted paper. There were also small items in the shop itself, like fifteen 'shop books', presumably ledgers, at 1*s* each, and nine dozen 'cards' at 1*s* a dozen. Last of all came the most valuable single item in the inventory, worth £45,[21] immediately after the printing press itself.

It is not possible, because of the appraisers' omission of the titles of almost all the stock on London Bridge itself, to do anything more than demonstrate the size of Tias's whole stock, the price-ranges of books he was producing, with at least some of their titles, and the relative emphasis he placed on chapbooks and ballads. Even this information is interesting enough.

In all, in his warehouse and house, he had just under 10,000 books ready to go out.[22] Only a very small minority of them, 642, or under 7 per cent, were priced at over 6*d*. These included Bibles at 10*s* and 4*s*, 'shop books' at 1*s*, eighty-six bound folios at 2*s* 6*d*, 212 bound quartos at 9*d*, Prayer Books at 8½*d*, and ninety-two large bound octavos at 8*d*.

Tias's emphasis was therefore almost entirely on books priced at 6*d* or less. Moreover, he concentrated more on books priced up to 4*d* than on the 5*d* to 6*d* range, although these were still well represented. Well over a third of his made-up books in stock[23] were valued at 2*d* or 2½*d* each. This category included the 500 copies of *Jack of Newbury* and the 475 copies of *Palladin of England* at 2*d* each, along with the 1086 copies of *Wise Virgins* and the 600 copies of *Books of Palmistrie* at 2½*d* each, stored in the warehouse. There were also 827 small octavos and duodecimos priced at 2½*d* each in the shop itself, along with fifty 'old' school books, and ten Testaments in sextodecimos at 2*d* apiece.

It is very tempting, and probably correct, to see the range of books valued at 2*d* and 2½*d* in the Tias inventory as earlier examples of the godly and merry books sold by all the specialist publishers at 2*d* each in the 1680s, when they were collected by Pepys. Pepys happened to have a duodecimo *Jack of Newbury*[24] and a pair of duodecimo *Art of Palmistry*[25] books from Tias's cheapest titles amongst his collection. However, a popular title could, and did, appear in several versions, as a broadsheet, a small book, a double-book or twenty-four page quarto, and in an extended quarto as a history.[26] A title registered with the Stationers' Company in one publisher's name could therefore presumably appear in many different formats. There is no necessary connection at all between the format and price at which Tias was publishing a title in the 1660s and the format and price at which the same title was issued twenty years later, in which it was perhaps collected by Pepys. This is true even when the same title was sold by Tias's direct heir Passinger, and his partner Thackeray.[27] On the other hand, there is the commonsense connection that a 2*d* or 2½*d* octavo title which sold well in the 1660s was liable both to be issued in the same format in the 1680s as in the 1660s, and also to be imitated by the other chapbook publishers. Hence the proliferation of *Art of Palmistry* chapbooks, amongst many others. Moreover an examination of survivals, and of the registers of the Stationers' Company, shows that small merry and small godly books were certainly being produced by the trade before the time of Tias. Anthony Wood collected a chapbook dealing with the execution of a 'Popish traitour', remarkably dated as early as 1581, as well as two others dealing with the adventures of pirates, produced in 1639.[28] A book of carols printed for Francis Coles survives from 1642.[29]

In 1656, Coles, Wright, Vere and Gilbertson entered the titles of 'ten little bookes' in the register of the Stationers' Company.[30] Actual examples of these little books produced by Vere and Gilbertson, who were known for their production of ballads, survive from the following year.[31] Small books as well as quartos were also produced for Francis Grove, who was freed as early as 1623 and died the year before Tias.[32] The establishment of the 'merry' book in popular esteem is forcibly testified by a song for chapmen printed in 1652, which opened 'Will you buy a new merry Booke' before moving on to sell ballads.[33] John Andrews of the White Lion near Pye-Corner had a godly trade-list of two titles selling at 3*d* and seven at 2*d* in 1659. All but one of these tracts survive (see pp. 105–6, n. 36); four of them were collected by Pepys in versions reprinted later in the century. Tias's small octavos and duodecimos in stock in 1664 are therefore very likely indeed to have been small godlies and merry books. By 1666, Gilbertson had a list of no less than thirty-one book titles.[34]

Tias was almost as heavily involved in the production of books at 3*d* and 4*d* as those at 2*d* and 2½*d*, however.[35] They included 375 copies of *Guy of Warwick*, with 166 of a title that has vanished beyond recall, both at 3*d* each in the warehouse. There were also 1235 copies of *Pathway to Health*,[36] 549 copies of a chapbook that was probably *Palmerin of England*,[37] 125 copies of a chapbook that was probably *Montelion*, and sixty copies of a work on *Comfort* which was almost certainly a godly chapbook,[38] all valued at 4*d*. These were augmented by 117 'paper' books in the shop at 3*d*, and 335 books described as 'small octavos bound' with another 200 'large octavos' and 166 'school books', presumably new this time, in the shop, all at 4*d*.

Just as it seems plausible to suggest that Tias's 2*d* or 2½*d* books

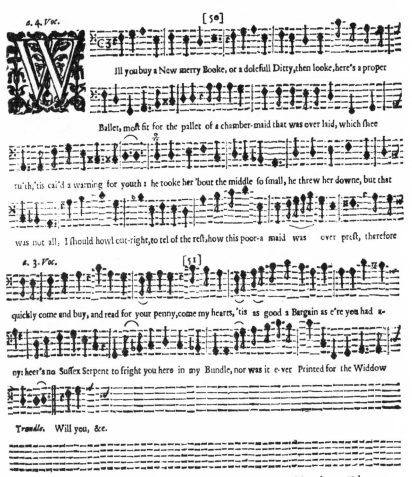

'Will you buy a New Merry Booke'

were small merry and small godly books, already a well-established line by 1664, so also does it seem plausible to suggest that many of his 3*d* and 4*d* books may have been the ancestors of the 'double-books' which figured on trade-lists in the 1680s (see below, pp. 130, 266). Again, the survivals show that the twenty-four page quarto was an established phenomenon by the date of the Tias inventory. Remark-

ably enough, since the survivals are by no means common, one of them
was produced for Tias himself.[39] An undated *History of Parismus*
remains to us as a tangible testimony to the existence of this seventeenth-century shop on London Bridge. However, it is by no means
alone. Jane Bell produced a *Guy of Warwick* in this format in 1659.[40]
The men who dominated the ballad trade were also producing books
in this format. An *Arthur* produced for Francis Coles survives from
1660, an *Adam Bell* for Francis Grove from 1661, and a *Robin Hood*
for Vere and Gilbertson from 1662.[41] The leading figures in the trade
had been, or were, all in the process of diversifying. Tias's *Guy of
Warwick*, *Palmerin* and *Montelion*, valued at 3*d* and 4*d*, are therefore
likely to have been in this format also.[42] Deacon's double-books were
priced at 3*d* in the 1680s. Pepys collected a group of them in the
Vulgaria including Deacon's *Bevis of Southampton* and *Robin
Hood*,[43] as well as Brooksby's *Guy of Warwick*.[44] If Tias's 2*d* and 2½*d*
books were small godly books and small merry books or octavos in
Thackeray's and Pepys's terms, and his 3*d* and 4*d* books were
twenty-four page quartos, made up of three sheets, it is at least
logically possible that some of his 5*d* and 6*d* titles were the forerun-
ners of the quarto histories of Thackeray's trade-list bound up by
Pepys in his *Vulgaria*. Tias had far fewer books priced at 5*d* and 6*d*.[45]
Amongst them were 375 *Soliliquies* and 221 of another title, again
erased by time, at 5*d*, and 673 of *Valentine and Orson* with 348 of
Amadis of Gaul[46] and 344 copies of *Poor Robin*, all at 6*d*. They were in
the warehouse when the inventory was made, and nothing in that price
range happened to be in the shop.

Survivals again show the active involvement of the predecessors of
the Ballad Partners in the production of this size of history earlier in
the seventeenth century.[47]

There is very little information in the Pepys collection on the
pricing of the histories. What there is, is on the shorter quartos of
forty-eight pages or more, which were made up of at least six sheets
of paper.[48] Deacon's quarto *History of the Gentle Craft* was advertised at 6*d*[49] and Pepys's copy contained sixty pages.[50] By inference,
Deacon's *Triumphant Weaver*, which appeared unpriced on all his
trade-lists, and was fifty-two pages long,[51] should have been approximately the same price. Pepys also had a copy of Passinger's
History of Argalus and Parthenia,[52] fifty-eight pages long, which
appeared advertised 'in quarto, stitcht, price 6*d*'[53] on a trade-list of

THE
Pleaſant Hiſtory
OF
PARISMUS
Prince of Bohemia.

DECLARING

Many Admirable Paſſages concerning his
Love to the Vertuous LAURANA,
onely Daughter to DIONYSIUS
King of *Theſſaly*.

WITH

A Narrative of His Wonderful Atchievements in
Feats of Chivalry, whereby he purchaſed to
Himſelf a Name Dignified with Honor
and Renown.

Very Pleaſant *and* Delightful *to* Read.

London, Printed by *J.B.* for *Charls Tyus,* at the Sign of the
Three Bibles on *London*-Bridge.

Tias's title page of 'Parismus'

John Williamson's. It looks very much as if forty-eight to sixty page unbound quartos were 6d each in the 1680s.

Whether or not it is fair to interpret Tias's inventory in terms of the prices of the 1680s for equivalent publishers, there is no doubt that in 1664 Charles Tias was putting his emphasis on the lower range of the chapbook market, and principally on the books priced at 2d to 4d, which made up over two-thirds of his stock. His attention seems to have been almost equally given to the 2d and 2½d books, which were probably octavos and duodecimos, and the 3d and 4d books, which were probably shorter quartos. But by no means all his stock was in book form.

The appraisers noted, as they searched the house on London Bridge, no fewer than 400 reams of books.[54] They sometimes specified whether these were small books. Two hundred and seventy-six reams were only listed as 'books', or 'in quires', ninety-four of them as small books, thirty as mixed duodecimos and twentyfourmos.

Four hundred reams represents about 200,000 sheets, reckoning 500 sheets to the ream.[55] If these were to be made up in the same proportions as the books ready to go out, these sheets in turn represent something in the order of 80,000 books printed and ready to make up.[56] Tias's total chapbook stock, including both the reams ready to make up and the 10,000 copies ready to go out, was probably around 90,000 books.

This compares very interestingly with the scale of operations of the French chapbook publishers. The rise of the Oudot family of Troyes, which produced the *bibliothèque bleue,* has been chronicled.[57] After 1672 Nicholas Oudot gave up his official position as printer to the Bishop of Troyes to concentrate on the more lucrative pedlars' booktrade. His son Jacques died in 1722. The inventory of his movables shows that he had at his death 36,000 books ready to go out, and over one-and-a-quarter million sheets[58] printed but not made up. Charles Tias had in 1664 only a quarter this number of books, and just under one-sixth the number of printed reams of paper. On the other hand, Tias is not known as an outstanding figure in the English trade: Coles, Vere and Wright, his contemporaries who were within the Ballad Partnership, are likely to have been much more substantial men. Furthermore, Tias died seventy years earlier than Jacques Oudot.[59] This seventy years coincides with the period in which the chapbook trade is generally supposed to have first expanded in England. If a relatively unimportant man outside the Ballad Partnership was operating on this scale in the 1660s, it seems safe to assume that the English chapbook trade was at least as flourishing as the French.

Tias's production of ballad sheets was relatively unimportant compared with his production of chapbooks. He had only seventy-five reams of ballads in the shop and stored about the house, which would convert into about 37,500 ballad sheets.[60] Chapbooks were between twice and three times as numerous as ballads in Tias's printing business at his death. Yet Thomas Passinger, who acquired his business, became known as one of the Ballad Partners. The question of whether the title is the most apt description of the activities of this group of men or whether it only reflects the interests of those first investigating the trade, is immediately raised.

The inventory of Josiah Blare,[61] taken on 16 May 1707, lists 31,002 'great and small bookes' in the shop. He had three times as many books ready to go out as Tias, and this part of his business was on a scale only slightly smaller than that of Jacques Oudot. On the other hand, he only had 257 reams of printed paper in stock,[62] compared with Tias's 400 and Oudot's 2578. The substantial profits made by Blare from his business have already been discussed (see above, p. 89). In the circumstances, it is particularly tantalizing that we shall never know whether Tias, forty years before, working on a larger scale, had also been able to save so comfortably.

Blagden wrote of the slow demise of the broadside ballad, which 'guttered out in the stronger light of the eighteenth century chapbook'.[63] Although recent writers have modified this to emphasize the gradual change in popular taste in the second half of the seventeenth century, which encouraged the growth of chapbook printing, the chapbook is still treated as a largely eighteenth-century development. As Victor Neuburg recently wrote,

> it was towards the publication of this kind of material that a number of leading men in the ballad trade had turned towards the end of the seventeenth century, so that by the 1690s chapbooks had begun to appear in quite considerable numbers.[64]

In the light of the Tias inventory, it is possible to revise the dating of this development, and to say that already by the 1660s chapbook production was far more important than ballad production. Indeed, it is also possible to suggest by inference that the Ballad Partners, at least by Passinger's generation, may well have kept this title because they held their stock in a building which was traditionally known as the Ballad Warehouse; and also because they have been studied almost exclusively by ballad specialists. The rare survivals from before the Civil War show, with the entries in the Stationers' Registers, that the diversification in the trade began long before Tias. Until inventories for the predecessors of the Ballad Partners turn up, showing the different importance that they placed on ballads and on books, it will be difficult to pinpoint the point in time at which the trade began to change its emphasis. It is now only possible to say that this change of emphasis had happened before 1664. It is impossible to see any reason why Thomas Passinger and his partner William Thackeray should have put the clock back and concentrated more on ballads than on chapbooks, since Passinger's master Tias had obviously found it profitable to concentrate more on the chapbook side of his business than on the ballads.

It would be interesting to know whether the growth of the paper industry in England stimulated the chapbook trade further. Rising imports of white paper supplied the demand for paper until the 1670s, when the major expansion for home production began. From then onwards, the production of coarse white paper at home increased.[65] Although Tias's attention was already fixed on the chapbook market before this development, it may well have urged the group of chapbook publishers whose work was collected by Pepys into greater activity. Certainly, survivals of the work of the Ballad Partners and their associates are much commoner from the 1670s on, but this may of course be nothing but an optical illusion, based on a combination of accidents and the work of collectors like Wood and Pepys.

The Tias inventory suggests not only that we should revise our ideas on the relationship between seventeenth-century ballad and chapbook production in a very radical way. It also adds another piece of evidence suggesting that cheap print may have been more accessible to the public in seventeenth-century England than has generally been realized. Blagden estimated the number of almanacs produced annually for the Stationers' Company in the 1660s at 300,000 to 400,000, or one for every three families.[66] In 1664, Charles Tias had around 90,000 octavo and quarto chapbooks in his shop, house and warehouse. There is no means of establishing his rates of turnover, but this is at least a fifth of the Stationers' Company production of almanacs and possibly as much as a third. Tias, of course, had no monopoly in the trade. If the Tias volume of chapbooks in stock is compared with Gregory King's estimate of the population in 1688, twenty-four years later, this is around one for every fifteen families. Josiah Blare had one chapbook in his shop for every forty-four families in the kingdom, even leaving all his reams of printed paper out of account.[67] And Blare was one of a quite considerable group of men supplying the market. It seems likely from the numbers and distribution of the chapmen through England that chapbooks had a quite high chance of being distributed over large parts of it. Even without evidence on marketing, however, Charles Tias's and Josiah Blare's shops between them provide enough evidence to modify the seventeenth-century history of cheap print somewhat. Thomas Back and John Love, who must have spent a very dusty time counting chapbooks and reams of paper on London Bridge and in Tooley Street in 1664, deserve our thanks.

NOTES AND REFERENCES

1 Blagden, C. (1953–4) *Notes on the Ballad Market in the Second Half of the Seventeenth Century*, Papers of the Bibliographical Society of the University of Virginia 6, 161–79, covers the period between 1655 and 1693. His work has recently been extended both forwards and backwards in time by Thomson, R. S. (1974) 'The Development of the Broadside Ballad Trade and its Influence upon the transmission of English Folk-songs', University of Cambridge PhD. I am indebted to Professor Thomson for his permission to refer to his work. He is at present engaged on the trade relationships of the Partners and their associates, he tells me by personal communication.

2 I would like to thank Dr Malcolm Kitch, who directed me to the records of the Court of Orphans, and Dr Marc Fitch, who searched, albeit unrewardingly, the slips from which the British Record Society volumes on the Archdeaconry and Commissary Courts of London are at present being prepared, for the wills of men involved in the trade that were not found by Blagden.

3 They may still be awaiting cataloguing in the Prerogative Court

of Canterbury, of course. It is particularly irritating that the original inventory of John Clarke, which according to the index exists in the Archdeaconry Court of London, is missing from the box in which it should be.

4 For Tias, Deacon and Blare, see Thomson, thesis cit., 61, 69–72; Bates, Brown, Norris and Midwinter, 74–5.

5 See also Blagden, art. cit., 178–9 for imprints and testamentary references, and 180 for apprenticeships.

6 Grassby, R. (1970) 'Personal Wealth of the Business Community in Seventeenth-Century England', *Economic History Review*, 2nd series 23, 224, 229. This is not a true comparison; Grassby's figures are drawn from the Court of Orphans, and it is therefore misleading to compare a figure drawn from a probate inventory with them. It may, however, give a minimum standard of comparison.

7 Public Record Office (PRO), Prob. 11 377, f. 133. There ought to be, and is not, an account of Wright's estate in the Court of Orphans.

8 The possibility that Blare's wealth was inherited has to be considered, but can probably be dismissed. The boy was apprenticed in 1675, and his father was a 'mealman' of Guildford, where his master Passinger's father was a 'gentleman' (Blagden, art. cit., 180). Mealmen, corn-badgers and maltsters, the middlemen in the corn trade, were normally more prosperous than husbandmen, but less prosperous than the most substantial yeomen in the countryside, although some examples of capitalistic maltsters have been found. The two maltsters whose inventories survive for the 1660s in the Lichfield area, for instance, left goods worth only £48 and £132 respectively. Vaisey, D. G. (ed.) (1969) 'Probate Inventories of Lichfield and District, 1568–1680', Collections for a History of Staffordshire, 4th series 5, Staffordshire Records Society, 124–5, 146–7. Other examples from before 1640 are to be found in Everitt, A. (1967) 'The Marketing of Agricultural Produce', in Thirsk, J. (ed.) *Agrarian History of England and Wales*, Cambridge, 549, 556.

9 Twenty-three different people owed him money, mostly in small sums. The proportionately very large sums owing to Tias and Deacon in good and bad debts arouse the suspicion that they worked through their distributors, the chapmen, on a sale-or-

return basis. The amount of money owing to them therefore probably reflects a blurred image of the amount of stock they had out. This list of small sums owing to Bates by so many different people, does something to confirm the suspicion that publishers did indeed work on a sale-or-return basis, or, at least, offered generous credit.

10 Gent, T. (1746) *The Life of Mr Thomas Gent, Printer of York, written by himself*, London, printed 1832, 10, 19, 22, 92–3, 97, 113–14, 137 and 140–1.

11 It is not clear whether the £216 17s 2d owed by Mr Osborn to Midwinter for 'books and copies sold to several Persons in the Testator's Lifetime' should be added to this. John Osborn also owed Midwinter £400 on bond, written off as a bad debt, but had paid the interest of £20 due on this.

12 The very large sum owing to him includes these private loans as well as all the money owed to him on small notes, presumably by chapmen. It is therefore far more comparable with Blare's total savings than with debts owing to him.

13 PRO, PCC, Prob. 4 3652.

14 Corporation London Record Office, Common Serjeants' Books, 6, f. 34.

15 ibid., 6, f. 162.

16 ibid., 5, f. 160b, Box 40.

17 PRO, PCC, Prob. 4 8224. This inventory would be worth publishing in entirety if it were not in such very bad condition. Parts of it have been obliterated beyond recall even under ultra-violet light. I here discuss only the portions at which a reasonable guess can be made. I am particularly grateful to Mrs Jane Cox, Mrs Helen Forde, Mr Christopher Kitching and Mr Irvine Gray of the Public Record Office, who between them made the inventory available, and helped check my partial transcript. Dr Christopher Harrison, of Keele, has also spent time examining photographs of the document.

18 It is very possible that the values per copy given in the inventory represent wholesale rather than retail prices. In the eighteenth century there is a record of a customer buying penny books wholesale at thirteen or fourteen to the dozen for 9d. Neuburg, V. (1968) *The Penny Histories*, London, 30–1. Also, the seventeenth-century chapbook specialists advertising for the

chapmen stressed the 'reasonable rates' at which they would be supplied.

19 Even here, the 'm' of Amadeus looks much more like 'en'.

20 This seems to have a trade term.

21 The description of this item has tantalizingly, almost completely disappeared.

22 A minimum of 9626.

23 At least 3548 copies.

24 *PM*, II (50), 1149–71. This happened to be W. Thackeray's dated 1684. He also had the long quarto version issued by Passinger and Thackeray, *Vulgaria*, III (19).

25 'The most Pleasant and Delightful Art of Palmistry', *PM*, II (8), 153–68, and 'The Whole Art of Palmistry', *PM*, II (9), 169–84. These were sold by Deacon and Dennisson, and Brooksby respectively. He had octavos of 'Seven Wise Masters and Seven Wise Mistresses', *PM*, III (5 and 6), 451–626 and 627–807, but he did not own a version of the 'Wise Virgins' which was, with the 'Pathway to Heaven', Tias's biggest line.

26 See, for instance, 'Dr Faustus', which was registered as a ballad in 1624 (Rollins, H. (reprinted 1967) *Analytical Index to the Ballad Entries in the Stationers' Registers, 1557–1709*, Hatboro', Penn., no. 615) and which Pepys had in a twenty-four page octavo version, *PM*, I (54), and in extended quarto, *Vulgaria*, III (14). 'Guy of Warwick' appeared as a ballad (Rollins, op. cit., no. 2119) and as a twenty-four page octavo (*PM*, I (44)). Tias's 375 copies of 'Guy' were priced by the appraisers at 2*d* each. Later in the century, Anthony Wood, like Pepys, also acquired a 'small merry' version of 'Guy' (Wood, 254(2)). Jane Bell's version of 1659 was a twenty-four page quarto (LC, 1284(2)). The early surviving version of the story printed for Thomas Vere of the Ballad Partners in 1649 was over a hundred pages long (Wood, 321(3)). It continued to be printed as a 'History' alongside the small merry versions, and was collected by Pepys in this format also (*Vulgaria*, III (9)). Such examples can be multiplied many times.

27 An immediate confirmation of this is given by examination of the printing of 'Jack of Newbury'. Tias's 500 copies were valued at 2*d* each in 1664. Passinger published a quarto 'Jack of Newbury' in 1682 with approximately eighty leaves which was bought by

Wood, possibly secondhand, for 6*d* in February 1677 (Wood, C.32(3)). I am grateful to Mr Paul Morgan of the Bodleian Library for looking at this book for me. Thackeray also produced a 'small merry' 'Jack' which survives as Wood, 254(8). Despite the variations in length and format of different versions, there was a high correlation between Tias's titles and those of Passinger's histories. Five of the six Passinger titles advertised in *Vulgaria*, I (4), and four of the six advertised in *Vulgaria*, II (2), had appeared in the legible parts of the Tias inventory.

28 Wood, 284(3 and 4).

29 Wood, 110A(2).

30 Eyre, G. E. B. (ed.) (1913) *A Transcript of the Register of the Company of Stationers, 1640–1708*, II, London, 55.

31 Wood had two, their 'biography' of Lilburne, 'The Self-Afflicter', Wood, 259(4) (1657), and the 'Most Sad and Terrible Narration of the Death of Michael Berkeley, Esq. . . .' who was tragically drowned in a duck pond, Wood, 284(9) (1658). The author of the former wrote 'to give you a view of his whole Life is to swell that up into a Volume which is meant for a single sheet'.

32 Blagden, art. cit., 169, 180; and 'The Famous History of Stout Stukeley . . .', Wood, 254(13) (nd). Grove's twenty-four page quarto *Adam Bell* was dated 1661, Wood, 321(6).

33 'Choice Collection of Catches . . .' Wood, 126 (1652), 50 (see illustration, p. 95).

34 Eyre, op. cit., 364. The system of registration seems to have broken down in the late 1650s; there are seventy pages of titles registered in 1655, forty in 1659–60, twelve in 1661–2 and only seven in 1665–6. It is therefore disappointing, but not surprising, to find no list of titles registered either by Sarah Tias on her husband's death or by Thomas Passinger on his assumption of the business, against which the titles given in Charles Tias's inventory could have been checked.

35 The appraisers noted at least 3475 of them.

36 It is difficult not to believe that the appraisers made a mistake here, and that this was not Arthur Dent's 'Plaine Man's Pathway to Heaven'. There were twenty-seven more copies, also at 4*d*, in the chamber on the street. The title this time was 'Dent's Pathway'. This was the book which made such an impression on John Bunyan, that omnivorous reader of chapbooks, when it came to

him in his wife's dowry. It had run through twenty-five editions before 1640 and seems to have reached literates at all social levels. A copy of a twopenny version of it produced in 1659 for John Andrews at the White Lion near Pye Corner survives in a group of nine godly chapbooks produced for Andrews in that year (LC, 2745).

37 The inventory probably reads '*Pelmiran* of England'. 'Palladine of England', listed further down, is also much clearer. Passinger and Thackeray jointly published in 1685 a 'Palmerin of England' collected by Pepys as his *Vulgaria*, I (1). It was in three parts, paginated consecutively, which together run to nearly 200 pages. Passinger, Tias's trade-heir, was advertising both of these 'histories' in the 'Destruction of Troy' (Part I), *Vulgaria*, I (4), which makes Tias's stock of both more likely.

38 There was another godly chapbook, on the Commandments, in the warehouse. The number of copies, the value of each, and most of the title have all vanished, but there were probably several hundred, since the total value of the stock of it was nearly £8.

39 LC, 1282(4). This title was, incidentally, registered to Francis Grove and William Gilbertson from March 1661 to August 1664. Blagden, art. cit., 169.

40 She earlier printed a much longer quarto version for Thomas Vere, illustrated below, p. 226 (Wood, 321(3)).

41 LC, 1282(2); LC, 1282(1); Wood, 321(6); and LC, 1282(3).

42 On the other hand, Tias also had 'small octavos' in the shop valued at 4*d*, which emphasizes the uncertainty of this sort of deduction.

43 *Vulgaria*, III (10), and *Vulgaria*, III (15), priced at 3*d* on the trade-list at back of 'Hocus Pocus or the Art of Jugling', *Vulgaria*, III (21).

44 *Vulgaria*, III (9).

45 A minimum of 1961.

46 The second letter is a dubious reading. It is partly erased but looks more like 'en' than 'm'.

47 One of the earliest survivals was produced for Henry Gosson, who was another of the dominant figures in the ballad trade, in 1616. It consisted of a set of unlinked stores thrown hastily together. 'The Honourable Prentice, or, this Taylor is a man . . .', Wood, C. 32(1).

48 'Sports and Pastimes', *Vulgaria*, IV (6) contains forty-eight pages. The author is describing a series of ways to fold a sheet of paper to resemble different objects, illustrated diagrammatically on the previous page, when on the last page of the text he suddenly writes, 'For the rest of the Figures I would have had cut, but I am tied to six sheets at present, which will not contain them'.

49 Trade-list, *PM*, I (4), 95.

50 *Vulgaria*, IV (12). The publisher of this appeared as Gilbertson at the Sun and Bible. However, Gilbertson and Deacon worked together sometimes. 'The Art of Legerdemain', which appeared on some of Deacon's trade-lists, which was collected by Pepys as *Vulgaria*, III (21). 'Hocus Pocus or the Art of Jugling' (eleventh edn) was brought out for J. Deacon to be sold by J. Gilbertson. It was sixty-two pages long. On the other hand, Anthony Wood noted that his 'Jack of Newbury' cost him 6*d* in February 1677 (see above, n. 27).

51 *Vulgaria*, IV (14).

52 *Vulgaria*, III (7).

53 At the end of *Vulgaria*, IV (15).

54 This figure is a minimum. I have adjusted the number of reams downwards when the lump sum given for their total value is lower than the numbers of reams specified indicates it should be. Thus seventy-five reams of quarto at 6*s* a ream 'in the Hall' priced at £17 2*s*, the value for fifty-seven reams, I have taken as the lower figure.

55 Blagden, art. cit., 175, tentatively suggests 510 sheets to the ream in his commentary on the 'Agreement' of 1689 between Thackeray, Millet and Milbourne. He does this by taking the ambiguous statement 'all future stock shall be reckon'd at ... 25 ½ Sheets to a Quire, and 20 Quires to a Ream' to mean that each quire contained twenty-five and a half sheets, rather than twenty-five half-sheets. The latter seems a more likely reading, and gives a ream of 500. Zupko, R. E. (1976) *British Weights and Measures: A History from Antiquity to the Seventeenth Century*, Madison, Wisc., 122, defines a ream of paper as containing 500 sheets. I have used 500 sheets to the ream. If Blagden's figures are right, I have, of course, underestimated Tias's numbers of books.

56 In view of Tias's strong emphases on his 2*d* and 2½*d* range and his 3*d* and 4*d* range amongst the books ready to go out, it seems right

to suppose that there were similar emphases amongst those standing in quires. If that supposition is correct, around 35 per cent (or
140) of his 400 reams were destined to be 2*d* and 2½*d* books. His
inventory in fact specifies that ninety-four reams were certainly
destined to be made up into small books. If these were twenty-
four page octavos, each printed on a sheet and a half, 140 reams of
500 sheets would have produced 46,666 of them. If they were all
to be made up into duodecimos, there could have been up to
70,000 of them. They are almost certain to have been mixed (see
above, p. 93) and the true total would therefore have been
between the two figures.

On the same assumption, a further 35 per cent (another 140
reams) of his unbound stock was destined to be 3*d* and 4*d* books.
If these were indeed double-books, twenty-four page quartos
each printed on three sheets, 140 reams of 500 sheets would have
produced 23,333 of them.

Similarly about ninety reams would have been destined to be
5*d* and 6*d* books. If these were six-sheet quartos, they would have
made up into some 7500 books.

Thirty reams would be left to make up into more expensive
books. The inventory in fact specifies that exactly thirty reams
were destined to be made up into mixed duodecimos and twentyfourmos. Elsewhere in the inventory it is apparent that these sizes
were used for thick little books, like Common Prayer books,
which sold at 8½*d* or 9*d*. These thirty reams would therefore not
make up into more than 4000 books at the most. In addition,
there were half a dozen 'Reders dictionarys' standing in quires at
10*s* each, and six Bibles in quires at 3*s*.

Even if the supposition that Tias's books made up, and those
standing in quires, were likely to bear a proportional relationship
to each other is wrong, the specific statements in the inventory
that ninety-four reams were of small books and thirty reams of
mixed duodecimos and twentyfourmos mean that the minimum numbers of books that these 400 reams could have represented was *c.* 50,000, and the maximum *c.* 190,000. The totals I
have given exclude completely twenty-four 'bundles' of 'small
books' and six 'bundles' of 'stitcht' quartos, as well as the numbers
of five of the twenty chapbooks stored in Tooley Street which are
completely illegible in the inventory. There were over a hundred,

and sometimes over 1000, of all but one of the other titles stored there.

57 Mandrou R. (1975) *De la Culture Populaire aux 17ᵉ et 18ᵉ Siècles*, Paris, 37–9.

58 Mandrou, op. cit., 39–40 and Appendix A, 199–201, for the inventory of Jacques Oudot. Mandrou followed the inventory and reckoned in dozens and reams. I have converted by 12 and 500 for comparative purposes.

59 A much more exact comparison would be between the fortunes of the Dicey family of Northampton and St Ives and the eighteenth-century Oudots. Unfortunately precision is impossible since there is no Dicey inventory to compare with that of Jacques Oudot, although there is plenty of general evidence both of Dicey prosperity and the scale of their operations. Neuburg, V. (1969) 'The Diceys and the Chapbook Trade', *The Library*, 5th series 24(3), 119–225.

60 Again, using a multiple of 500 sheets to the ream.

61 Corporation of London Record Office, Common Serjeants' Books, 5 (1694–1713), f. 160b, Box 40.

62 There is no means of telling definitely how much of this printed paper was ready to make up into the chapbooks with which Blare's name is generally associated, and how much of it represented ballad sheets. If it was intended for twenty-four page octavos, it would have made up into 85,667, again working on multipliers of 500 sheets to the ream, and one and a half of these to an octavo. Blare is likely also to have had relatively small stocks of double-books and histories at one end of the scale, and ballads at the other, however.

63 Blagden, art. cit., 179.

64 Neuburg, V. E. (1977) *Popular Literature: A History and a Guide*, Harmondsworth, 108. See also 76–8, 94–5, 103–5.

65 Coleman, D. C. (1958) *The British Paper Industry, 1495–1860*, Oxford, 50–6.

66 Blagden, C. (1960) *The Stationers Company*, London, 188, and (1958) 'The Distribution of Almanacs in the second half of the Seventeenth Century', *Studies in Bibliography*, Charlottesville, Va., xi. This is really one for every four families, using Gregory King's estimate of 1,360, 586 families in 1688.

67 If these are taken onto account (see above, p. 109, n. 62) he

had at least one for every twenty-six families, and maybe as many as one for every twelve families. As Professor J. Holt points out to me, the number of chapbooks actually printed and circulating gives an absolute minimum readership, since such cheap books almost certainly passed from hand to hand until they fell apart. I also have a suspicion that they were available for casual reading at the alehouses which formed the local bases for their vendors, the chapmen, much as old magazines are today to be found in dentists' and doctors' waiting-rooms.

V

The distributors: pedlars, hawkers and petty chapmen

❧

One vital link in the chain between the publishers of small books and histories who proliferated in late seventeenth-century London and made comfortable livings, and the audience at which their efforts were aimed, remains undiscussed. Unless a distribution network did indeed cover the kingdom and reach its tentacles across the country-side to supply the potential readership, arguments from probability remain unconvincing.

The publishers of the chapbooks and the ballads were quite clear about the way in which their wares were to be marketed. They did not set themselves up in the more reputable parts of London. They established their shops with an eye to their distributors, the chap-men, at whom all their advertising was aimed. Deacon, for instance, ended a quarto in 1686, 'Courteous Reader, these Books are Printed for, and sold by, J. Deacon, at the sign of the Angel in Guiltspur Street; where any Chapman may be Furnished with all sorts of small Books and Ballads'.[1] John Back's *Danger of Despair* of 1686 ended with a trade-list of further octavo and duodecimo books for sale at 2*d*,[2] and four more expensive bound quartos, all of which were 'Books printed for and sold by J. Back at the Black Boy on London Bridge, who Furnisheth any Countrey-Chapmen, with all sorts of Books, Ballads, and all other Stationery-Wares at reasonable Rates'. Thomas Passinger simply proclaimed that at his shop on London Bridge 'English and Irish chapmen . . . may be well-furnished, and have good Penniworths'.[3]

Nearly all the specialist publishers were congregated in two areas (see Map 1 p. 114). They either set up shop in the very rough part of town all round the Market at West Smithfield, where chapmen would con-gregate anyway for general trading purposes, or on London Bridge itself, which also had a general reputation as a popular and rather low

BOOKS Printed for, and are to be sold by J. Deacon, *at the Sign of the* ANGEL *in* Guilt-spur-street, *without* Newgate.

THe Art of Legerdemain, 4to

Markhams faithful Farrier, wherein the depth of his skill is laid open in all those principal and approved secrets of Horse-manship, in 8vo.

The History of the Gentle-Craft; containing many matters of Delight; very pleasant to read, in 4to. price 6 d

The Triumphant Weaver; Or, The Art of Weaving, in Verse; 4to.

The noble birth and adventures of *Robin Hood Bevis* of *Southampton.*

The Seven Champions of Christendom, in 4to.

Wisdoms Cabinet opened; Or, The Seaven Wise Masters of *Rome,* in 4to. price 3d.

Noble birth and adventures of *Robin Hood.*

The life and death of *Sheffery ap Morgan.*

The loyal Garland of mirth and pastime; to which is added the *Bellmans* loyal Verses.

A Groatsworth of Wit for a penny, Or the interpretation of dreams.

The True Tryal of Understanding; Or, Wit newly Revived: Being a Book of Excellent New Riddles. Very pleasant and Delightful to read.

At the above-mentioned place, any Countrey-Chapmen *or others, may be Furnished with all sorts of small* Books *and* Ballads.

Deacon's trade-list

J. Back, at the Sign of the Black-Boy on London-Bridge, near the Draw-Bridge, Furnisheth Country Chapmen or others, with all sorts of Small Books, Ballads, and all other Stationary-Wares at Reasonable Rates,

Back's advertisement

shopping area in the seventeenth century. So outside Newgate, between Holborn and Aldersgate Street, Thackeray, Clarke, Wright, Brooksby, Kell and Deacon were to be found. Passinger, Gilbertson, Back and Blare were all on London Bridge. Only Joshua Conyers, further out on Holborn, and Charles Dennisson, just inside Aldgate, amongst the specialist publishers, chose sites away from these two main concentrations.[4]

The next logical step in the enquiry therefore is an investigation into the numbers of these chapmen, and, if possible, their stock in trade, to see if the goods they carried really did include books. Few figures in Restoration England are quite as elusive as the peripatetic pedlar, but, as it happens, some information does survive from the very end of the century. In 1681, the author of the *Trade of England Revived* suggested that the proliferation of hawkers travelling the kingdom to sell goods both wholesale and retail, was, with the proliferation of small unspecialized shopkeepers, one of the main causes of the 'decay of trade'.[5] By 1685, an almanac called the *City and Country Chapmans Almanac*[6] was especially produced with this trading audience in mind. It contained lists of the fairs in England and Wales, arranged for each month of the year, a list of market towns in England and Wales arranged by county, to which the day of the week on which the market was held was added, and, as an aid to travel, a list of the stage towns on the roads out of London, with the distances between each. The arterial north road to Edinburgh, the north-west road to Chester and Holyhead, the 'middle west' road to Gloucester and to Pembroke, the west road to Plymouth and on to Cornwall, the south roads to Rye and to Dover, and the east road to Yarmouth, were all described, together with their branches. Road books for the

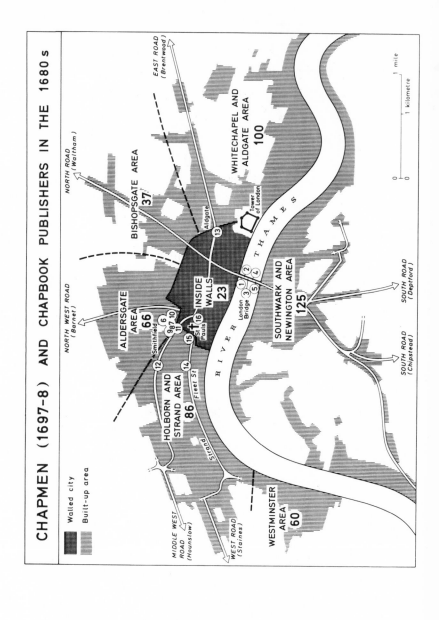

CHAPMEN (1697-8) AND CHAPBOOK PUBLISHERS IN THE 1680s

Walled city

Built-up area

NORTH ROAD (Waltham)

NORTH ROAD (Barnet)

NORTH WEST ROAD (Barnet)

BISHOPSGATE AREA **37**

EAST ROAD (Brentwood)

WHITECHAPEL AND ALDGATE AREA **100**

Aldgate

ALDERSGATE AREA **66**

Smithfield

6
9 8 7 10
11
St. 16
15 Pauls
14

INSIDE WALLS **23**

13

Tower of London

MIDDLE WEST ROAD (Hounslow)

HOLBORN AND STRAND AREA **86**

12

Fleet St.

Strand

London 1 2
Bridge 3 5 4

T H A M E S

WEST ROAD (Staines)

R I V E R

SOUTHWARK AND NEWINGTON AREA **125**

SOUTH ROAD (Chipstead)

SOUTH ROAD (Deptford)

WESTMINSTER AREA **60**

0   1 mile

0   1 kilometre

gentry had appeared early in the century, and itineraries giving fairs as early as 1625,[7] but this was the first publication of its kind. It continued to be printed annually for the benefit of traders, and was joined in the eighteenth century by regional guides to market towns.[8]

Hawkers and pedlars were not, as the author of the *Trade of England Revived* wanted, suppressed. Indeed, the reasons offered to the Lords in Parliament[9] against a Bill banning any trading by pedlars outside markets or fairs included the argument that such a suppression would be a danger to government, since there were about 10,000 pedlars and nine out of every ten of these were 'lusty stout, young fellows'. There were also economic arguments that pedlars were too important to trade to suppress, both because 'dealing with pedlars etc., is become a particular trade and many wholesale dealers have been bred up to it alone and have no other customers', and also

---

Map 1   Chapmen licensed in London, 1697–8, and chapbook publishers in the 1680s

> Bold numbers on the map represent chapmen licensed according to the Act of 1696–7 in each area
> Ringed numbers on the map represent publishers of octavo and duodecimo chapbooks bought by Samuel Pepys, 1661–88

1 THOS. PASSINGER, The Three Bibles, London Bridge
2 CHARLES PASSINGER, The Seven Stars, London Bridge
3 JAMES GILBERTSON, Sun and Bible, London Bridge
4 JOHN BACK, The Black Boy, near Drawbridge, on London Bridge
5 JOSIAH BLARE, The Looking Glass on London Bridge, near the church
6 WILLIAM THACKERAY, The Angel, Duck Lane, near West Smithfield
7 JOHN CLARKE, The Bible and Harp, near the Hospital Gate, West Smithfield (?formerly, James Bissell, The Bible and Harp in West Smithfield)
8 PHILIP BROOKSBY, Golden Ball, near Bear Tavern, and near Hospital Gate, at Pye Corner in West Smithfield
9 RIC. KELL, Blew Anchor in Pye Corner in West Smithfield
10 JOHN WRIGHT, next to the Globe in Little Brittain
11 JONAH DEACON, The Angel, Guildspur Street, without Newgate in St Sepulchre's parish
12 JOSHUA CONYERS, Black Raven in Fetter Lane a little above St Andrew's Church over against Ely House
13 CHARLES DENNISSON, Stationers Arms within Aldgate
14 M. WOOTON, Three Pigeons in Fleet Street
15 GEORGE CONYERS, Golden Ring on Ludgate Hill
16 ED. BREWSTER, The Crane, St Paul's Churchyard

because of the scale of their seasonal operations.

> This sort of men having been tolerated or connived at for 40 yrs last past are grown very numerous & into great credit & in the months of March, April and May buy commodities to the value of several hundred thousand pounds upon 6 or 8 months credit.

However, if such a noticeable group of men were not to be suppressed, an alternative suggested by both their numbers and the size of their trade was to treat them as a potentially profitable source of revenue. In 1696–7, an Act to license all hawkers and pedlars and petty chapman travelling on foot or with a pack animal at £4 a head for both man and beast was passed.[10] Each individual trading outside a market or fair was to carry a licence, on penalty of a £12 fine. Examination of the register of licenses under the Act of 1696–7 shows that by the end of the century the hawkers and pedlars were indeed worth taxing. Just over 2500 of them were licensed in the first year's operation of the Act.

The pedlar may have been a common figure in the 1690s, but he had already been well known for over a century. The pedlar had been the hero of ballads by the 1560s, when the song of the 'Pedlar and his Pack' was registered with the Stationers' Company.[11] A licensing procedure had been thought of as early as 1571–2.[12] A very real pedlar of little books was selling them in Balsham churchyard in Cambridgeshire in 1578.[13] When *The Winter's Tale* was written in 1611, Autolycus was therefore a character the audience was likely to know. Shakespeare gives a very full account of the pedlar's stock in trade.[14] Autolycus was, of course, a singer of the ballads he carried, which treated of courtship and of monstrous births and fabulous fish. The Register of the Stationers' Company, which deals, at one brief period in the 1560s, with the phenomena of monstrous fish in Holland, monstrous pigs at Market Raison in Lincolnshire and Salisbury, and a monstrous child at Maidstone, show how accurate this brief glimpse of popular taste was.[15] Autolycus carried tablebooks as well. But he also carried all the wares which were so important as courtship gifts, looking glasses, gloves, ribbons all the colour of the rainbow, necklets, bracelets, brooches, quoifs, stomachers and headgear. He did not carry perishables; the rustic who was unlucky enough to meet this plausible pick-pocket on the way to buy the food for the sheep-shearing feast had to go elsewhere for spices, sugar, rice and currants. But he did carry a wide range of textiles, cambrics and

A petty chapman

lawns, caddisses for garters, as well as trimmings like lace, and the inkles, tape and points that were so necessary a means of closing garments before the button became widespread, to be replaced in turn by the zip-fastener. The pins and thread in his pack were also absolutely essential tools to the housewife before ready-made clothing became widely available. Although this literary pedlar was shown selling to the poor, he also carried goods fit for the gentry. There were masks, perfume and poking sticks for ruffs in his pack. His counterpart in reality probably also had suitable patter and goods for the back doors of the gentry as well as the front doors of the village street. Sir Nicholas Le Strange, son of the High Sheriff of Norfolk, recorded in his jest book that 'a gentlewoman lov'd to buble away her mony in Bone-laces, pinnes, and such toyes, often used this short Ejaculation; God love me, as I love a Pedlar'.[16]

Autolycus is not said to have carried godly books, even though his audience amongst the feasting shepherds did include one man who 'sang psalms to hornpipes'. The pedlar who knocked on Richard Baxter's yeoman father's door in the village of Eaton Constantine under the Wrekin in Shropshire in the 1620s, was better provided for

Puritan readers. He carried 'some good books' as well as ballads.[17] The anonymous author of *The Downefall of Temporizing Poets*, who was concerned to castigate the ballad writer and his trade, estimated the total number of hawkers and ballad singers resident in London in 1641 at 317, of whom only forty were hawkers.[18] In 1668, there were still only forty-four officially approved hawkers selling mercuries in London. These figures, focused as they are on ballad singers and approved hawkers, cannot be compared with confidence with those of the 500 hawkers and pedlars selling all goods who gave London as their place of abode when they took out licenses under the Act of 1696–7. Common sense does suggest that a very considerable expansion had taken place in the numbers of such people between the 1640s, or even the 1660s, and the 1690s. A petition made by booksellers to the Stationers' Company in 1684 complained that the great number of hawkers selling great quantities of books both in London and at country markets was damaging the booksellers' retail trade.[19] The names of some of the hawkers licensed in 1697–8 suggest forcibly that although they might be catering for many other tastes and types of consumption as well as the audiences for ballads and books, they were still recognizably linear descendants of Autolycus. 'Homer' Roden was licensed for Kingston in Herefordshire, 'Dionysus' Brunt for Macclesfield, and the more simply nicknamed 'Merry Merry' for Charlbury in Oxfordshire.

The returns made to the Exchequer as a result of the Act of 1696–7 survive in a very detailed form.[20] They give the name of the hawker licensed, his, or often her, place of abode and county, number of pack-animals he or she had, and the total sum paid. It therefore seemed well worth analysing these returns, to see how these hawkers and petty chapmen who failed to evade the tax were distributed across the county in the late 1690s.

The pattern suggests that the licensing procedure may have been uneven; relatively few chapmen are licensed for East Anglia, for instance. Whatever the inaccuracies and vagaries of the licensing procedure, they were still distributed all over the country (see Map 2). The largest concentration was, of course, in London, where there were over five hundred of them. Over a fifth of these were based immediately south of the river, in Southwark and Newington Butts. They presumably worked on the southern roads to Rye and Dover, and presumably bought their stocks of chapbooks, if indeed they did carry such things, from the publishers like Thomas Passinger and

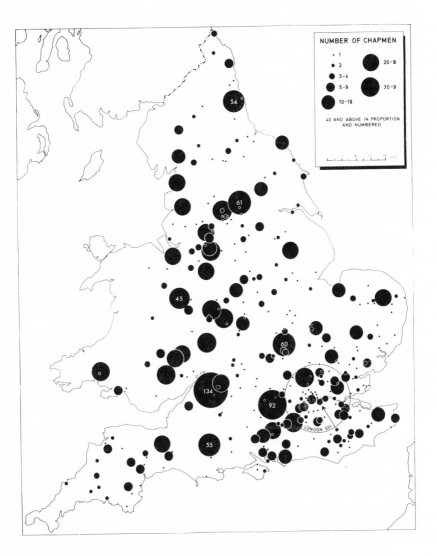

Map 2   Chapmen licensed in England and Wales, 1697–8

Josiah Blare on London Bridge. The other concentration of publishers round Smithfield Market was ideally sited to serve the needs of the considerable group of hawkers and pedlars living in the Holborn and Strand area, where the western roads to Cornwall and to Wales left London (see Map 1, p. 114).[21] Smithfield was equally convenient for travellers working the north-western road to Chester and so to Ireland.

A fifth of the chapmen licensed were in London, but many provincial towns from Newcastle-on-Tyne southwards had major groups of over forty of them. There were particularly large concentrations of them in the textile manufacturing areas of the West Riding and Lancashire, and on the edge of the Cotswolds. The same was true of the west Midlands metal area. A large number of them worked out, therefore, from the centres of manufacturing from which they acted as the distributors. Regional analysis of their inventories may well show groups of them specializing in the sale of the products of the region concerned.[22]

Just over half the chapmen licensed were based on the market town.[23] They were presumably stallholders there, bringing in a wider variety of goods from outside the area than had been familiar before. The little town of Cleobury Mortimer in the Clee Hills of Shropshire had a resident chapman, according to the parish registers, between 1622 and 1634.[24] In the same area, silks, laces, holland and tobacco became more readily available. It seems likely that chapmen like these licensed in a market town and actually resident there extended their activities over the marketing area during the rest of the week, in the manner of a peripatetic village shop. In any case the pattern of registration shows the extension of the web of travelling traders well beyond the old marketing centres. Consumer goods could certainly be bought away from the market towns then, just as the author of *The Trade of England Revived* had complained. Moreover there was a concentrated scatter of chapmen licensed in non-manufacturing areas of denser population. The Home Counties were noticeably well served by small groups of these distributors. But even in the most isolated areas, indefatigable individuals were also licensed as hawkers and pedlars. When Alston Moor in Cumberland, Allandale in Northumberland, and Padstow on the Cornish coast all had licensed chapmen in 1697–8, it is not unreasonable to say that the distribution network at which the specialist chapbook publishers aimed their advertising did indeed cover the remotest areas of the whole kingdom. If the chapmen bought books as one of their specialities purchased for a return journey from London, these books had a real, if highly erratic, chance of spreading even to the highest Pennines.

A preliminary survey of the items listed in the inventories of chapmen for the end of the seventeenth century and the beginning of the eighteenth century show some of them did have books in their packs. As common sense would suggest, this speciality was only one, and a small one at that, of the tremendous range of consumer goods available by the end of the seventeenth century. Not only were chapmen relatively poor, and highly mobile, but also appraisers were unlikely to list their goods in any detail. Even if books were generally not listed, other 'small wares' of low value were often lumped together in the inventories to make negative evidence of the absence of books as inconclusive as it was for the potential purchasers for them. No ballads at all have yet been found, although patently they continued to be printed and marketed in large numbers. They must simply have been too cheap for an appraiser to bother with. A basket of about two hundred ballads was stolen in 1696 in Kirby Lonsdale in Westmorland from a man who was highly likely to have been an itinerant, since his name does not appear in an exhaustive *index nominum* of all records for Kirby Lonsdale.[25] However, with all their omissions, enough itemized inventories exist to demonstrate something of the range of diverse goods available at the door in the 1690s. Amongst them, one possible selling line was the book.

John Cunningham, chapman of Great Chard in Kent, was only worth £26 2s 11d when his appraisers listed his goods in 1690.[26] He seemed, like many of the chapmen, to have no fixed abode at all, for he had no furnishings of even the most meagre sort. His clothes and ready money were his most considerable asset. Despite his poverty, he represented one of the minority of chapmen who had a pack animal licence in 1697, for his old horse, old pack-saddle, pair of hampers and packing cloth were worth £2 5s 0d. His hampers were full of textiles to be made up presumably by the purchasers at home, scotch cloth, over a hundred yards of holland in six different qualities, flaxen cloth, blue linen, striped dimity, narrow muslin, wide muslin, and his only made-up goods, muslin neck cloths at 9d each, and three shirts. Amongst all this cloth, the appraisers listed one Bible and 'some other books' at a total value of 3s. The entry is scarcely illuminating, but the books were there.

George Pool, of Brampton in Cumberland was almost as poor as
John Cunningham. His goods were worth about £30 in 1691, including £3 of ready money, and his only suit of clothes, consisting of one
coat, one waistcoat, the rest of his clothes and his watch, a very
precious object which was separately bequeathed in his will. He was
on foot, for he had no horse, but he did have a pack sheet and wrapper
worth 4s. The sheer weight and bulk of this pack makes the reader
more disposed to think that the carriers of such loads were likely to
be young men. The goods contained in George Pool's pack were
more varied than Cunningham's. By far the largest item was 'hair' presumably for wigs, valued at £7 8s 0d. He had no less than seventy-six
and a half yards of scotch cloth, various remnants, a parcel of sewing
silk, a parcel of bone lace and other lace, silk handkerchiefs in different
sizes and qualities, silk ties and tippets, an old wig, a dozen combs, a
hatband and fringe and eleven books valued at 9d each. The Cumberland farmer's wife had a chance then of buying one of the lengthier
histories (see pp. 96–8 and n. 51, pp. 255–6), if she so desired.

Thomas Allen, of Petworth in Sussex, had in 1692 a wider variety
of reading matter for sale than George Pool. He had thirty-seven
books priced at from 5d to 7d each, valued together at 17s 7d, as well
as a dozen Bibles priced from 1s to 2s, totalling £1 8s 2d.[27] Robert
Griffen, of Canterbury,[28] according to his appraisers, had more
again. Griffen, unlike Cunningham and Pool, was a man who occupied a house. This had three rooms and a washhouse, and was
furnished in very reasonable comfort, with a bed with curtains and
feather mattress and a chest of drawers in the best chamber, joint
stools and looking glasses and pewter in the hall. Griffen had £30
of ready money, as well as household furnishings arguing some
prosperity. His horse, with two pack-saddles, was in the yard. Not
only was he another mounted chapman, but his goods also included
four hampers, and 'tilts and boardes for the stall'. So his trade was
obviously based on his own stall, which he could presumably
assemble at any market. In his case, stall holding and a pack animal
went with much greater prosperity; he was worth £74 17s 4d in 1707.
His 'selling goods' were separately listed from his household effects;
they included a small trunk of lace, linen cloth, 'made' linen, and
handkerchiefs, knives and sheaths and other 'small toys', five small
looking-glasses 'and other selling ware'. He also had two and a half
dozen books at 10s, or 4d each; one and a half dozen books at 4s 6d,
or 3d each; and one dozen Bibles at £1. So those who went to market

within reach of Canterbury where Griffen set up his stall, certainly had the opportunity of buying books at $3d$ and $4d$.

The biographer of a chapman born in Galloway in 1783, who took to the road at the end of the century, and 'blended the departments of stationery and drapery ... vending muslins and poem-books by turns' suggested that there was a natural sequence in a chapman's career from carrying a pack to owning a shop.

> The first step was to save a little substance; the second, to extend their credit and augment their wares; the third, to bundle the pack on the back of a horse, with the view of remaining longer *out*, and displaying a more imposing stock of goods; the fourth, if they throve, to harness the said horse to a wagon; and the fifth and last to take a shop in a county town and vegetate tranquilly behind the counter.[29]

The case of William Johnson of Lincoln, who was born in Scotland where his father died insolvent and became a pedlar in England, is an instructive one. He carried a pack of linen as a pedlar and by 1718 was able to take up a small shop in Lincoln where he at first sold hardware, caps, handkerchiefs and other ready-made wear in linen. He became a wholesale linen draper and a freeman of the city and eventually left a fortune of between £8000 and £9000.[30] William Johnson's successful career from pedlar to freeman and shopkeeper suggests that the nineteenth-century Scottish model of a successful chapman's career may well hold true for earlier periods.

If this is so, then George Pool of Cumberland, travelling on foot carrying his pack, would have been near the beginning of his career. This seems very likely from the combination of evidence in Pool's will and inventory. Not only did he possess no household goods, but he also left his meagre effects to his sisters and brother, and his father was his executor. He is likely to have been a young man living, or at least based, at home. John Cunningham, still without household goods, but with a pack horse, was one step up on the ladder. The comfortable Robert Griffen, who had a horse and travelled the markets with his stall ready to put up, was far advanced in his career and was probably also a much older man.

The strong connection between chapmen and the market towns where so many of them were licensed in 1697–8 is witnessed not only by the physical evidence of the frames of market stalls appraised amongst the goods of the most prosperous of them, but also by market records. Lists surviving from Beccles in Suffolk of the trades represented at fairs include 'chapman' and 'bookseller', and the annual rentals of stalls at the three fairs from 1675 onwards show at least one chapman and sometimes as many as six were at each fair. Some of the names re-occur as regulars for years. In 1696 one Magg paid a stall rent as 'chapman and bookseller'.[31] It seems likely that chapman carried a medley of best-selling lines, which, as in the case of Cunningham and Griffen in Kent, Allen in Sussex, and Pool in Cumberland, may have included some books. The tradition continued into the nineteenth century. In the 1820s, pedlar dolls became popular. Examples survive of both men and women, carrying a miscellany of goods that Autolycus would have recognized immediately (see Plates 3 and 4).[32] Amongst the variety of goods displayed in the baskets or bags of these dolls were books. The connection between popular reading and markets and fairs still existed as late as the end of the nineteenth century. The late Alison Uttley, who was born in 1884 and grew up in a remote farm in Derbyshire, looked forward eagerly as a child to the books her mother brought her home from the market.[33]

Some chapmen were specialists in books and ballads. A good account of the trade survives in the reminiscences of an itinerant bookselling specialist travelling to Lochbroom in 1820. He carried stock of three 6*d* books and six 3*d* ones, six collections of songs and a quantity of almanacs. He disposed of his stock for sale at inns and sold at village shops as well as at private houses. He added to his attractions, as many other such salesmen did, by playing the Jew's harp.[34] Even in the late seventeenth century, as Maggs of Beccles indicates, there were chapmen who specialized more in the cheap books published with these vendors in mind than in the whole range of possible stock in trade.

The packman who called at the door, and those who were still stallholders at market, were not, of course, the only distributors of these cheap books. Just as shopkeepers in London might also travel with wares for sale at fairs,[35] so also might the relatively rare provincial bookseller who made such an impecunious living in the late seventeenth century. Michael Johnson, Samuel's father, who was a bookseller of Lichfield and found it extremely difficult to make a living, ran stalls at Birmingham, Uttoxeter and Ashby-de-la-Zouche in this fashion (see above, p. 75). Provincial booksellers like Johnson might sell some of the histories at their market stalls. Others, like the stationer of Norwich whose inventory was taken in 1629, might have some small books amongst their grander stock. He had nine primers and eleven small books valued at 2s together. By the 1690s, there were already provincial booksellers who specialized in one area of interest. Nevill Simmons of Sheffield was a specialist printing nonconformist authors, as befitted a man who was probably the son of the bookseller of Kidderminster and London who published over fifty of Baxter's works. The first evidence of his trade in Sheffield survives from 1692, when he held a very sizable book auction there. The auction catalogue shows Simmons courting the trade of 'Gentlemen and others', but he also depended on selling his books from door to door in the countryside. Otherwise he would not have spent £4 on a licence legalizing him as a hawker in August 1697. Simmons published books in Sheffield until 1724, often co-operating with George Conyers at the Golden Ring in Little Brittain, whose trade-list of 1688 shows him publishing quarto histories and octavo merry and godly books collected by Pepys in the *Vulgaria* and *Merriments* as well as longer works. Conyers advertised his books and ballads for country chapmen. Some of the books issued by his trade connection Simmons in Sheffield were very substantial works, but Simmons' list also included sermons selling at 2d and 4d. It seems likely that this specialist in nonconformist books made his living providing the important dissenting congregation in and around Sheffield with reading matter of many different levels of price and complexity. He was a respected member of the dissenting community, for his daughter married the minister of the chapel in 1724. Hawking books on foot was just one of the methods he was willing to use to reach his customers.[36]

There were other retailers of cheap books apart from the chapmen and the specialist booksellers. Some, like the widow of Lowestoft who had cheap books in 1590, might have a few books amongst completely different stock. In her shop she had seventy-nine volumes worth only 22s 2d together. They included twenty-two primers in English and eighteen ABCs.[37] Primers at 3d were stocked by mercers at Charlbury in Oxfordshire and in Ormskirk in Lancashire in the second and third decades of the seventeenth century, along with a whole range of general necessities including ironmongery and groceries as well as cloth.[38] Thomas Greenwood of Burton in Kendal called himself a blacksmith in his will in 1683.[39] But his inventory showed that he ran a shop as well as his smithy. It was a general store and in it, amongst bridles and stirrup leathers, silk and inkle, tape and thread, white sugar, salad oil, combs and tobacco were books worth £1 12s 0d. They were sandwiched between ribbons and woollen cloth, and were closely succeeded by almanacs, which in turn were jostled by looking glasses, hooks and eyes, ginger, starch and nutmegs. The general shop might also carry reading matter.

The distributive network of chapmen and chapwomen, at whom the Ballad Partners' and cheap book publishers' advertising was aimed, did, then, spread all over the kingdom. Some few of those whose inventories have been examined did indeed carry books. The values of those so far found varied from 3*d* to 9*d*. The evidence of the prosperity of some of the publishers, the increasing numbers of those attracted into the business, and the spread and functioning of their distributors does therefore permit us to say with some confidence that the chapbooks were available to the reader who wanted them, even in very remote areas.

NOTES AND REFERENCES

1 *Vulgaria*, III (21).
2 *PG*, 24, 508–9.
3 *Vulgaria*, I (4).
4 The other exceptions, G. Conyers, M. Wootton, and Edward Brewster, in the respectable publishing area of Fleet Street and St Paul's Churchyard itself, were also more reputable publishers who only dabbled in the cheap end of the market, from whom Pepys only very rarely picked up octavos and duodecimos. I am very deeply indebted to Mr Cedric Parry who, out of his close knowledge of seventeenth-century London, placed all the shops of the specialist cheap publishers on the map for me.
5 Thirsk, J. and Cooper, J. P. (eds) (1972) *Seventeenth Century Economic Documents*, Oxford, 392–3, 397.
6 Capp, B. (1979) *Astrology and the Popular Press: English Almanacs, 1500–1700*, London and Boston, 355.
7 Morgan, V. (1979) 'The Cartographical Image of "The Country"', *Transactions of the Royal Historical Society*, 5th series 29, 150 and n. 64. Thomson, R. S. (1974) 'The Development of the Broadside Ballad Trade and Its Influence on the Transmission of English Folksongs', University of Cambridge PhD, 180.
8 For instance 'A Book of Fairs; Or, A Guide to the West-Country Traveller . . .', LC, 2737 (19).
9 Leicestershire Record Office, Finch Mss, PP 159. The document

is undated, but possibly of the 1690s. I am very grateful to Dr Peter Clark for this reference.

10 *Statutes of the Realm*, VII, 266–9, partly reprinted in Thirsk and Cooper, op. cit., 423–6.

11 Rollins, H. (1924) *Analytical Index to the Ballad Entries in the Stationers' Registers, 1557–1709*, I (reprinted 1969), Hatboro', Penn., 178.

12 Historical Manuscripts Commission (1872) *Third Report*, London, 96.

13 Spufford, M. (1974) *Contrasting Communities*, London, 208.

14 *The Winter's Tale*, Act IV, Scene ii, and Scene iii, 133–327 and 600–23.

15 Arber E. (1875) *A Transcript of the Registers of the Company of Stationers of London*, 1554–1614, I, London, 311–37.

16 Lippincott, H. P. (ed.) (1974) Sir Nicholas Le Strange (1603–55) *Merry Passages and Jeasts: A Manuscript Jest Book*, Salzburg Studies in English Literature: Elizabethan and Renaissance Studies 29 (117), 44.

17 Keeble, N. H. (ed.) (1974) *The Autobiography of Richard Baxter*, London, 3, 7.

18 Reference from Thomson, thesis cit., 178.

19 Information on approved hawkers of 1668 and the booksellers' petition of 1684 from McKenzie, D. F. (1976) 'The London Book Trade in the Later Seventeenth Century', Sandars Lectures, typescript, Cambridge University Library, 25–6.

20 PRO, AO, 3/370.

21 Chartres, J. A. (1977) 'The Capital's Provincial Eyes: London's Inns in the early eighteenth century', *The London Journal* 3 (1), 29–33, demonstrates the way London inns at the end of these arterial routes served specific regions of the country and acted as bases for the regional carrying trades. These carrying trades expanded notably between 1681 and 1715. Chartres, J. A. (1977) 'Road Carrying in England in the Seventeenth Century: Myth and Reality', *Economic History Review*, 2nd series 30 (1), 78–9. It seems very reasonable to view the increase in the number of hawkers and pedlars on the roads noted by contemporaries in the 1680s and 1690s as part of the same phenomenon.

22 I am at present (1980) engaged in such an analysis, which I hope to complete shortly.

23 From comparison with the lists of market towns given in Everitt,

A. (1967) 'The Marketing of Agricultural Produce', in Thirsk, J. (ed.) *Agrarian History of England and Wales*, IV, 1550–1640, Cambridge, 467–76.

24 Goodman, K. W. G. (1978) 'Hammermans Hill: The Land, People and Industry of the Titterstone Clee Hill Area of Shropshire from the Sixteenth to the Eighteenth Centuries', University of Keele PhD, 111–12.

25 Kendal Quarter Sessions Indictment Book, 1692–1724. I owe this information to the kindness of Sarah Harrison.

26 Kent Archives Office, Maidstone, PRC/27/32/113.

27 Kenyon, G. H. (1958) 'Petworth Town and Trades, 1610–1760', *Sussex Archaeological Collections* 96, 70. I am grateful to Dr Claire Cross for this reference.

28 Kent Archives Office, Maidstone, PRC/11/67/89.

29 A memoir prefixing the second edition of the poems of William Nicholson (1828), Dumfries.

30 Lincolnshire Record Office, Ecclesiastical Court Papers, Box 69/8. I am very grateful to Dr Peter Clark for this reference.

31 Microfilm in Suffolk Record Office, Ipswich, JC1/41/4 from original in Beccles Town Hall, Rix Div. 4, 365, 366 ff.

32 Notably in the collection of Bethnal Green Museum, e.g. Misc. 4 48–1925 and Misc. 2/1924.

33 Personal communication.

34 Magee, W. (1830) *Recollections of a Personal Interview with the Late Laird of Dundonnell at his Cottage in Lochbroom, during a tour through the North Highlands in 1819–20*, Edinburgh.

35 Historical Manuscripts Commission, op cit.: Letters of Robert Gray, shopkeeper of London, who travelled with wares for sale at fairs, 1606–18.

36 I am very grateful to Dr David Hey, who identified Nevill Simmons for me, and gave me the information on his family connections from the Sheffield parish register, as well as the reference to Hester, G. (1893) *Nevill Simmons, Bookseller and Publisher: with notices of Literature connected with Old Sheffield*, London.

37 I am grateful to Nesta Evans, Rachel Garrett, Ursula Priestley and Helen Sutermeister, for these and other examples.

38 Vaisey, D. G. (1965) 'A Charlbury Mercer's Shop 1623', *Oxoniensis*, 108.

39 I owe this reference to the kindness of Dr John Marshall.

VI

The contents of Samuel Pepys's collection and the *bibliothèque bleue*

❧

In 1964, Professor Robert Mandrou wrote his *De la Culture Populaire aux 17ᵉ et 18ᵉ Siècles*,[1] a study of the content of the little blue-covered paper books sold at two sous a time, from the early seventeenth century onwards. Although his work has been amended and modified, his book swung the whole current of thought amongst French social historians. He may truly be said to be the founder of the *'mentalité'* school, which seeks both to examine popular attitudes, and to put such examinations on a sound quantified base. Although the English material exists for a comparative study, it has not yet been made, although the attention of English social historians has recently turned to popular print.[2]

Troyes was one of the old Champagne fair towns which had a revival in the sixteenth and seventeenth centuries based on the making of cotton caps and the knitting of stockings. It therefore acted as a natural distribution centre from which pedlars worked. The town had a group of just under a dozen printer-booksellers at the end of the sixteenth century. One of these, Nicholas Oudot, had the idea of issuing a cheap series of simplified fairy stories, rewritten medieval romances and saints' lives. This series was so successful, that, when he died in 1636, he had already issued 100 titles. His own son, Nicholas Oudot junior, gave up his official role of printer to the Bishop of Troyes to concentrate on the more lucrative pedlars' book trade. It was his son, Jacques, whose scale of business has already been compared with that of Charles Tias and Josiah Blare in England (see above, pp. 98–9), who had, at his death in 1722, 36,000 books ready to go out, and one-and-a-quarter million sheets printed, but not bound. Moreover, the Oudot family was not alone, by the end of the seventeenth century; rivals in Troyes itself had followed a lead which led to great prosperity. By the mid-eighteenth century, every French provincial town had its publishers of pedlars' literature.[3]

Professor Mandrou based his analysis upon a group of about 450 items from the *bibliothèque bleue de Troyes.* Unfortunately, the dates of publication of the series cover a period from the seventeenth century right through to the nineteenth, and some of them are also longer, presumably therefore much more expensive, than the little twenty-four page, two sous, publications with which the Oudots were principally concerned.[4] However, the material undoubtedly exists for an English comparison. The seventeenth-century prose chapbook in England has been little studied.[5] The collection of chapbooks made by Samuel Pepys and now surviving in the Pepys Library at Magdalene College, Cambridge, is the best English collection on which to base a comparison of cheap little paperbacks sold in England with Mandrou's classic study of those sold in France.

It is a more limited but also a more concentrated collection. Pepys's *Vulgaria* bound up in four volumes, *Penny Merriments* bound up in three volumes, and *Penny Godlinesses* bound up in one volume, contain altogether 215 items. There are fifty-five quartos in the *Vulgaria*, and 160 surviving octavos and duodecimos[6] in the *Merriments* and *Godlinesses*. The question of what constitutes a chapbook is of course a very real one. There is no doubt at all that the religious publications bound separately by Pepys in the *Penny Godlinesses* were chapbooks to their publishers. Small godly books made up as much as 31 per cent of all the specialist publishers' titles on their trade-lists (see below, Table II, p. 134), and this pious group of chapbooks formed numerically one of the largest groups collected by Pepys. The identification of the little twenty-four page quartos in the third and fourth volumes of the *Vulgaria* with the 'double-books' on the trade-lists (see above, pp. 95–6, and Appendix, pp. 262–7), and the identification of the medium-length quartos with 'histories' priced around *6d* (see above, pp. 96–8), means that at least some of the items in the *Vulgaria* should certainly be classified as chapbooks also, and included in a consideration of the contents of the collection. I have, however, excluded twenty-two of these items, all those with over seventy-two pages, on the grounds that they would have cost over 6*d*, and are far too long to be considered as works that could sell at a really 'popular' price.[7] I can be faulted in this decision on the grounds both that the really long 'Histories' did appear on Thackeray's trade-list of chapbooks (see below, Appendix, p. 267) and that they were also advertised for chapmen to market. However, I have, rightly or wrongly, taken the probable selling cost of the books as the decisive criterion in whether to include them.

I have only therefore included 193 items in my analysis of the contents of Pepys's collection. To them I have added the forty-five almanacs also collected by Pepys, solely for the purpose of numerical comparison with Mandrou's findings on the *bibliothèque bleue*, since the latter contained almanacs in his analysis.

Despite its smaller size compared with the *bibliothèque bleue*, the collection is big enough to give a basis for a quantitative as well as a qualitative idea of the themes of the chapbooks in circulation, particularly since it was mainly accumulated in a single decade. This is so providing always that Pepys collected both a random, and a sufficiently wide selection of the material on the market.

Over half of Pepys's chapbooks are dated.[8] From these dates it seems that he began to collect, in a very sporadic way, in the early 1660s.[9] From 1661, he collected one or two dated chapbooks at least every second or third year, until 1676. In the next six years, he collected at least one, sometimes as many as four, dated chapbooks annually. Then in 1682, the number of dated examples in the collection suddenly jumped to thirteen. Every year from 1682 to 1687, he acquired at least a dozen dated chapbooks, and once as many as twenty-one. Then in 1688, he suddenly lost interest, and only bought two.[10] These were the last in the collection, with a solitary exception in 1693.[11]

The bulk of the collection was therefore acquired in the six years between 1682 and 1687.[12] The best method of testing its comprehensiveness seems to be to compare the number and nature of the items that Pepys acquired from each publisher-bookseller with those which the same publisher-bookseller advertised in his trade-lists.

If it can be shown that Pepys obtained a reasonable selection of the chapbooks put on the market by each of the specialist publishers in business by the time he was collecting (see above, Chapter IV), and if any kind of bias in the types of chapbook he acquired, or avoided, from each of them can be demonstrated, the Pepys chapbooks can be used with more confidence for a study of popular taste.

In 1682, when Pepys began to collect seriously, four of the Ballad Partners, Wright, Clarke, Passinger and Thackeray, were printing together. By 1688, when Pepys lost interest, the only one of the partners still alive was William Thackeray. In about the middle of the following year, Thackeray issued a broadside trade-list of stock. This comes so conveniently immediately after the intense period of activity by Pepys that it seems reasonable to compare all the titles of the imprints issued by the various combinations of partners in his collection, in which the last remaining partner, Thackeray, had presumably now acquired the rights, with the full list of titles that he was advertising in 1689.

Thackeray advertised, in the chapbook section of the trade-list, thirty-seven small godly books, sixty-four small merry books, twenty-one double-books[13] and twenty-three histories. Pepys's division of his collection into *Godliness, Merriments* and *Vulgaria*, then, follows trade practice, once Thackeray's double-books are identified with the twenty-four page quartos included by Pepys in the *Vulgaria*, and his histories with the more substantial quartos of the *Vulgaria*.[14]

Pepys had in his collection no fewer than forty-five, or 70 per cent, of the sixty-four titles of small merry books on Thackeray's list. The vast majority of them bore one of the partnership imprints, although a couple, Deacon's *Second Part of Tom Tram* and Deacon and Dennisson's *Dr Faustus*, were versions of the same title issued by a rival.[15] His collecting of the small godly books was less thorough: he only had fifteen of the thirty-seven, or 40 per cent. He had ten of the twenty-three histories on Thackeray's list, but only six of the twenty-one double-books[16] amongst the *Vulgaria*. From this it seems, then, that his coverage of the duodecimos and octavos was excellent, although he was, perhaps predictably, much less interested in the religious chapbook trade than in the secular. His collection of quartos was less comprehensive, but still contained over a third of those sold by the main partnership.

The Thackeray broadside list cannot be matched for any other chapbook publisher. But the Pepys chapbooks occasionally carry, at the end, as either an alternative or an addition to the colophon, a list of further titles printed for, and sold by, the same bookseller. These lists obviously did not purport to be as inclusive as Thackeray's broadside. They were presumably made up of the dozen or so titles the bookseller concerned believed to be his best-selling, or most popular lines.

There are trade-lists of this brief kind for Philip Brooksby, Jonah Deacon, Charles Dennisson, John Back, and Joshua and George Conyers amongst the *Merriments* and *Godlinesses*. Only Josiah Blare, amongst the more important chapbook and ballad specialists, was missing. In every case except Dennisson's, over a score of titles was concerned. The six men were advertising, between them, 133 titles. There were twenty-one histories, forty-two godly titles and seventy other merry books. Pepys's coverage of them was not as good as his coverage of the main partnership, but it was still good. He had sixty-one, or 45 per cent, of all titles. Amongst them, he had just over half the histories, as against a third of the histories on Thackeray's trade-list, but his comparative lack of interest in the small godly chapbooks was even more marked. He only had twelve of a possible forty-two, or under 30 per cent, against his 40 per cent of Thackeray's godly books. His collection included over half of all the other non-religious titles advertised by the six publishers.

These non-religious titles included fifteen practical books on horsemanship, gardening, cookery, arithmetic, medicine and etiquette.[17] Another of Pepys's predilections becomes evident when these guides to practical living are considered. They did not interest him and, in general, he did not collect them, with the single exception of cookery books, which obviously caught his attention. If all the practical titles are excluded from the total being advertised by the six men outside the main partnership, Pepys had 65 per cent of the rest of the merry books on their lists.

This is impressive evidence of Pepys's thorough coverage of the small secular octavos and duodecimos. The evidence is even more impressive when his coverage of individual booksellers is considered (see Table II, p. 134). He collected from all the known specialists. He may not have acquired so many godly books, but he still bought some from each of the publishers in the field, just as he acquired the *Merriments* from all of them. When the number of imprints he had collected from the different combination of the Ballad Partners to give him 70 per cent of the whole of Thackeray's merry list of 1689, as well, are taken into account, it is clear that he must have set himself

TABLE 2 Books advertised by the specialist chapbook publishers compared with those collected by Samuel Pepys

Name of bookseller	Date of lists	Histories and double-books		Small merry books		Non-godly		Small godly books		Total on trade-lists	Total of trade-list titles in Pepys's collection
		Number advertised	Number collected	Number advertised	Number collected	Total advertised	Total collected	Number advertised	Number collected		
Philip Brooksby	1684 1685	2	2	9	5	11	7	12	2	23	9
Jonah Deacon	1676 1686 1687 three not dated	5	3	11	8	16	11	10	3	26	14
Charles Dennisson	undated list (no 'godly' list)	2	2	4	3	6	5	?	–	6	5
John Back	1686(2)	1	–	13	5	14	5	11	5	25	10
Joshua Conyers	two undated lists (no 'godly' list)	2	1	19	10	21	11	?	–	21	11
George Conyers	1687 1688	9	3	14	7	23	10	9	2	32	12
Total of six		21	11 (53%)	70	38 (54%)	91	49 (54%)	42	12 (29%)	133	61 (46%)
William Thackeray	1689	44	16 (36%)	64	45 (70%)	108	61 (56%)	37	15 (41%)	145	76 (52%)
All seven booksellers		65	27 (42%)	134	83 (62%)	199	110 (55%)	79	27 (34%)	278	137 (49%)

quite systematically to buy from all the main publishers catering for the chapbook trade.

This point is made even more plain when the chapbooks collected by Pepys that do not appear on the trade-lists are taken into account.[18] In the case of all the non-Ballad Partners he had items that were not on the relevant trade-lists. Sometimes, as with Jonah Deacon, he had a considerable number of additional items. Deacon had fourteen titles on his trade-lists, but Pepys collected twenty-one productions of his alone, together with six small books published jointly with Charles Dennisson, two quartos published jointly with William Thackeray and three small books 'printed for WT to be sold by Jonah Deacon'. Not only did Pepys apparently buy regularly from all the main booksellers dealing in chapbooks whose names are already familiar from Blagden and Robert Thomson's work, but he also bought from men, and women, whose names are not so familiar. Charles Passinger at the Seven Stars on London Bridge, whose relationship with Thomas Passinger at the Three Bibles a few doors away is not clear, supplied him. So also did a dozen more.

Samuel Pepys's collection of chapbooks can therefore be taken confidently as a well-balanced, and very high, proportion of the chapbooks in circulation in the 1680s, providing always that the under-representation of the small godly books and the practical guides is remembered. A comparison with the contents of the *bibliothèque bleue* is abundantly justified.

The most important single line amongst the French pedlar's literature was religious booklets. Twenty-six per cent of those surviving from the *bibliothèque bleue* were pious little booklets designed to reinforce faith. Hagiography, miracles in the lives of the saints, the ever-present miraculous so comfortingly near to everyday life, spiritual songs and hymns, devotions and catechismal books, and, above all, the retelling of the birth and passion of Christ, formed over one-quarter of the stock in trade.[19] The trade-lists of the English chapbook publishers suggested that the religious twopennies dominated their printing policy and sold even better than the French; 31 per cent, nearly a third, of the books issued by the five publishers for whom we have both godly and secular trade-lists, were religious.[20] Even though Pepys was much less thorough in his collection of them, 19 per cent of his chapbooks were still small godlies. Their content was, of course, completely different from the French,

TABLE 3 The *bibliothèque bleue* compared with the Pepys collection

The *bibliothèque bleue* 17th to 19th centuries(?)	After Mandrou subtotal	no.	%	Morin, after Martin no.	%	Pepys's chapbook collection: mainly 1680s	subtotal	no.	%
PIOUS WORKS									
Carols and songs about saints				161	11½	Carols		1	
Instruction				?	?	Instruction		4	
Saints' lives, etc.				69	5	Death and judgement		9	
						Death-bed testaments		7	
						'Awful warnings'		4	
						Calls to repentance		9	
						Consolation		9	
						Other		3	
Bible stories and religious tracts				161	11½				
Total		c.120	26	391	28		46		19
POPULAR CULTURE									
Novels: adventure and romance	'few'			184	13	Novels		5	
Burlesques and parodies	c.30			24	2	Jest-books, burlesques		24	
Morals, satires on sexes, etc.				73	5	Anti-female satire		8	
						Satirical moralities		6	
Secular songs				40	3	Secular songs		17	
Theatre				74	5	Theatre		—	
Classical literature	c.10					None (see novels?)		—	
Crime						Crime		5	
Courtship-manuals	c.30					Courtship and lovers' dialogues		16	
Death						None, see 'pious works'		—	
Total		c.120	26	395	28		81		34

Trades, miseries of apprentices						Trades, miseries of apprentices	–		
Games						Games, cards	–		
	c.50					Riddle-books, etc.	8	13	
						Tricks and practical jokes	2		
Education, letter-manuals				74	5	Letter-manuals	3		
Historical legends, chivalric and subchivalric novels, including any in an historical setting	c.40		9	190	14	Robin Hood, Dick Whittington, etc.	13		
						Chivalric, Arthur, etc.	11	34	14
						'Roman' myths	3		
						'Realistic' novels of trades, etc.	7		
Total		c.90	20	264	19			47	20
EVERYDAY LIFE									
Calendars and almanacs	c.44?			not included		Almanacs	45		
Arithmetic and spelling				36	3	Arithmetic	–		
Medicine	20					Medicine	1		
Itineraries						Itineraries (in almanacs)	?		
Gardening						Gardening	–		
Cookery	6			42	3	Cookery	4		
Blacksmiths						Blacksmiths	–		
Law	–					Law	1		
Black and white magic	10			75	5	Dreams, palmistry, prognostication, etc.	12		
Newssheets, satirical pieces, politics				80	6				
Total		c.80	17	233	17			63	27
FAIRY MYTHOLOGY									
Fairy stories				76	6	Fairy stories	–		
'Grands mythes', Fortunatus etc.						'Grands mythes', Fortunatus	1		
Total		c.50	11	76	6			1	–
GRAND TOTAL		c.460	100	1359	98			238	100

with the exception of books of carols, books about Christmas, and seasonal songs for other feasts, which survived the Civil War in England[21] and were therefore popular in both countries. The English godly books laid immense stress on the importance of bringing the reader to repentance, and so to a fit state for conversion, and to his, or her, desperate need of the justifying grace of God. Their emphasis was laid on justification through faith, and a subgroup of them which I have classified as 'comforting' paid some attention to the worries of those unfortunates who found themselves without the convinction that they possessed this justifying faith. There was a lack of emphasis on the life, and redeeming bloodshedding of Christ. His chief role was as Judge. The most striking thing about the religious chapbooks is their domination, both in words and woodcuts, by the skeletal figure of Death. Death has been removed, in the English chapbooks, from its place as a separate tonic in popular culture, stemming from the medieval Dance of Death, and has become a pedagogue within the small godlies pointing a bony finger at the way to conversion. There is indeed some case, looking at the evidence of these chapbooks, to ask whether the third quarter of the seventeenth century in England and Wales[22] was not as death-dominated as in Puritan New England, and as Italy had been in the third quarter of the fourteenth century.[23]

Although there is no pre-Civil War collection of chapbooks as such to compare with Pepys's post-Restoration set, it is interesting, though in no way exactly parallel, to look at the contents of the collection of fifty-two books owned by Cox of Coventry, and re-membered and listed by Robert Laneham, the mercer of London.[24] Some shifts in popular taste between 1570 and 1680 are shown by the comparison. Cox had none of this religious cheap literature, although he did have Colin Clout's mockery of the Church. After the Interregnum, religious pulp dominated the cheap market. This is a startling conclusion, which inevitably suggests that popular interest in religion spread widely amongst conformists, as well as the 4 per cent of non-conformists in society (see below, pp. 194–5), who might justifiably have been expected to take a special interest.

The second most important category amongst the French chap-books, which, indeed appears with equal importance with the religious, was the group which Mandrou called simply 'popular culture'.[25] It was composed of a heterogeneous mixture of a few

1 The cultural mediators: K. du Jardin (1662–78)
'The Strolling Ballad Singers'

2 The reality of elementary education in the
seventeenth century: Jan Steen (1626–79) 'A
School for Boys and Girls'

romances, thirty-odd burlesques and parodies, secular songbooks which mainly concentrated on love-songs and drinking-songs, texts of plays, farces, tragi-comedies, comic operas, religious dramas, with some pieces descended from the classical theatre, and thirty-odd texts dealing with crime, courtship and death.

Thirty-four per cent, over a third, of Pepys's chapbooks fell into one or another of these categories, and there is no reason to suspect his own inclinations of biasing the number in any particular way. The proportion is the more impressive because two of the French sections were non-existent amongst the English chapbooks. There were no plays at all. Despite the popularity of rural and town drama in the sixteenth century, and right through to the 1630s, judging from the Pepys collection alone it had not yet recovered from the Commonwealth interdict. Certainly plays did not appear on the trade-lists of the specialist chapbook publishers displayed on the back of the other chapbooks. The exceptions are the songs in the books of 'Garlands', which are frequently recommended as the latest tune from the playhouse. However, it seems likely that there were plays in print obtainable cheaply from other publishers. The romantic Francis Kirkman, who spent his youth dreaming of chivalric adventure, devoted part of his adult life to cataloguing, unfortunately without prices, the plays printed and published to 1671.[26] He counted no less than 806 of them. Mrs Pinchwife, in Wycherley's *Country Wife*, asks for 6d worth of ballads and, failing those, buys *The Covent Garden Drollery*, which was presumably a garland, and two plays, *Tarugo's Wiles* and *The Slighted Maiden*.[27] In these circumstances, it is impossible to understand the absence of drama from Pepys's collection, unless he was confining himself to the output of the chapbook specialists, who certainly did not publish it.

Death, which still appeared in France as a leader of the *danse macabre*, in England assumed the role of a teacher of religion. In this capacity, he dominated the godly books, but disappeared from the small merries. Crime formed a surprisingly small category in the Pepys collection, despite its popularity in the earliest of all small merry books that survive.[28] Yet other categories flourished quite enough to compensate for these omissions. There were few novels, but the important members of the English 'popular culture' group were, like the French, the burlesques and parodies, and, possibly even more than the French,[29] the courtship manuals and lovers' dialogues. Thirty-eight, nearly half the whole section, were jest-books, burlesques, anti-female satires and satirical moralities. The reprinted jest-books of *Scogin* and *George Peel*, which had been very popular in the sixteenth century, and still were, if their appearance in the Pepys collection is evidence, had no continuous narrative line at all. They were a series of disconnected anecdotes about the merry doings of central figures, who acted as link devices. Both Scogin and Peel were Oxford students, and therefore moved at least on the fringes of educated society. The 'heroes' of the burlesque, which replaced them, did nothing of the kind. *Tom Stitch the Tailor*, *Robin the Merry Saddler of Walden*, *The Unfortunate Son* and the *Unfortunate Welshman* moved from one drunken and very frequently scatological amorous adventure into another. There was no concept of marriage in the burlesque or in the group of anti-female satires; the chapbook version of that supposedly honourable estate was to equate it with cuckoldry.

The art of compliment chapbooks and the courtship dialogues giving instructions that were very frequently satirical, on how to woo both virgins and widows, tell a somewhat different story. There were no less than sixteen of them, a fifth of the popular culture section, and no less than 17 per cent of the whole chapbook collection. The importance of courtship, whether in deadly earnest or in mockery, was obviously an extremely important, almost obsessive topic to the humble in Restoration England. It was therefore a best-selling line

Death Triumphant

CUPID'S

Soliciter of LOVE

With Sundry Complements.

Wherein is shown the deceitfulness of Loving & Lovers, now a days commonly used.
With certain verses and sonnets, upon several subjects
that is Written in this BOOK.

By *RICHARD CRIMSAL*

No Laie no Life.

FC

Printed by *J. M.* for W. T. and are to be sold by T. Back at the
of the Black-Boy on London-Bridge.

The Unfortunate SON;

Or, A kind WIFE is worth Gold.

Full of Mirth and delightful Reading.

Good Reader, let thy Patience brook,
But to Read over this small Book;
Which will thee satisfie a while,
And surely force from thee a Smile;
A Story of such Fortune bad,
Had never sure poor Harmless Lad.

Printed by J. M. for J. Deacon and C. Dennisson,
and are to be Sold at their Shops, at the Angel in
Giltspur-street; and at the Stationers-

Hero of burlesque

for the publishers for the humble. The god of the merry books was Cupid, whose pretty, lethal figure appeared in many woodcuts dominating stockyard and city alike, slaying Somerset bumpkins and court fops with equal zest. His representations in the woodcuts seem frequently to have a conscious iconographic reference to his brother Death of the godly books and the implication was that his reign, also, was universal.

Secular songs, important in France,[30] were as important in England as the art of compliment books. Another fifth of the 'popular culture' section of the collection was made up by books of 'garlands'. In England, as in France, no musical notation was ever given for the words of the new songs set out; but they were always said to go to a known, old tune, like 'As May was in her Youthful Dress' or 'Caper and Jerk it'. The celebratory functions of music and its importance were quite frequently referred to in the chapbooks in general, as well as in the songbooks in particular, so the Pepys collection generally emphasizes the social importance of music as entertainment in the 1680s.

A glance back a hundred years at Cox's collection, shows that half his books, rather than a third, can be categorized under the various headings classed by Mandrou as popular culture. He had four novels, eleven jest-books and burlesques, two anti-feminine satires, four satirical mediations on the state of society, and one book on crime. He also had four of the plays that Pepys did not collect in the 1680s, but no courtship books. Songbooks were not yet in fashion, but he had instead seven titled ballads 'and a hundred more he hath, fair wrapt up in Parchment, and tied with a whipcord'. So music was as important to him as to his seventeenth-century descendants. The changes in popular fashion were the apparent disappearance of plays, the appearance of quite fresh burlesques with humbly-born heroes, and a new wave of art of courtship books, reflecting a new fashion, and perhaps a new preoccupation.

Mandrou called another of his major groups 'Portraits of society'.[31] Into this he subsumed two subsidiary parts of the *bibliothèque bleue*. The booklets dealing with trades and, particularly, the misery of apprentices within them, those teaching the rules of cards, piquet and dice, and educational treatises, ABCs and letter-writing manuals, formed half.[32] The historical novels, which gave a colourful and somewhat startling insight into the way French society looked at its own past, formed the other.[33] Together they made up a fifth of the whole collection.

The English equivalents of the first part of this group of Mandrou's are entirely missing. There was not a single chapbook on the miseries of apprentices, whereas there were plenty on the amorous adventures of apprentice-heroes. It seems unlikely that Pepys would have missed chapbooks on the misfortunes of apprentices if they existed. None are identifiable on the trade-lists, so it looks as if English apprentices, as opposed to their French counterparts, were at least supposed to be happy. There were no books dealing with card-games either; Pepys would surely have collected these if they existed also, so perhaps the card-playing so often found in alehouses[34] was confined to traditional and relatively simple games. Instead there were a couple of books dealing with conjuring and magic tricks, and a set of riddle-books. Riddling had obviously not lost its attraction as a pastime since the days of the Saxons,[35] and some of those reprinted here were very old.

Cox had had a pair of riddle-books, including an earlier version of one of Pepys's collections, in the 1570s.[36] Out of the riddle-books had developed a set of related proverb and puzzle-books on the *Five Strange Wonders of the World*, the *Figure of Seven* or the *Figure of Nine*, which were lists of proverbs, or of five, seven or nine sets of related objects.

There were no educational books as such in Pepys's collection. Certainly there were both ABCs and treatises on education about in abundance,[37] but it is probable that he would have regarded such things as 'practical' and of no interest. He did collect a few letter-writing manuals, on the other hand.

The first part of Mandrou's 'Portraits of Society' section was therefore almost entirely missing in Samuel Pepys's collection. This reflects Pepys's lack of interest in education as a subject, but it also reflects a genuine difference in the amusements of the two cultures, as well as the way they looked at their trades. The second group of Mandrou's social portraits, the historical tales and fables through which the French saw their own past, was a very important one. Nine per cent of the *bibliothèque bleue*, about forty books, were of this type. Three-quarters of them were chivalric, and based on the Charlemagne cycle. Right through to the nineteenth century, the Carolingian epic of noble dealings, aided by magic, with stories of a feudal society combating the infidel, engaged in vast battles and demonstrating its military virtues in splendid hunting-parties and jousts, dominated the historical reading of the poor in France.

The English version of their own past also figured largely in their reading; in fact, it formed an even larger proportion of the chapman's stock in trade than in France. Fourteen per cent of the whole Pepys collection was devoted to tales with an historical setting. Such tales had already been very important in the 1570s. A third of the books belonging to Cox had been historical novels, and no less than thirteen of these were chivalric. But between the 1570s and the 1680s, a very important development had taken place in the writing of historical fiction (see below, Chapter IX). The popularity of medieval chivalric works had continued and was, indeed, so great that a whole wave of pot-boiling 'neo-chivalric' works had been added to the genuine medieval survivals. The end of the sixteenth century saw, however, the beginnings of the 'realistic' novel in Deloney's works with clothier heroes. Their cut-down versions were especially adapted to appeal to the poor, and the poor were especially encouraged to see their way to success in a trade, however low their birth. Alongside these, again, another little group of chapbooks appeared with heroes or heroines drawn from somewhere near the bottom of society, vagrants, servants, and day-labourers, who had all, at some time in a past which was often mythical, made their fortunes.

So although, in both France and England, the historical chapbook was important, the English chapbooks, however unreal they were, made a much greater attempt to adjust to social reality than did the French. The English reader could imagine himself a hero against the Turks; but he could also imagine himself a wealthy clothier, a Lord Mayor of London, or even making good as a minor country gentleman.

It is in the field of publications acting as guides to everyday life, calendars, almanacs, and practical booklets on medicine, gardening, arithmetic and farriery and so on, that Samuel Pepys proves little help to us. Seventeen per cent of the *bibliothèque bleue*, nearly a fifth, comes into this category.[38] Pepys did collect almanacs quite assiduously for two years, although he did not collect practical guides, with the exception of cookery books, and books of prognostication and palmistry. The inclusion of Pepys's almanacs means that despite the shortage of practical booklets, 27 per cent, over a quarter, of the English collection, still covered everyday living. Almanacs in England have now received magisterial and exhaustive treatment.[39] It was they, not the chapbooks, that gave practical guidance and running commentary on every aspect of the everyday world. Politics, religion, science, medicine and current events were to be found in the almanacs; the chapbooks were fiction for pure relaxation. In view of Pepys's neglect of practical books, apart from the almanacs, I have not made any further comparison with this section of the *bibliothèque bleue*.[40] It is, however, necessary to notice in the briefest terms the only group he did collect, apart from the almanacs, which come under this heading of 'guides to practical living', and in fact extended the prognostications of the almanacs. He had a dozen books of fortune telling, and black and white magic, ranging from a copy of the perpetual almanac *Erra Pater* so much scorned by the more professional astrologers,[41] with its gentle weather-lore and practical hints on husbandry:

> If Swallows fly upon the Water low
> Or Wood-lice seem in Armies for to go
> If Toads hie home, or Frogs do croke amain
> Or Peacocks cry, soon after look for Rain,

through *A Groats Worth of Wit for a Penny, or the Interpretation of Dreams* by Lilly, sold by Deacon,[42] and its inevitable rival *Two Groats Worth of Wit for a Penny* by 'those Famous Astrologers Mr Rich. Saunders and Dr Coelson'[43] sold by Conyers. These were followed by a couple of books on palmistry;[44] *The Strange and Wonderful History of Mother Shipton*, with the truth of her prophecies from the Henry VII's reign onwards until 1684, appeared in small book and middle-length quarto format, although again the more reputable astrologers felt that she brought them into disrepute.[45] The more sinister histories of *Doctor Faustus*[46] and the closely related history of *Frier Bacon or the Three Famous Conjurers*, again in small book and mid-length quarto format[47] demonstrated again popular belief in magic and the desire to read stories of the supernatural, that had nothing to do with either emergent scientific interest on the one hand, or religious belief on the other. Amazingly, though, Mandrou's last category of all, the myths and fairy stories that made up 11 per cent of the French *bibliothèque bleue*, was, with the single exception of *Fortunatus*[48] and his inexhaustable purse of gold, completely missing in England. Queen Mab and her train, Puck and his followers, did not in the 1680s appeal to the public. The twopenny publications of the 1680s show that both religion and cheap astrology were flourishing, and indeed there was no necessary conflict between them. There was as much need, judging from the religious tracts, to propitiate God as there ever had been, although the saving faith that would certainly do so was perhaps less easy to come by than the older means offered by the pre-Reformation church. Nor was the minister, whose stern figure predominated in the woodcuts only less frequently than that of Death, shorn of all his powers, although these were now much more the ability to convey the assurance, or conversely, to feed the doubts, of the faithful about possession of that faith. As for astrology, it may have lost its intellectual status, and a gap may have widened between its qualified acceptance by Calvin and Perkins, and 1700,[49] but it is highly unlikely that either intellectual doubt or tension between religion and astrology was necessarily felt by the humble in the late seventeenth century. It is academic to suppose that such categorizations were necessarily taking place.[50]

In general, then, the English chapbooks were differentiated from the French by their comparative lack of interest in crime, in the theatre, in the card-games of high society, and their lack of emphasis on the miseries of, as opposed to the benefits of, trade. They were also differentiated by their abundance of humble, if risible, heroes and heroines, and the much wider scope of their historical novels, which were not confined only to the courtly. Sadly also, the English appear not to have believed in fairies. On the other hand, they shared the tremendous emphasis on religion as a best-selling line, though it was of course completely differently interpreted. They also shared the interest in burlesques and in farce, be it expressed in the language of Billingsgate or Les Halles, the courtship dialogues, or the pastime of music. Both societies watched the stars in their courses, and shared a magical interest that was not necessarily in conflict with a religious one. Publishers of all these lines in both countries seem to have found themselves comfortably participating in a trade on the increase, in which fortunes were to be made.

NOTES AND REFERENCES

1 Mandrou, R. (1964, 1975) *De la Culture Populaire aux 17ᵉ et 18ᵉ Siècles*, Paris. My references are to the paperback edition of 1975. Bollème, G. (1971) *La Bibliothèque Bleue*, Paris, mainly considers the eighteenth and nineteenth centuries, and, in (1965) *Les Almanachs Populaires aux XVIII Siècles*, Paris, the almanacs that made up, with the calendars, about one-tenth of the collection.

2 See, for instance, Burke, P. (1978) *Popular Culture in Early Modern Europe*, London, and Capp, B. (1979) *Astrology and the Popular Press 1500–1800*, London and Boston. Victor Neuburg's critical bibliography in (1977) *Popular Literature: A History and a Guide*, Harmondsworth, is a very useful starting point. His bibliography forms a guide to the work already done on popular print before that date.

3 Mandrou, op. cit., 37–9.

4 Mandrou discusses, for instance, on p. 128, a letter-writing manual 216 pages long, which he describes as one of the longest in the collection. No idea is given of how many such lengthy works the collection contains. Since Mandrou wrote, and at about the time I started work on the Pepys collection, A. Morin brought out a catalogue including 1389 separate editions definitely known to exist, representing several hundred titles of the *bibliothèque bleue* (Morin, A. (1975) *Catalogue Descriptif de la Bibliothèque Bleue de Troyes*, Geneva and Paris). These editions have been analysed by subject by Henri-Jean Martin in an article that first appeared in the *Journal des Savants* and was translated as (1978) 'The Bibliothèque Bleue: Literature for the Masses in the *Ancien Regime*', *Publishing History* 3, 70–102. Unfortunately, Martin used a different set of categories from Mandrou, so his detailed figures cannot be set against Mandrou's approximate ones with any ease. However, I have reorganized them into Mandrou's original categories; the results appear on Table III, pp. 136–7. Oddly enough, the results of the impressionistic analysis and the exhaustive one appear very comparable. Religious works made up 26 per cent according to Mandrou, 28 per cent according to Martin. 'Popular culture' made up 26 per cent according to Mandrou, 28 per cent according to Morin. 'Portraits of society' made up 20 per cent and 19 per cent respectively, and 'everyday life' accounted for 17 per cent in

both cases. The difficulty remains, of course, that the collection is still not broken down according to date. Like the English chapbooks, they can be approximately dated by someone with a close knowledge of the publishers, but not by someone without this knowledge. I have not, therefore, attempted to extract seventeenth-century items from Morin's catalogue, to arrive at a French group truly comparable with that assembled by Samuel Pepys.

I have arrived at the figures deduced from those given by Martin on Table III (pp. 136–7) by combining his headings 'letter writing' with 'etiquette'; and 'tales of chivalry' with 'history, travels'. I have not included his 2 per cent of 'unclassified' under any heading, so his percentages do not now add up. It is noticeable both that he excludes almanacs, which are included by Mandrou, and, *vice versa*, has a heading 'newssheets, satirical pieces, politics', which Mandrou does not include. Since the 'satirical pieces' include some satirizing of the professions, it is possible that their omission may help account for the relative blandness of the French collection, on which I comment above (see p. 71).

5 There is no full study yet of the seventeenth-century chapbook, although Neuburg, V. (1971) *Chapbooks: a bibliography* (second edn), London, is indispensable for the eighteenth century. I would like to thank the trustees of the Marc Fitch Fund for their generous grant in 1975 which made it possible for me to start work, on the Pepys collection. Meanwhile, Thompson, R. (1976) *Samuel Pepys's Penny Merriments*, London, has reprinted extracts from some eighty of Pepys's octavos and duodecimos taken from the first two volumes of the *Penny Merriments.* His selection is slanted towards the more entertainingly bawdy, a treatment to which some of the chapbooks readily lend themselves. His paper, (1976) 'Popular Reading and Humour in Restoration England', *Journal of Popular Culture* 9 (3), 653–71, attempts some analysis, but again concentrates on the very high sexual content of a group of the chapbooks. Both this paper and his (1976) 'Samuel Pepys's *Penny Merriments*: A Checklist', *The Library*, 5th series 31, 223–4, are misleading. They purport to be a consideration of all the chapbooks collected by Pepys, but in fact omit his *Penny Godlinesses* from all mention, except a very slight passing reference in the 'Checklist', p. 233, n. 30. They also completely

omit to mention the items contained in the four volumes of Pepys's *Vulgaria*. The first omission by Mr Thompson is serious, since it unbalances his consideration of the content of the twopenny works available, by omitting the largest single group, and thereby excluding Death, the hero of the godly books, entirely, in favour of Cupid, the hero of the merry ones. The omission of the shorter quartos in the *Vulgaria* exaggerates the bawdy chapbooks at the expense of the various forms of novel. It also means that Mr Thompson's numbers of items in the collection, as well as the numbers in each category within it, and the numbers of dated works collected by Pepys, are all wrong. For example, there are 114 dated items in the collection, not fifty-one, as 'Popular Reading' states, p. 654. He has expanded his work on the bawdy chapbooks further in (1979) *Unfit for Modest Ears*, London.

6 This compares with between sixty and seventy items datable over a much longer period from 1581 to the 1690s in the Wood collection in the Bodleian Library, and just over thirty from before 1700 in the Lauriston Castle collection in the National Library of Scotland.

7 See above, pp. 96–7 for the prices of the shorter histories. The prices of some of the twenty-two, printed by the same bookseller a decade or so earlier, can be found in Foxton, D. E. (ed.) (reprinted 1965) Robert Clavel, *The General Catalogue of Books printed in England since the Dreadful Fire of London, 1666*, English Bibliographical Sources, Series 2, Farnborough: Part 3, 'To the end of Michaelmas Term 1672'; and Part 4, 'To the end of Trinity term 1674'. The two parts of 'Don Belianis of Greece', *Vulgaria*, I (2), were priced jointly at 3s bound. The first two parts of the 'Seven Champions', *Vulgaria*, II (1) cost 3s likewise, as did the two parts of 'Parismus, Prince of Bohemia', *Vulgaria*, II (3). So also did the three parts of the 'Destruction of Troy'. 'Montelion', *Vulgaria*, III (2) was priced at 1s. 'Valentine and Orson', *Vulgaria*, III (2) was 1s 6d 'sticht'. The cheapest of the works I have excluded for which I have found a price was the long version of 'Guy of Warwick', *Vulgaria*, III (9), which was sold by Brewster at 10d 'sticht' in 1674. This may not be relevant since Pepys's copy was sold by Brooksby.

The decision to exclude these longer histories on the grounds of cost seems amply justified. Most of the items in Pepys's chapbook collection simply do not appear in Clavel's catalogue, although we know they were being produced by Tias's trade-heirs (see above, pp. 132–5). He listed, for instance, seventy-three miscellaneous small octavos in 1674. No less than fifty-nine of these were priced at 1s 6d or above; only eight cost 6d or less, and the list included only two at 3d (Clavel, op. cit., Part 4, 53–6). If this is compared with the prices of Tias's stock in trade in 1664 (above, pp. 93–8) it is obvious that chapbooks, the majority of which Pepys bought for 2d, were simply not worth including in a respectable catalogue, which therefore leaves the base of the iceberg invisible. These invisible substrata of really cheap books have misled Dr Sommerville into thinking that popular religious books after the Restoration averaged 1s in price (Sommerville, C. J. (1977) *Popular Religion in Restoration England*, Gainesville, Fla., 21), whereas, of course, the religious chapbooks collected by Pepys were almost all sold at 2d.

There is a bibliographical problem in the study of the seven-teenth- and, indeed, sixteenth-century chapbooks. Just as many of them escaped the attention or were too inferior for the atten-tion of booksellers like Clavel, so also many of them escape the cognizance both of Pollard, A. W. and Redgrave, G. R. (1926) *Short Title Catalogue* (Vol. II covering titles I–Z, second edn revised 1976) for the period 1475–1640, and of its continuation by Donald Wing (1945–51) from 1641–1700 (Vol. I, A–E, revised 1972). Since they often escape the *Short Title Catalogue*, either because they do not survive at all, or are not yet included, they also escape the attention of studies based on it, like Sommerville, op. cit., 11, n. 35. The dates of first registering, if not printing, of the chapbook titles are presumably in the unindexed volumes of Arber, E. (ed.) (1875–94) *Transcripts of the Stationers' Company Register,* 5 volumes, London, continued by Eyre, G. E. (1913–14), 3 volumes. Until a scholar as dedicated to chapbooks as Hyder E. Rollins was to ballads produces the equivalent of the *Analyti-cal Index to the Ballad Entries (1557–1709) of the Register of the Company of Stationers of London* (2 volumes 1924, reprinted 1967) it will be impossible to gain a clearer impression of their history. It would, for instance, have been particularly interesting to have been able to trace the date of first printing of a group of the chapbooks making a particular appeal to a humble audience. Examples of the group are 'The Lovers' Quarrel or Cupid's

Triumph' (known in the trade as 'Tommy Potts'), 'Long Meg of Westminster', 'Aurelius, the Valiant London Prentice', 'Thomas Hickathrift', 'Sir Richard Whittington' and 'Honest John and Loving Kate' (see below, pp. 244–9). Of this group, only 'Long Meg' appears in the *Short Title Catalogue*.

8 114 of 215.

9 With the exception of a single stray quarto, *Vulgaria*, III (22), printed for Henry and Moses Bell in 1637.

10 It was at this point that his attention switched to almanacs, which he collected for 1688 and 1689.

11 It was about this time that the *Vulgaria* and the *Merriments* and *Godlinesses* were bound up for Pepys to construct his catalogue. The handwriting of the clerk who wrote the indexes to the volumes is the same as that of the clerk who wrote most of the catalogue. It is of course possible that he bought the chapbooks as a collection, as he did the ballads, rather than as they came out, but there is no evidence of such a purchase. The *Diary* only mentions the purchase of a single isolated chapbook, the *Montelion*, on 10 November 1660, although the copy of it now in the collection is dated 1687. I am indebted to Mr Robert Latham for all this information.

12 This is an interesting contrast with the dating of his ballad collection, which seems likely to have been begun in 1665, and was continued right through to 1702. Goldstein, L. M. (1966) 'The Pepys Ballads', *The Library*, 5th series 21, 291. On the other hand, it fits exactly with the dating of his Spanish chapbook collection to the early 1680s. Wilson, E. M. (1955) 'Samuel Pepys's Spanish Chapbooks', Part I, *Transactions of the Cambridge Bibliographical Society* 2 (2), 127–54.

13 Only the double books had mixed religious and secular titles. Thackeray's list is printed as the Appendix, p. 262 onwards.

14 For instance, Pepys's version of the 'History of Montelion', which was on the Thackeray trade-list, had been issued by Thackeray and Passinger in 1687. It had 186 pages. *Vulgaria*, III (I).

15 *PM*, I (42), 905, and (54), 1153. I have included them in my total as if they had been published by the main partnership, since it seemed unreasonable to suppose that Pepys would have bought the same title twice.

16 Pepys's comparative lack of interest in godly books accounts in

part for his relatively low numbers of double-books. Nine of them, from their titles, were godly. Three of the remaining twelve, 'The Seven Champions', 'Reynard the Fox' and 'Paris-mus', he had in longer versions as histories, *Vulgaria*, II (I) (in three parts), *Vulgaria*, IV (8), and *Vulgaria*, II (3). Of the nine possible titles reamining, he had six.

17 The Thackeray list only includes two practical books, both of them on cookery, which Pepys happened to have. He did collect one or two other useful books which do not happen to be advertised on the publishers' short trade-lists, and which are therefore not discussed here.

18 These do not appear on Table II, which only examines items on the trade-lists.

19 Mandrou, op. cit., 45, 87–110.

20 Seventy-nine out of 251, see above, Table II, p. 134.

21 See Wood, 110 (A) which includes as item (2) an early example from before the Civil War.

22 Jenkins, G. H. (1978) *Literature, Religion and Society in Wales 1660–1730*, Cardiff, 141–4.

23 Stannard, D. E. (1977) *The Puritan Way of Death*, New York, and Meiss, M. (1951) *Painting in Florence and Sienna after the Black Death*, Princeton.

24 Furnivall, F. J. (ed.) (1871) *Captain Cox, His Ballads and his Books; or, Robert Laneham's Letter*, London.

25 A recount of the figures he prints suggests that there were 120 titles involved; or, again, 26 per cent of the whole literature. Mandrou, op. cit., 45–7, 111–33.

26 See above, pp. 72–3. His catalogue was collected by Anthony Wood, Wood, E 27 (3). A later catalogue of plays printed up to 1688, Wood E 28 (5), suggests that Kirkman's catalogue was the first of any merit.

27 Wycherley's *Country Wife* (1675) in Jeffares, A. N. (ed.) (1974) *Restoration Comedy*, I, London, 449. Bernard Capp tells me that the *Drollery* books he has seen are larger and up-market. Perhaps Mrs Pinchwife was driven to lay out more than *6d*.

28 Four of the eighteen small merry and small godly books I have found surviving from before 1660 were concerned with crime, the largest single group except for the dominating godlies. They included the earliest of all, the death of a 'Popish traitor' pub-lished 1581, and the serialized exploits of two pirates in 1637

(Wood, 284 (3 and 4) (a and b)). The low number of criminous chapbooks in Pepys's collection was partly, but only partly, a by-product of his habit of including stories of violent death following murder with the godly warnings to the wicked of the reward of smaller sins. 'The Wicked Life and Penitent Death of Thomas Savage' and a similar account of the death of Gabriel Harding, both of whom had committed murder, *PG*, 37 and 45, were therefore cheek by jowl with the 'Warning to Wicked Livers' and the 'Allarum from Heaven', *PG* 6 and 46, which warned the faithful that the penalty of telling lies denying the theft of a Bible, and the sale of one's own hair for gain, might result in the rotting off of the hands and the swelling of the tongue, respectively. Anthony Wood followed the opposite course, and put his pair of copies of the 'Wicked Life of Thomas Savage', along with an affecting account of a gentleman who died in a duck pond, into his volume of criminous chapbooks (Wood, 284 (5, 6 and 9)). However, even if Samuel Pepys's copies of chapbooks dealing with murder are classified with the 'criminous' chapbooks rather than his godlies, crime still forms a surprisingly insignificant group.

29 It is difficult to be sure about this; Mandrou gives no separate figures for the courtship manuals, but puts them together with crime and death. He had thirty booklets out of 460, or 6 per cent on all these three subjects. Pepys had sixteen out of 238, or 7 per cent, 'art of compliment' chapbooks alone.

30 Mandrou gives no figure for the number of books of songs. He has 160 separate songs, op. cit., 118. Other British collections demonstrate the same point. Anthony Wood's volume of books of carols contains an early merry book of 'Good and True Fresh and New Christmas Carols' printed for Francis Coles in 1642, as well as books of carols printed for Thackeray, Passinger and Deacon late in the century (Wood, 110 A (2, 4 and 5)). The Lauriston Castle collection in the National Library of Scotland contains at least another thirteen books of garlands dating from the 1670s to 1700 (LC, 2958–70).

31 Mandrou, op. cit., 47, 135–63.

32 ibid., 135–45.

33 ibid., 146–63.

34 Emmison, F. G. (1976) 'Tithes, Perambulations and Sabbath-breach in Elizabethan Essex', in Emmison, F. G. and Stephens, R. (eds) *Tribute to an Antiquary*, London, 199.

35 See, for instance, Crossley-Holland, K. (trans. and ed.) (1978) *Exeter Riddle Book*, London, which includes seventh-century riddles.

36 Furnivall (ed.) op. cit., xlii, xliv. *The Book of Riddels* is identified with the twenty-four page octavo *Book of Mery Riddels*, printed by Edward Aldee (1600), cx. The Pepys version is the 'Book of Merry Riddles', *PM*, I (24), 521–44.

37 See those cited in Cressy, D. (1975) *Education in Tudor and Stuart England*, London.

38 Mandrou, op. cit., 44–5, 64–72.

39 Capp, op. cit.

40 Pepys's single book on medicine and his cookery books will be found briefly considered in 'Readership', p. 61 above.

41 *PM*, II (19), 441–64. See Capp, op. cit., 31, 210.

42 *PM*, I (49), 1073–88.

43 *PM*, I (50), 1089–104.

44 *PM*, II (8 and 9), 153–84.

45 *PM*, I (56), 1201–24 and *Vulgaria*, IV (7); Capp op. cit., 211.

46 *PM*, I (54), 1153–75. Pepys also had another 'Faustus' in the *Vulgaria*, III (14), too long for the scope of this survey. The first part of the *History* was first printed in 1592, five years after the German original, and three after Marlowe's play, and went through numerous editions. Baker, E. A. (1929) *History of the English Novel*, II, London, 53.

47 *PM*, I (1), 1–23, and *Vulgaria*, III (13). The earliest known prose edition of the story was licensed in 1594. Baker, op. cit., 196. Robert Greene's play written in 1589–90 was influenced by Marlowe's *Faustus* and published in 1594.

48 *PM*, I (18), 401–24. Pepys also had a quarto version too long for inclusion in this analysis, *Vulgaria*, III (3).

49 Capp, op. cit., 276–80. Dr Capp shows the continuing importance of astrology amongst the lower social classes in the eighteenth century and indeed later on, pp. 281–3.

50 I write this out of personal experience as editor of an Anglican parish magazine, who, amongst other offerings, has recently been given a piece on the significance of the Cross, and its influence on unidentified flying objects. I believe it to be extremely easy for academics to over-emphasize the degree to which the majority of ordinary people are either aware of, or bothered by, different categories of belief.

VII

Small merry books:
courtship, sex and songs

❧

AUNT
Its impossible that Biddy should have desires,
she's but newly come out of the country and just
turn'd of sixteen

TAG
That's a ticklish age, Madam!

DAVID GARRICK (1748) *A Miss in Her Teens*

Over a third of Samuel Pepys's collection was made up of the 'small merry books' that also figured so largely on the publishers' trade-lists. The major groups of these were the jest-books and burlesques, the courtship and lovers' dialogues, and the secular songs. There was a very small group of novels. *Patient Griselda* survived from the middle ages in England, as in France, to be a model, and unbelievable, wife. She appeared in England in the 1680s as a twenty-four page quarto or double-book selling at 3*d*.[1] Robert Greene's *Dorastus and Fawnia*, by an author so jealous of the success of the young Shakespeare's *Henry VI* plays that Greene described him as 'an upstart crow beautified with our feathers',[2] was popular enough to be still appearing both in quarto and in small versions[3] in the 1680s. Quarles's *Argalus and Parthenia*,[4] which with its idyllic shepherds' life and palace of the heroine's uncle could have figured for both Bunyan's shepherd's valley and the Interpreter's House, and the little three-penny quarto *Antonius and Aurelia*,[5] close the group. These were the only chapbooks, with the chivalric stories, to have descended from élite culture.

Seven per cent of the whole chapbook collection and a fifth of the 'popular culture' section was on courtship. It was therefore a subject that was guaranteed to sell well, and was known to be a popular preoccupation. Demographers have shown that the average age of brides at their first marriage between 1550 and 1750 was at its highest after 1650. It could be late as thirty, and that of the first marriage of grooms was as late as twenty-eight. It is possible that the proportion of those who remained unmarried was rising. This combination of late marriage and a high proportion of single people is so unusual for a pre-industrial society that it has been described as 'unique or almost unique in the world'.[6] Perhaps, in the circumstances, it is not surprising that the whole subject of courtship should have been a source of major preoccupation amongst the humble, which the chapbook publishers found it worth their while to feed. Nor is it difficult to imagine that the twopenny print stressing marital and extra-marital intercourse or cuckoldry as themes may have had a considerable ready-made audience in a society with such a large proportion of bachelors. The prevailing themes of pin-ups in Army barracks come to mind. The stress on sexual adventure in the chapbooks may perhaps be accounted for as a compensatory device in the current demographic situation in Stuart England, more readily than by complex explanations suggesting an anxious re-assertion of male dominance after the comparative Puritan emancipation of women and the elevation of marriage under the Commonwealth.[7]

Literary evidence of social custom[8] is always a dubious and possibly heavily distorted source of evidence of actual practice. The courtship chapbooks do, however, provide evidence of attitudes in society which conveniently supports recent work by social historians interested in courtship, sexual behaviour and marriage in the seventeenth century. They sometimes answer questions that more factual and strictly acceptable historical evidence, usually drawn from the ecclesiastical courts, cannot provide.[9] They show, for instance, that the concept of romantic love as a basis for marriage was very much present in seventeenth-century humble society. This, reflected in its own twopenny literature, was not a world in which people married for economic interest rather than inclination. Above all it was not a society that had to wait to fall in love until it learnt this new 'cultural expectation' from the spread of the late eighteenth-century novel.[10] The art of compliment chapbooks are full of speeches by passionate swains threatening to die of love for the beloved.

> I told you in part, my mind at the last meeting we had, and your answer was to me, that you would resolve me at our next meeting, now is the time or never, for I am in flame; or else you will destroy the whole substance of my heart

writes one lover.[11] The tradition is very frequently mocked in the chapbooks, either by a sensible girl who does not believe a word of her lover's protestations that she will bring him to his grave, or, on the other hand, by one particularly dramatic episode when a young gentleman actually succeeds in dying of love, to his mistress's total astonishment and considerable vexation.[12] But it is still the tradition, and it holds good for all social levels. Doll the Dairymaid and Dick the Ploughman in their own fashion are as love-lorn as the 'gentle folk' who write such elaborate speeches (for other examples, see above pp. 68–71). William the apprentice of London says to Susan the serving maid, 'Tell me not of Beauty, thou art the most beautiful Virgin in my eye that is living upon the Earth, therefore delay not to ease my burning heart'.[13]

The tradition in the courtship chapbooks is also that sex is pleasureable, for women as well as for men (see above, pp. 63–4). Kate is reluctant, as she and John plan their wedding, to think even of walking down the street to church with all eyes upon her yet she, with him, will look forward to the 'gossiping' to celebrate the birth of their first child. Unskilled advice is offered to the bridegroom, which warns him of the bride's fear on their wedding night.

> Let not the Bridegroom be afraid,
> Though he encountered with a Maid;
> She'll squeak, she'll cry,
> She'll faint, she'll die,
> She'll fear as she did tremble;
> But take her and rouse her,
> And mowse her and towse her,
> For she doth but dissemble.[14]

A slightly more sophisticated dialogue between a bridegroom and a bride on their wedding night takes more account of her fear, and reaches a happier conclusion.

Bridegroom	Will you not come to bed my heart, why do you so delay? Come let me help you.
Bride	To bed! Sweetheart, why are you so sleepy?
Bridegroom	No, but I shall be worse if you are so sad and melancholy; come prithee my dear heart to bed: why dost thou blush, let me undress thee, be not coy, but smile.
Bride	Alas I feel myself not well my love.
Bridegroom	It's only bashfulness my dear, know you well there's no such Physick as your husband's warm harms [sic].
Bride	Be not so hasty my Dear 'tis time enough.
Bridegroom	Do you then already cease to love me?
Bride	No think not so, for I love thee dearly.
Bridegroom	To bed, then I shall give better credit to thee, be not so cold a Lover.
Bride	My passion is now over, and now my dearest I haste to thy embraces.
Bridegroom	Welcome my comfort and delight, and thus I fold my Arm about thee.
Bride	And thus about thee my dearest bliss, I twine like the Female Ivy.[15]

A fake shepherd from the pastoral tradition promises his girl contentment: 'I will play you love's delight, which if you will dance over with me, I know you will have heart's content in doing so.'[16] An even more bogus shepherd rejoices with his girl in the consummation of their marriage:

> How happy Celia is it, now we are
> In Wedlock joyn'd and made a happy pair, . . .
> This has not been if you had prov'd unkind,
> This true content you ne'er before could find;
> 'Tis true my Strephon, I had been,
> In Ignorance till now,
> These happy days I ne'er had seen
> Till I had kept my vow:

But now I find such sollid bliss,
That i'd not be a Virgin now.[17]

The delights of the marriage-bed are, in this 'literature' for the poor, the reason why widows must be wooed and won quickly. The long drawn-out amorous speeches are not for the widow; as one of them says briskly:

> A thousand bashful Coxcombs might have come and I should have dasht them out of all countenance, but thou hast hit the nail on the head, and hadst not thou tired me with tedious Wooing, thou hadst never got me, but now be as brief to procure a Licence speedily (that shall be your charge) for tomorrow I must be wedded, and bedded, or I am gone again.[18]

There is no hint in any of these chapbooks of the economic reasons, valid in any period of high population, why widows and their land might be eagerly sought after,[19] or the reasons why they might as eagerly be seeking a husband to run their tenements. The reasons for speedy remarriage in the twopennies are all amorous. The young man says to the old widow:

> Tell me truly, from the bottom of your heart, had you not better content in bed when you lay with your husband, than you have now you lye alone. I know if you speak true you cannot say the contrary: a man is a complement to a woman and a woman the like to a man being joyned together in hymens bands: Now tell me widow, have I spoke the truth or no?

She replies:

> Truly you have touched me to the quick: I cannot say, but I had more pleasure in one night's lodging with my husband, than I have ever had since he dyed, which is the space of one whole month.[20]

Courtship is, then, in this convention, a process leading onto fulfilment for both partners, although the fulfilment is strangely underwritten, and there is an abrupt transition to the convention of the insatiable woman of the anti-feminine chapbooks, and the wholesale cuckoldry of the burlesques. The progress of courtship is surveyed in some detail, and these details fit surprisingly well with what is so far known of the historical reality.

The questions raised by Dr Macfarlane in 1968 included whether anyone but the young couple themselves was implicated in the decision to marry, whether once engaged they were allowed to meet alone, and whether sexual intercourse was permitted once they were betrothed. He concluded that the literary evidence that the consent of all the involved parties was needed was clear; parents, friends and the young couple should all consent, and no child should be forced. But he felt on the scanty evidence then available that the consent and goodwill of parents and friends was possibly less necessary the further down the social scale one went. The prevailing custom of adolescents leaving home before fifteen and spending the ten years before their marriage away from home inevitably led to lack of parental control. He also concluded that there was a high degree of tolerance in Essex village society of pre-marital pregnancy, since most of the cases that can be deduced from the parish registers never appeared in the church courts. The couples who did end up in the church courts were enjoined to confess their fault at the wedding. So pre-marital conception was regarded as a sin in the church courts, but was tolerantly treated, as indeed was adultery after marriage, with the exception of the 1650s.[21] The proportion of brides who were pregnant at their marriages could vary enormously from village to village in the same period, but Dr Macfarlane's investigations produce no proportions higher than the 20 per cent suggested as a norm for up to 1700 by Dr Hair.[22]

Dr Ingram shows in practice the wide involvement of a network of kin in betrothals in Wiltshire. He discusses the literary evidence of the conduct books, which enjoined strict chastity on women, but also appeared to accept that much unchaperoned contact between the sexes was normal. He then shows that, in reality, from the details given in church court cases, the sexes enjoyed a great freedom to meet in public places, in household service, in agricultural labour, and in buying and selling, as well as in periods of leisure at village festivities and fairs, in alehouses and at inns. Private meetings did not normally in themselves give rise to suspicion of immorality, although they might do so if they were frequently repeated, or displeased an angry spouse. They were certainly permitted to engaged couples. Kissing was permitted in dancing. He concluded on the basis of his village studies and church court evidence alike that pre-marital pregnancy was running at an average of about 22 per cent, very close to the average postulated by Hair, but that its prosecution in the church courts was patchy, and depended very much on the parish of the couple concerned. The prosecution rate, particularly of the poorest members of society, was higher in the increasingly impoverished, populous, partly-industrialized areas of Wiltshire. There the production of bastards, or even of the poor born in wedlock, would put a further strain on poor relief. Even so, he concluded, with Macfarlane, that the attitudes of the courts and of society in general to pre-marital intercourse and pregnancy were tolerant. He also examined in some detail the suggestion that, since in legal theory the contract between the parties, rather than the solemnization of marriage in church, was binding, the popular custom in some areas may have been to consummate the contract, rather than wait for the marriage, as the church required. He found that in ecclesiastical court cases brought against antenuptial fornication an intention to marry was frequently argued as a plea in mitigation, but that the promises given had usually been of an informal kind, made privately, rather than before witnesses. He suggested, in conclusion, an ambivalent situation, where a good deal of freedom between courting couples was permitted, and the ambiguities in the legal situation were appealed to in mitigation if this freedom resulted in pregnancy, and happened to be prosecuted.[23]

The art of courtship books support the pictures drawn by Macfarlane and Ingram with surprising accuracy. The protagonists in the lovers' dialogues, including young and shy girls, are free to make new acquaintances and to renew old contacts in public places. The degree of this freedom, both to meet and to make any contract to marry without the consent of kin, depended on the social background of the parties. A very wide range of custom is therefore demonstrated in the dozens of different dialogues contained in the courtship books. A girl might be as fearful of criticism as the young maid who timorously accepts a stranger's escort home, and meets his declaration of love at first sight by inviting him to visit her at her father's house. She is however unwilling to stand outside discussing the pangs of anguish he feels at leaving her, pointing out that 'There be many jealous eyes, that do watch on occasion to expose me to censures for maintaining you with such unusual familiarity. Let me entreat you, as you tender my Credit to leave me.'[24] A gentlewoman, as she points out very correctly to the young gentleman who begs her in many florid words to grant him life in her love, is not free to choose her own mate:

Indeed Sir, I dare not enter the state of Marriage without discretion: and furthermore I am under the government of my parents whom I dare not, nor will not offend: As they have performed their duty with care and cost in bringing me to this age, so I must in like manner perform my duty in obedience to them, as fits a child to do: I must not cast the Reins of the Bridle on the Horses neck, and let him run where he pleaseth; such as do so, are to ride out of their way.[25]

It is notable, however, that even the most strictly brought up girls are free to have these preliminary discussions alone, before there is any question of an engagement. Even when a dower is to be considered, and parental approval therefore had to be obtained, the personal feelings of the couple for each other is paramount. In this literature, even when it deals with a 'peasant marriage contract', economic considerations are not overriding.[26] Cisley, the Lancashire farmer's daughter, meets Simon at a wedding. He bestows a 'smacking kiss, after his own Countrey fashion' on her in return for help tying a favour in his hatband, and escorts her home. When he declares his love for her, she thanks him, but points out that she can not dispose of herself without her widowed father's consent. Simon, 'being a little elevated with the Wedding Ale, began to wooe her Father . . . until at last the old man persuaded him to get his daughter's consent, and then he would tell him more'. The young people immediately arrange to meet next market day, and Simon departs to tell his mother 'the good news', since, as the chapbook carefully explains, his father

Cisley and Simon

is dead. Simon and Cisley, who both come from farming backgrounds, feel a need to obtain the approval of both sets of parents. Cisley's father is equally unwilling to act without his daughter's approval. Once parental consent is given, they plan, and conduct their courtship entirely themselves. Simon helps Cisley finish selling her father's hemp at the market, and then they resort to the alehouse together to collect the money for the oats Simon has sold on his own account. From the alehouse they move to the grander tavern, where they celebrate their engagement with sack. Patently, this mingling of the sexes in agricultural business and in relaxation at the alehouse is as normal in Simon and Cisley's literary world,[27] as it was in reality in seventeenth-century Wiltshire. It is also normal, however, for the suitors of farmers' daughters to be brought home in the first place. There is a connection between this custom, and the possession of any possible dower. One 'willing Maid' replies to her lover: 'I must not be so bold as to dispose of myself without my Parents consent: you must therefore at first obtain my Parents good will in respect of my patrimony. . . . I then am wholly yours.'[28]

Another whole series of dialogues covers the progress of a courtship from the first avowal of love at a private meeting, through the girl's insistence that the consent of 'her friends' must be obtained, to the suitor's interview with her father, who carefully examines his status, and, as a result, invites him to make frequent visits to his daughter at home.[29]

Girls with no prospects were less insistent on the claims of their kin, and less nice in their behaviour. Sarah eventually replies to her insistent wooer Thomas, 'If you love me as you say, let us be married as soon as you will, and then do as you please, as for our Fortunes you know are but mean'.[30]

The apprentice William of London is of better family than the serving maid, Susan, whom he is courting. This worries her a little, for as she says,

> Neither am I furnished with that which you look for, which is Riches; and I also am of low degree, and of mean parentage, and therefore may in some measure bring disparagement to you, and you may bring upon yourself a prejudice in matching contrary to your Parents good liking.

He feels able to disregard this, however. He replies:

Were thou the richest in worldly treasures in this City, my love could not be firm to thee than now it is: as for my Parents dislike, I need not be troubled at it, for they will prove no hindrance to me.[31]

It is apparent that she, from her mean background, has no need to seek consent of any kin, and he, who is of slightly higher status, will disregard the claims of his own. Servants are commonly drawn, in this literature, as free in this way. Andrew calls on the in-servant, Joan, after her deaf old master is asleep at night.[32] The only restrictions on John and Kate, who are both in-servants, are those imposed by their hours off work, and John's dislike of calling at the house where Kate works, and where is 'such a flickering of laughing amongst the maids and children' when he comes. They, like Simon and Cisley, conduct their wooing in an alehouse. They begin this with a tiff. Kate is suspicious because John has just demonstrated the freedom of the sexes to meet, not only by sharing a pot of ale with one Peg Ramskin on a cold morning and being kissed by her in consequence, but also by responding to a widow's advances, and calling upon her at her home. He points out in response to the second charge that he took a friend with him to visit the widow 'because I would not be seen with her alone' and that they only went to eat her gammon of bacon, although they did kiss her in thanks. This explanation is quite acceptable, and the couple make peace and pass on to discuss whether they can manage to make ends meet if they marry. Kate's father is dead, and the £10 he left her are in her uncle's hands; but she feels no need to obtain his approval. John's father is still alive, but gave him his portion of £10 when he left home. Again, they are not concerned to obtain his consent. They are far more dependent on Kate's mistress's good humour, for she may give a 'money dinner'[33] for them at her house. They also depend on John's master's favour as well, since they hope to obtain the lease of a house from him in which they may set up an alehouse of their own; they only need a few benches to do this. They also hope to obtain his permission to keep a stock of malt going in his malthouse with which to supply this. So the restrictions on their marriage are purely economic rather than those imposed by kin. Their planning is principally concerned with the business of making a living as, in fact, the planning of servants must have been.[34] The evidence of the courtship dialogues seem, in their emphases on freedom of meeting, on the necessity for the consent of kin when a portion was involved, and the increasing lack of need for the good-will of parents and friends amongst the poorest sections of society, to mirror reality closely.

They also mirror reality in their ambivalence towards pre-marital intercourse. They demonstrate a whole range of responses once the courting pair have agreed on marriage. Interestingly, these seem to be more controlled by individual and personal reactions than by the social level of the participants. At one extreme there are the some-what stilted remarks of the coy maiden who promises her lover:

> You may entertain a resolution that you shall enjoy me; but by a legal way, I prise you as my self, and would not you should miscarry either in health or sickness for a Million: . . . so take a freedom that was never granted to any (a chast kiss) for our pledge according to your own unspotted desire.[35]

Other maidens, who made no bones at all about being kissed, still do not dream of anticipating their weddings. Neither Cisley the farmer's daughter, nor Kate the servant do so; one model reply from a young maid to an over-bold lover runs 'Let no shadow of Repentance steal into the sweet consideration of our mutual happiness, I have pro-mised to be your Wife, stay then till the time that I may rightly be so'.[36] The servant-girl Susan was persuaded to allow her apprentice much more, however:

S William, if your Words and deeds prove real, I am contented to become yours; I mean in a lawful way, that is, in Marriage: you may obtain that which you say you have so long desired.

W Than Susan, my time being now short to serve as an Appren-tice, I hope you will not seem nice to let me enjoy the fruition of your love.

S Nay, be not too hasty, hot love is soon cold: it may be you may meet with a Beauty more pleasing to your fancy, and then your old love will be cast off for a new one.

W Tell me not of Beauty, thou art the most beautiful Virgin in my eye, that is living upon the Earth, therefore delay not to ease my burning heart, which burns with love to thee and thou shalt find me faithful to the end of my life.

S Well then, seeing you are so earnest, I have no power to resist, I am at your disposing: do with me as you please.

> So being night they went to bed,
> 　not making any strife,
> He did obtain her Maiden-head,
> 　before she was his Wife
> But afterwards they Married were,
> 　as Lovers ought to do,
> And now they live at hearts content,
> 　and long may they do so.[37]

She was not alone. A whole group of girls in the chapbooks behaved in a similar way. To these heroines, a promise of marriage gave adequate security for intercourse. And they at least hoped that the contract, rather than the marriage service, was binding. The couples who pleaded a private agreement to marry in mitigation of pre-nuptial fornication before the ecclesiastical courts in Wiltshire[38] and elsewhere, thus have their literary counterparts.

There were also more cynical, and frequently much more experienced, young women in the chapbooks, who refused their lovers' embraces not out of any exalted notions of chastity, but because they had been caught that way before. The forty-year-old maid-servant Joan flatly rejected Andrew's suggestion of intercourse before their wedding. Their dialogue was very revealing.

Joan　No, indeed that must not be, for if I should have a Child before I'm married, what do you think people would say? they'l call me whore, and the Child bastard.

And.　O ye simpleton, if I should call every one Whore that has had a Child before they were married, I see enough every day to scratch my eyes out of my head.

Joan　Fy, fy, it is time to talk of better things, for say what you will, Honesty is the best policy, for if all Maids were of my mind, they need not be so long without Husbands as they be.

And.　Why Joan, what would have them do for to get Husbands sooner?

Joan　What would I have them do, I would have them to be nice and wise, not to be so fond of a sweetheart, as to let them lye with him first before they are wedded, for those that do such things, not one in a thousand are married to that man which gets her maidenhood, for when he has had his will, away he is to another, and leaves his Old Love sick of a two-legged Tympany.[39]

A very wide range of sexual behaviour before marriage is therefore demonstrated in the twopenny chapbooks which seem to comprehend the whole spectrum of actual pre-marital behaviour, from the large proportion of brides who married before conception, through the 20 per cent for whom a promise of marriage was enough, who therefore perhaps married when they were already pregnant, to those unfortunates who not only bore but were actually prosecuted in ecclesiastical courts for bearing a bastard, or, in Joan's phrase, a 'two legged Tympany'.

The progress of courtship was marked by gifts which seem to have been traditional. One 'may-day Song' briefly sketched an outline of courtship which is amplified many times in the lovers' dialogues.

> Next we will act how Lovers wooe;
> And sigh and kiss as Lovers do:
> And talk of Bride, and who shall make,
> The Wedding-Smock, this Bridal Cake:
> What Posies for our Wedding Rings,
> What Gloves we'l give, and Ribonings.[40]

The complimentary chapbooks contained suitable rhymes to be

Cupid's Masterpiece

given to the sought-after girl with a variety of objects. The favourite presents were bracelets, looking-glasses, gloves, purses, scarves, handkerchiefs and ribbons, although thimbles and bodkins also appear. These seem to have been offered in reality, as well as in the courtship literature, since breach of promise cases in the ecclesiastical courts required the return of presents of this kind, given in vain.[41] The verses written to accompany them include the inept:

> Would that love
> (by his great Power) would change me to a glove
> your fair hand then should evermore be kist
> and I would ever dwell about your wrist.[42]

They also include the direct, written upon a silver bodkin:

> My dearest sweet, like this is Love,
> It must be thrust in, and then it must move.[43]

A mocking glance is thrown at the impecunious farmer's son, who can only afford a yard of blue ribbon for his girl:

> I send you here of Ribbon a whole yard,
> And money goeth with me very hard;
> For else this yard two yards should be,
> Since I do hold nothing too dear for thee.[44]

These gifts culminated, of course, with the supreme offering of a gold wedding ring, just as the courtship dialogues freqently culminated in marriage. The couplets to be written with rings occasionally had a theological twist:

> My faite is given, this pledge doth show
> A work from Heaven perform'd below.[45]

Their usual theme was life-long constancy:

> Such liking in my choice I find
> That none but death can change my mind.[46]

The importance of the wedding itself as a ritual event was emphasized in the dialogues, which sometimes devoted much space to the plans for it. The most impecunious lovers could not afford new wedding clothes. The servants Andrew and his sweetheart Joan and Honest John and Loving Kate all decide to forgo the expense of these, even though John is determined to give Kate a gold ring, unlike the

burlesqued Andrew, who is willing to use a ring from a sow's nose
instead. Simon and Cisley, as befit a couple from a farming background, both have new clothes for their wedding. Simon's are
ordered from the tailor on market day, and Cisley's new high-heeled
shoes are the cause of her ludicrous fall into the river on her way to
her wedding.

However poor the couple are, they are determined, in the literature, to celebrate their wedding in style. They may not have new
clothes, but they will certainly have a wedding feast, even if it is given
by a master or mistress instead of by parents. Simon's mother made
Simon and Cisley's wedding dinner, which was followed by a 'Cup
of good ale of their own brewing and a lame fiddler to make them
merry, with which they past on the time till Supper', and the cer-
emonial bedding of the bride. The feast, the dance, and the bedding of
the bride, with the ritual consumption of sack posset and 'throwing
of the stocking', are the constants in wedding celebrations. John and
Kate intend to have their house ready to sleep in the night after their
wedding. They also intend to lay in ale,

> That we may be able to invite all the wedding people to drink with
> us, and then we shall have good Handsel indeed, and we will also
> have a good Gammon of Bacon, and that will make the drink go
> down merrily.[47]

Dancing is the element which is even more stressed than ale in the
celebrations. Kate laughs to think 'how the young men will turn the
Lasses about in dancing, and how they buss them', although she is
abashed by the thought of the competition there will be to dance with
her. Andrew and Joan plan tabor and pipe music at their wedding.[48]
Even the veriest hayseed of a country farmer says at the successful
conclusion of his clumsy wooing, 'I'll get my Leather-doublet new
furnisht, and a pair of Wisps to sadle my legs, for we mun dance on
that day sure; and who can dance in boots?'[49]

Here again the chapbooks mirror reality. The non-conformist
minister Oliver Heywood was somewhat dubious in 1678 to find
dancing at a Puritan wedding.[50] His contemporary the Reverend
Giles Moore, who was rector of Horstead Keynes in Sussex from
1665 to 1679, had no such scruples. He attended five weddings
between 1661 and 1669,[51] at all of which he paid the fiddler 6*d*. He
also gave a fiddler 6*d* at a non-wedding feast, and once paid a bagpipe

3 Nineteenth-century pedlar dolls

4 Nineteenth-century pedlar dolls and market stall

player *6d*, as well as contributing *9d* towards a drum for the 'Parish Boyes'. His normal custom at a wedding was to make a small money gift to the groom, as well as the payment to the fiddler. Thus on 30 June 1661 he noted 'Giv'n Ja: Browne beeing then newely marryed *5s.* Collection 1–6*d*'. This journal gives conclusive evidence of the normality of the wedding dance, played for by the local fiddler, who might, as Simon and Cisley's musician was, be a crippled man drawn to music as a livelihood, much as cripples were drawn to the 'sheltered' occupation of schoolteaching.[52]

The chapbooks draw attention to the importance of music in country life, both to celebrate weddings and on other occasions. Seventeen of the chapbooks were 'garlands' or books of ballads (see Table III, pp. 136–7). So song-books made up another fifth of the 'popular culture' section of the chapbooks, and 7 per cent of the whole collection. Music and courtship were equally important in the chapbooks collected by Pepys.

Music, like all leisure activities, leaves little trace behind it when the notes have died away. This is particularly true because the instruments of the poor, like the books of the poor, are not listed in probate inventories. Flageolets, tabors and pipes, and even the old fiddles that were so vital a part of alehouse culture, were not recorded. It is impossible to believe, however, that they were not there. Because of the sparse evidence it is convenient to look at popular music in the nineteenth century, while it was still a living tradition, and then try to read the palimpsest.

Thomas Hardy was the son of a village mason, who had built up a successful business. His father and grandfather before him had created a choir of instrumentalists, in which Hardy senior played the 'cello and his sons and son-in-law, including Hardy's father, played the violin. Hardy's father was also much in demand as a singer and fiddler at country dances. He taught young Thomas the fiddle very early, and he learnt to play hundreds of country dances from his father's and grandfather's old music books. As he grew up, and began to play at village weddings and dances himself, sometimes with and sometimes without his father, parental tension mounted, possibly over the boy's exposure to dances that could easily develop into the setting for drunken lovemaking.[53]

Hardy drew extensively on his own experiences in his writing. In his preface to *Under the Greenwood Tree*,[54] he wrote of choirs like his grandfather's. The members 'brought fiddle strings, rosin, and music paper, which they ruled themselves' from a pedlar, who travelled in such wares from choir to choir. 'He was generally,' Hardy wrote, 'a musician himself, and sometimes a composer in a small way, bringing with him new tunes and teaching each choir to adapt them for a consideration.' This music was transcribed by the musicians themselves, 'copied out in the evenings after work, and their music books were home bound'. They contained hymns at the front, ballads and bawdy songs at the back. If Hardy is writing of his grandfather's choir, musical notation was no secret to this group of masons and agricultural labourers in the 1820s and 1830s.

Hardy's fiction also demonstrated the importance of both ballad singing and dancing. *Tess of the D'Urbervilles* had a mother who sang ballads endlessly to the latest inmate of the cradle as she laboured at the wash tub. 'Mrs Durbyfield was a passionate lover of tunes. No ditty floated into Blackmoor Vale from the outer world but Tess's mother caught up its notation in a week.' Hardy draws a strong contrast between 'the mother with her fast-perishing lumber of superstitions, folk-lore, dialect and orally transmitted ballads, and the daughter, with her trained National teachings and Standard knowledge under an infinitely Revised Code' whom he suggested were 200 years apart. Even so, Tess, in the days of her grief, spent some of her time trying to perfect the ballads which had most pleased the husband who had deserted her, when she worked on a diary farm and sang with the other milkmaids. She had a considerable repertoire.

Tess was also present at one of the dances that ended as a grand carouse on the day a fair coincided with the market at a local town. It culminated in so much tipsy lovemaking that poor Hardy was pushed into Greek mythology to convey his meaning without offence. The outhouse in which it took place ended up peopled with Pan and Syrinx, Priapus and Lotis and a general group of Sileni.[55]

There is a body of other nineteenth-century evidence demonstrating the importance of music in the lives of the humble. The history of the Copper family, farm carters and bailiffs of Rottingdean in Sussex, has been written, unembellished by fiction, and shows a singing tradition stretching from the end of the Napoleonic War via the foundation of the English Folk Dance and Song Society, to the present day. It was important as a family amusement, but was also tied to the village inn, which acted as the centre for the singing of the men of the farming community as it also did for the Mummers' Play.[56] John Clare, who was also inside the tradition as a day-labourer's son (see above, pp. 3–5), had a grandfather who was an itinerant fiddler and taught in the Helpston village school in Northamptonshire for a time. Clare himself had to learn to play the fiddle from the gypsies, however, and did so partly to earn money at the 'annual feasts in the neighbourhood and at Christmas'. Despite his poverty-stricken background and patchy education, he succeeded in learning musical notation, so that when from 1817 onwards he began to collect, first tunes for his violin, then ballads, he could write them down more 'literately', it is suggested, than his poems or prose. Despite his collecting as a known figure of equal status with those from whom he collected, he already had problems before 1828 familiar to collectors who were more remote socially from their material. He was impeded by the shyness of 'old people who sing old songs only sung to be laughed at'. Yet he managed to acquire songs from a ploughman, a shoemaker and other villagers as well as his own parents, who both had considerable repertoires.[57]

The Hardy family in Dorset, the Coppers in Sussex and the Clares in Northamptonshire were not unusual. The unpublished notebooks of Doctor Percy Manning suggest that, until the 1860s, every district had its piper, a shepherd or labourer who played for his own and surrounding villages.[58] The extent of nineteenth-century evidence for the survival of ballad-singing and dancing suggests very strongly that the vehement late sixteenth- and early seventeenth-century Puritan campaign against it, from which most earlier evidence comes, had been only temporarily successful at best.[59]

A survey has been made of the cases concerned with music and dancing brought before the ecclesiastical courts in sixteenth-century Essex. Most of these naturally referred only to music and dancing on the Sabbath, particularly in service time. Even so at least thirty cases appeared in the records. The most scandalous deposition in Puritan eyes must have been the one made in 1566, by a woman who averred that

> John Clark, rector, would have her dance upon the green at their door, and took her by the hand and kissed her, and whistled the dance with his mouth . . . which was but in pastime, and the dance was flowers in the broom.

A variety of instruments were used. In 1571 a Waldon man who was a 'minstrel' piped the people to dancing in the sermon in service time. In 1579, a man was presented for 'playing on his fiddle unseemly dances'. In the 1590s, a man was presented for 'playing on his tabor and pipe in a beerhouse yard', and Thomas Baker of Terling was said to 'often play upon the sabbath day upon the green upon his tabor and pipe, and sometimes continue(s) till night'. Terling produced several presentations. In June 1600, there was a 'general dancing upon the green, when one Belstead's wife did kneel down eight or nine times for the kissing of a young man'.

Another group of Essex presentations concerned the dancing of the morris. The most interesting concerned a wedding celebration in 1603, when musicians were presented for 'making preparation . . . to dance the morris in sermon time, and they met with the bridegroom, and came dancing the morris home with him'.[60]

This kind of Sunday entertainment and wedding celebrations spread all over the country. Of sixteenth-century Lancashire, it has been written, 'in the view of the preachers, pipers represented an even greater threat to the spread of the Gospel than ale-sellers'. There a curate was reported in 1581 for dancing on Sundays and holy-days 'amongst light and youthful company, both men and women, at weddings, drinkings and rush bearings', and in 1597, a parish clerk took a piper into the church to organize dancing in service time.[61] In Shropshire in the late 1620s, Richard Baxter wrote:

> in the village where I lived, the reader read the Common Prayer briefly, and the rest of the day even till dark night almost, except eating time, was spent in dancing under a maypole and a great tree not far from my father's door, where all the town did meet together. . . . So that we could not read the Scripture in our family without the great disturbance of the tabor and pipe, and noise in the street.[62]

In Yapton in Sussex a fiddler enticed all the village youth to dance on the green instead of going to catechism each week.[63]

The professional disapproval of musicians like Thomas Whythorne, who was an early madrigalist and taught music in great houses, of those to whom he would have denied the title of musician, that

Do use to go with their instruments about the countries to cities, towns and villages . . . for such as will hear them, either publicaly or privately: or else to markets, fairs, marriages, assemblies, taverns, ale-houses and such like places and there . . . will sell the sound of their voices and instruments,[64]

Dancing to tabor and pipe

combined with the disapproval of Puritans. But despite the Puritan efforts to suppress dancing and music on the sabbath, and to produce more suitable alternatives to secular ballads,[65] popular music still seems to have survived to flourish again after the Civil War.

The Pepys family, like so many others, sprawled across the social scale from country gentlemen to London tailors, and holders of government office to much humbler country cousins. In 1661, Samuel Pepys wrote in his *Diary*:[66]

> Today I received a letter from my Uncle to beg an old fiddle off me for my Cosen Perkin the Miller, whose mill the wind hath lately broken down and now he hath nothing to live but by fiddling – and he must needs have it against Whitsuntide to play to the country girles. . . . I entered to morrow to send him one.

So the girls of the Isle of Ely were, in 1661, going to celebrate Whitsun as they always had. Moreover a living could be made by playing at seasonal feasts, for the skill was in demand, as it still was in John Clare's time.

Only the Quakers amongst the Puritans really disapproved of music as such. John Bunyan may have taken a year to give up dancing, but he, with a similarly limited education to John Clare's, may also have known musical notation, and music was obviously very important to him. The tin flute and fiddle he made for himself in jail are well known, but he also possessed a chest decorated with inlaid musical instruments.[67] The spiritual autobiographers, who became Quakers and therefore persuaded that music was inherently evil, themselves provide evidence of the hold that music had on them.

Josiah Langdale of Nafferton in Yorkshire, who was born in 1673, shows both how dancing still flourished as an adolescent and courting pastime in the 1680s, and also how it was learnt after school at night.

> Dancing took much with the young People of our Town. . . . Much Evil was committed at this School. . . . The Dancing Master was a Fidler and Jugler, and after we broke up School every Night he went to play his Tricks. I did not learn many Dances before it became an exceeding Trouble to my Soul and Spirit. . . . After some time my Playfellows would entice me to Feasts, where young

men and women meet to be merry . . . and such Like was I invited to, under a Pretence to improve our Dancing.[68]

The crippled barber, John Mulliner of Northampton, writing at the end of the 1660s, not only found himself obliged to give up his sheltered employment of periwig-making, since it catered to the vanity of man, but also burnt his musical intruments and gave up his music 'which was a great Delight to me'.[69] But the most interesting testimony to the social importance of music and the standing that the ability to play could therefore give to a member of a community came from a Leicestershire miller, writing sadly from Leicester County Jail in the 1670s of the ways in which he upset, or was upset by, the inhabitants of his community of Nether-Broughton:

remember, dear Friends, the Testimony which I was constrained to bear . . . against the vain Custome of feasting and banqueting; O the hurt that that hath done in the Town of Nether-Broughton: It hath drawn many into idle Discourse foolish Jesting, and Laughter.

What seemed to hurt him most, however, since it reflected the false values of his friends, was that when he first opened his house in Broughton for meetings, those who declared the Gospel to the curious who came '*were esteemed by some of you as them that could play well of an Instrument*'.[70] This desirable state of affairs did not, however, last.

Musicians in a community were therefore people in demand by the locals, who had a rarity value despite their, often dubious, alehouse connection, which did not necessarily please their social superiors. The little so far known about their incidence suggests that a market town might expect to have one, and that a considerable village might also do so. The parish register of Cleobury Mortimer in the Clee hills of Shropshire, which gives occupations between 1622 and 1634, refers to a minstrel as well as a chapman. Cleobury was a market town which was reviving in importance in the early seventeenth century.[71] The Bishop of Lichfield noted musicians in his census-type description of the market town and parish of Eccleshall in Staffordshire in the 1690s. Eccleshall parish contained over 20,000 acres, and was one of the largest in Staffordshire. It had at least twenty-two separate townships with a minimum of 615 families there in 1693.

The Bishop had antiquarian tastes, and was not content to note only current activities in his manor. One burgage in Eccleshall itself housed a labourer in receipt of poor relief, whose great-grandfather and grandfather had lived in the same tenement in the 1650s and before, and were both musicians. Dorothy Oliver had, also before the Civil War, married a 'fiddler and trumpeter' as her second husband. In the 1690s a labourer called Thomas Smith lived in Eccleshall itself. He was a drummer, and probably responsible for most of the current tabor and pipe playing that the town needed. One John Smith, of whom the Bishop thoroughly disapproved, also lived in Eccleshall. He had been a miller, farmer and a smith before becoming a joiner, then a bagpiper and then a fiddler. He next became a soldier, presumably using his music, but he disliked the army also, and bought himself out and returned to the miller's trade. James Bird of Croxton, one of the hamlets on the main road through Eccleshall to Chester, was a fiddler 'gaming at cards for any, showing tricks', and Robert Hodge of Croxton Bank was also a musician, who kept an alehouse. The musicians of Eccleshall may have been a useful social asset; and it is noticeable that all three of them had married women who had inherited at least a cottage in their own right. They obviously had some attraction. However, they were not particularly liked by their lord. Another reference to Wilkinson, 'the fiddler of Stone', the next market town, is significant both because it implies that every market town might have a fiddler, also because of the social context. He was mentioned only because he had fathered the bastard of the daughter of a labourer who lived in Eccleshall itself.[72] The Bishop's prejudice against fiddlers was shared by the gentry, not because of their immorality, but because the music they provided was common. Sir John Dalton pronounced that 'Fidlers, and all bad Musicke are like the Cocke; when they crow, every Man rises, and away'.[73]

Prejudice on moral grounds was felt even more strongly by non-conformists. Oliver Heywood persuaded one old man 'to seek advice about salvation' but as he went

> he called at an alehouse, fell to drinking at night was found drunk with some fiddler and idle company about him, afterwards being discoursed with he said now he need not goe for he was . . . pretty quiet in his mind. . . . O dreadful state!

wrote the would-be instrument of his salvation.[74]

THE NEW
𝕵𝖔𝖇𝖎𝖆𝖑 𝕲𝖆𝖗𝖑𝖆𝖓𝖉
Of MIRTH and DELIGHT;
Or Banquet a of the Choicest
AND
NEWEST SONGS;

Fitted for the Diverfion and Satisfaction of all Ingenious young Men and Maids, who take Delight in Mirth.

Printed for T. Conver near St. *Andrews* Church in *Holbourn*

The fiddler

It looks, from the Bishop's reconstruction of the Eccleshall population, as if it had had at least one, and sometimes more, resident musicians for most of the seventeenth century. In the next century, Hawkeshead, in the southern Lake District, marked its development as a market centre by supporting both a fiddler and a dancing master.[75] If one of the distinctions of a market town was to support a musician, it is no wonder that such people both had a rarity value, and yet were common enough to provide the most important element in wedding celebrations. Nor is it surprising that the books of garlands were laid out as they were. A considerable repertoire of tunes, presumably known to the reader or at least to the local musician, was assumed. Each new song was introduced by the simple expedient of giving the tune to which it went. Even the ubiquitous Honest John was capable of inventing a song to Kate while he was working in the malthouse, and played it over to her on his flageolet. She responded to him by singing 'My Love is to New England gone'. Jointly they agreed that their alehouse should be called the 'Three Fiddlers' so that their customers would 'judge they may have Musick'.[76]

No musical notation was ever used in the garlands.[77] The books of songs in Pepys's collection referred to 108 different tunes. Amongst these, there were favourites. Eight 'new songs' went to the tune of 'When Flying Fame', six to 'My Life and My Death', and five to 'Oh Mother Roger'. Four new songs apiece were written to tunes of the 'Thundering Cannons Roar', 'Maids a-Washing', 'The Country Farmer' and 'The Two English Travellers'. The favourites for which only three new sets of words were composed are already too numerous to mention; they varied in mood from 'Caper and Jerk It' to the 'Doubting Virgin' and from 'Fortune my Foe' to 'Joy to the Bridegroom'.[78] It seems highly improbable that rural readers can really have had so wide a range of tunes at their disposal, yet it is worth remembering that the Corporation of the Poor, responsible for training London foundlings and poor children, instructed them in music as well as reading, writing and a trade.[79] It is too long a leap from mid-seventeenth London to late eighteenth-century Northamptonshire and the musical expertise of John Clare's labourer father with his repertoire of over 100 ballads even via *Honest John and Loving Kate*. We need to know much more about the range of tunes known to ordinary, non-grammar-school educated, rural

The GOLDEN
GARLAND

Of most Delightful Mirth and Merriment.
Containing Variety of Excellent New SONGS.

This may be Printed, R. P.

Printed for J. Blare, on London-Bridge.

Songs for rustic courting couple

people in the seventeenth and early eighteenth centuries. Unfortunately for these purposes, there is no reason why anybody should be presented in an ecclesiastical court after the Restoration for singing. Only some non-conformists were likely to object. One tiny fragment of information therefore comes from the Bedfordshire borders in the 1720s. John Bunyan's Open Baptists disliked drunkenness very much. They also disliked 'Light, unbecoming actions . . . about the maypole'. The affiliated church at Gamlingay just into Cambridgeshire took offence, first at Thomas Cooper for the 'childish exercise of pipeing and useing of musick in his Common Conversation', and then at the behaviour of widow Rose Robinson in February 1721. She 'became disordered with drink at goodman Chesham's on the night on which the shoe-makers keep a feast, and their did they often urge and presse on other carnal people to sing vain heathenish Love Songs'. Widow Robinson's sin was compounded because she described it as 'so small a thing'.[80] It does not sound as if celebrating a feast with a combination of drink and song in a mixed company was at all unusual to Widow Robinson. There is enough evidence to suggest the tremendous importance of both singing and dancing as a means of relaxation in late seventeenth-century life. There is not nearly enough, however, after the main Puritan attacks were over, to be specific about the occasions of such festivities, apart from weddings.

There were almost as many burlesques and anti-female satires amongst the 'small merry books' as there were courtship and songbooks (see above, Table III, pp. 136–7). These have been treated elsewhere.[81] There are still some elements in them which deserve attention, however. One of these is the way they reflect prejudice against immigrants, who are usually poor. They were, therefore, in the literature, invincibly stupid. The very real menace of the poor beggar was coped with by mockery.

Four of the burlesques have the wanderings, mishaps, mispronunciations and misadventures of their Welsh 'heroes' as their main theme.[82] Young Shon ap Morgan travels to London. On the way he puts up at a pastry cook's and is served with a groat's worth of cold pork and mustard sauce. 'What,' he asks 'is that child's turd?' 'Oh,' says the cook, 'it is Sauce; Mustard is good for your eyes, Sir.' So, inevitably, he anoints his eyes with the mustard. He caps his misfortunes by asking for a 'pice Possitt'. The mistress and her maid are unaccustomed to Welsh dialect, and after anxious consultation over why he should want a piss possett, they decide 'this may be a well-approved Welsh Medicine for a queazy Stomach', and duly send him one up. His adventures reach an unexpectedly happy ending; he gets a job with a merchant, negotiates his marriage for him and lives happily ever after. But he is a well-known figure, for his own wooing is independently burlesqued in one of the art of compliment chapbooks.[83] Welshmen and Scotsmen and their lovemaking are frequently mocked in the wooing dialogues. Nicholas Le Strange records as frightful a 'Welsh' joke as any 'Irish' joke today, about a Welshman who thought he might have sixteen wives, 'for the Priest told him when he married "foure better, four worse, foure richer, four poorer"'.[84]

The historical background to these literary figures of fun is the sixteenth- and seventeenth-century pattern of long-distance migration. In the Clee hills area of Shropshire there was only one Welsh surname in the 1524–5 subsidy returns. The parish registers indicate a steady flow of Welsh immigrants from the second quarter of the sixteenth century. The registers of Neen Savage record the highest number of Welsh immigrants between 1575 and 1616. Twenty-six new names were recorded, and eighteen of the people concerned were beggars. Many of the names only occur once in the register, and so their owners presumably moved on eastwards into England. There was also a steady flow of Welsh immigrants into the small town of Burford in the late sixteenth century.[85] The records of the Draper's Company of Shrewsbury showing the origins of their apprentices show an increase in immigration in the seventeenth century. Between 1572 and 1609, only two drapers' apprentices came from Wales although over a third of the men in the shearman's guild were Welsh by 1587. Between 1609 and 1639, forty-three apprentices came from Wales, more than from any other area except Shrewsbury itself and Shropshire.[86]

It seems clear that the effects of this late sixteenth- and seventeenth-century immigration filtered through into popular consciousness and was reflected in the tradition of anti-Welsh jokes so freely used by the chapbooks. There is an exact parallel between the waves of immigrant labour from Ireland from 1817 onwards to its climax after 1846, and the appearance of the jokes about stupid Irishmen still current in our own time. Perusal of *Punch* for the first half of the nineteenth century shows that the first 'Irish' jokes appeared at exactly the right point in time for that particular influx of Irishmen.[87]

The chapbooks are perhaps most alien to the reader three hundred years later in their lack of compassion. Slapstick aimed at an immigrant group would not be accepted by most twentieth-century readers, and that aimed at simpletons would probably not be acceptable to any readers. The chapbooks present another problem. They are often funny, and richly funny at that, but the humour is frequently of the dung-hill variety. Nothing was more amusing than to empty a full chamber-pot upon the head of a passer-by, unless it was also full of faeces. Here the subject matter comes up against a twentieth-century taboo. Jokes about defecation and urination are, on the whole, relegated to the junior school, and are certainly not printed. People in the sixteenth and seventeenth centuries did not share this inhibition. Adults, including the gentry, patently found such jokes acceptable, and laughed at them. Dame Alice Le Strange felt quite able to tell her son, who recorded the story in his jest-book, how as a little girl travelling with her mother, she exclaimed 'There(s) Ice yet I the Ditch', and the gentleman accompanying them teased her by saying 'Fye, what a beastly girl is this, she cryes to me and Points saying look etc. "there I shit I the Ditch" '.[88] Perhaps the story that illustrates this shift in humour best is the one that combines two currently unacceptable elements, mockery that includes both stupidity and shit. It is the history of an Essex bastard, who was simple-minded. He was taken into a knight's house to become a fool. One of the anecdotes about him relates how he took a purge, and then shit so vigorously that he befouled himself and stank the parlour out. The lady of the house could not 'forbear laughing to see him so surprized and crying so greviously'.[89]

The chapbooks are full of such jokes.[90] A significant group of these jokes suggest the use of both piss and shit to express contempt. A maid-servant will piss into a pot of beer for a disagreeable customer and a boy will serve up a pudding of turds for his mother's lover.[91] There is other evidence for this usage. The most unpleasant slur that could be thought up to vilify one group of local Quakers, who aroused the hostility of their opponents, was apparently the story that they had defecated on an altar in Norwich. They therefore broke a taboo by defiling a holy place.[92]

There seems to be remarkably little written in psychological literature about defecation since Freud propounded his theories. Nor is there a great deal in modern anthropological literature, although there is enough to show that the attitudes of primitive peoples vary widely, and that the learnt attitudes of disgust towards excrement, which logically extend to using it for the ultimate gesture of contempt, are by no means universal.[93] Therefore this usage in the chapbooks of the 1680s can only be stated as a puzzle. The English were well aware of the utility of human excrement; the contents of the privies of London filled the night soil carts that manured the market gardens of Hertfordshire, and which as 'returning empties' brought back London vegetables.[94] The practice has continued right through to the twentieth century in some remote places.[95] Why the people of Stuart England, who were in no way removed from the physical realities, since they still coped with the perennial problems of emptying the privy and had something extremely useful to do with the proceeds, should have used a language of contempt based on these proceeds, is a problem that can only be stated here. It was already very old in the seventeenth century.

The 'small merry books' were, then, much concerned with courtship, sex, music as a pastime, and scatalogical jokes. They mirror social reality in some ways far more accurately than the reader would at first suspect. They revel in slapstick and in satire and in the misadventures of unfortunates. The quality that they totally lack to a modern reader is compassion. They lack, also, any sense of time, as they lack any real sense of the romantic love so much parodied and mocked in them. For this last quality, the seventeenth-century reader had to turn to the smaller quartos.

NOTES AND REFERENCES

1 *Vulgaria*, IV (2).

2 Craig, W. J. (ed.) (1911) *Comedies of Shakespeare*, Oxford, 990.

3 *Vulgaria*, III (2). This had a more elaborate vocabulary, mythology, and conceits than the *Merriments* version, *PM*, I (17), 377–98.

4 *Vulgaria*, III (7).

5 *Vulgaria*, III (5). This appears, in part at least, to be a straight plagiarization from Forde's 'Ornatus and Artesia', *Vulgaria*, III (4).

6 Wrigley, E. A. (1969) *Population and History*, London, 86–7; Hajnal, J. (1965) in Glass, D. V. and Eversley, D. E. C. (eds) *Population in History*, 101; Laslett, P. (1965) *World We Have Lost*, London, 83; and Wrigley, E. A. (1966) 'Family Limitation in pre-Industrial England', *Economic History Review*, 2nd series 19 (1), 86–109. Earlier in the century, age at first marriage was younger, but still remarkably late. The mean age of grooms was 28.7 years, and of brides 25.2 years in South Elmham. Evans, N. (1978) 'The Community of South Elmham, Suffolk, 1550–1640', UEA MPhil. Findings from family reconstitutions are summarized by Smith, R. M. (1978) 'Population and its Geography in England, 1500–1730', in Dodgshon, R. A. and Butlin, R. A. (eds) *An Historical Geography of England and Wales*, London, New York and San Francisco, 216–17. I have leant very heavily in this section on the general surveys of the demographic literature, and the particular findings of Alan Macfarlane and Martin Ingram in their theses on 'The Regulation of Marital and Sexual Relationships in Seventeenth Century England, with special references to the county of Essex' (1968), University of London MPhil, and 'Ecclesiastical Justice in Wiltshire, 1600–40, with special references to cases concerning sex and marriage' (1976), University of Oxford DPhil, in order to put the chapbooks in a realistic historical context. I am very grateful indeed to Dr Macfarlane and Dr Ingram for allowing me to use their work in this way.

7 Thompson, R. (1976) 'Popular Reading and Humour in Restoration England', *Journal of Popular Culture* 9(3), 665–7.

8 I have not treated the courtship chapbooks as if they had descended in the social scale. In fact they seem very likely to have been adjustments for a different audience of the tradition of courtship dialogue initiated by the twelfth century *Art of Courtly Love* of Andreas Capellanus (Parry, J. J. (trans. and ed.) (1941) Records of Civilization Sources and Studies 33, New York). These conversations are frequently between lovers of different social rank. Some passages in the compliment books are very close indeed to medieval writing. The whole tradition of romantic love expressed and often mocked in the chapbooks, is magnificently and succinctly parodied in Robert de Blois's thirteenth-century 'Advice to Ladies' in Shapiro, N. R. (trans.) (1971) *The Comedy of Eros: Medieval French Guides to the Art of Love*, Urbana, 80–1.

9 Dr Macfarlane, for instance, wondered whether the romantic love complex was present in seventeenth-century society and whether sex was looked on as pleasurable, thesis cit., 88–90, 144.

10 Stone, L. (1977) *The Family, Sex and Marriage in England 1500–1800*, London, 93, 98–9, 284–6.

11 'Cupid's Soliciter of Love', *PM*, I (46), 1013.

12 ibid., 1010–13.

13 'The Lover's Academy', *PM*, II (35), 837.

14 ibid., 840.

15 'Cupid's Masterpiece', *PM*, I (33), 718–19.

16 'Cupid's Soliciter of Love', *PM*, I (45), 1020–1.

17 'Art of Courtship or the School of Delight', *PM*, II (16), 358–9.

18 'Cupid's Court of Salutations', *PM*, II (37), 898.

19 Ravensdale, J. R. (1981) 'Deaths and Entries: the Reliability of the Figures of Mortality in the Black Death in Miss F. M. Page's *Estates of Crowland Abbey* and some Implications for Land Holding', in Smith, R. M. (ed.) *Land, Kinship, and Life-Cycle*, London, and Spufford, M. (1974) *Contrasting Communities*, London 116–17.

20 'Cupid's Soliciter of Love', *PM*, I (45), 1015.

21 Macfarlane, thesis cit., 67–83, 107–15, 124–7.

22 Hair, P. E. H. (1966) 'Bridal Pregnancy in Rural England in Earlier Centuries', *Population Studies* 20 (2), 237 and *passsim*.

23 Ingram, thesis cit., 112–13, 116–18, 165–6, 169–74, 174–6, 178–87, 191–5, 370–1.

24 'The Lover's Academy', *PM*, II (35), 844.

25 'Cupid's Soliciter of Love', *PM*, I (45), 1006.

26 The evidence of the chapbook fiction is therefore in complete contradiction to Professor Stone's interpretations of lack of affection or even knowledge of that emotion between couples in humble society. Stone, op. cit., 98–9, 191–3. He is of course right that the poorer the couple, the fewer were the constraints on them, pp. 292–3, 297, as the couples chosen from the courtship literature show. Even here, though, the compliment books certainly do not maintain his suggestion that 'The absolute poor were more or less free to select their own mates. . . . But they looked for an efficient economic assistant rather than an affectionate companion', p. 193. Romantic love, personal liking and the satisfaction of sexual desire were all elements the courtship

books expected their readers to seek. The in-servant was no exception to these expectations.

27 'The Merry Conceits and Passages of Simon and Cisley, Two Lancashire Lovers', *PM*, I (57), *passim.*

28 'Cupid's Love-Lessons', *PM*, I (47), 1044.

29 'Cupid's Court of Salutations', *PM*, II (37), 887–92.

30 'The Art of Courtship', *PM*, II (16), 349–50.

31 'The Lover's Academy', *PM*, II (35), 836.

32 'Merry Dialogue between Andrew and his Sweetheart Joan', *PM*, I (5), 101, 111.

33 If this custom of taking up a collection from the wedding guests was found in a chapbook, referred to in this brief fashion, it may have been quite common. Dr Macfarlane drew attention to it, thesis cit., 74, since at one wedding attended by Josselin in 1647, £56 was raised. Macfarlane, A. (ed.) (1976) *Diary of Ralph Josselin, 1616–1683*, London, 98.

34 'A Pleasant Dialogue between Honest John and Loving Kate', *PM*, I (10), *passim.*

35 'Cupid's Court of Salutations', *PM*, II (37), 895.

36 'Cupid's Love-Lessons', *PM*, I (47), 1031.

37 'The Lover's Academy', *PM*, II (35), 836–7.

38 Ingram, thesis cit., 192.

39 'A Merry Dialogue between Andrew and his Sweetheart Joan', *PM*, I (5), 109.

40 'Cupid's Masterpiece', *PM*, I (33), 723–4.

41 Macfarlane, thesis cit., 71.

42 'Cupid's Masterpiece', *PM*, I (33), 724. A collection of these rhymes is to be found in Evans, J. (1932) *English Posies and Posy Rings*, London.

43 'Cupid's Love-Lessons', *PM*, I (47), 1047. This contains a section devoted to verses to accompany various gifts, pp. 1045–7. The whole of 'Cupid's Posies', *PM*, I (21), 465–80, is made up of these.

44 'Cupid's Posies', *PM*, I (21), 477–8.

45 'Cupid's Love-Lessons', *PM*, I (47), 1046.

46 ibid.; see also, 'Cupid's Posies', *PM*, I (21), 476–7.

47 'A Pleasant Dialogue between Honest John and Loving Kate', *PM*, I (10), 223.

48 'A Merry Dialogue between Andrew and his Sweetheart Joan', *PM*, I (5), 106.

49 'Cupid's Masterpiece', *PM*, I (33), 723.

50 Horsfall-Turner, J. (ed.) (1881) *The Rev. Oliver Heywood, BA, 1630–1702: His Autobiography, Diaries, Anecdote and Event Books*, II, Brighouse, 253.

51 Bird, R. (1971) *Journal of Giles Moore*, Sussex Record Society, Lewes, 322–33. I am very grateful to Victor Gammon for giving me this reference.

52 See above, Chapter II, p. 29 for Thomas Tryon's writing master. Vincent, D. (1981) *Bread, Knowledge and Freedom*, London, Chapter 5, draws attention to the way schoolteaching offered a possible 'sheltered' occupation for a crippled man.

53 Gittings, R. (1978) *Young Thomas Hardy*, Harmondsworth, 26–7, 47, 50–1. Hardy himself said the coming of the railway in 1847 was responsible for killing the orally-transmitted ballads, p. 40.

54 To the new edition of 1896.

55 Hardy, T. (1974 edn) *Tess of the D'Urbervilles*, London, 46–8, 50–1, 94–7, 391.

56 Copper, B. (1975) *A Song for Every Season*, St Albans, 11, 183–4. See also above, p. 15.

57 Grainger, M. (1964) *John Clare: Collector of Ballads*, Peterborough Museum Society, Occasional Papers 3, 5, 17, 6–7, 14–15.

58 Baines, A. (1943) *Woodwind Instruments and their History*, London, 224–6. Plate xvii illustrates Joe Powell, described as the last of the old taborers in England *c.* 1870, together with an Oxfordshire pipe and tabor of 1886, both in the Pitt Rivers museum in Oxford.

59 For this campaign, see Burke, P. (1978) *Popular Culture in Early Modern Europe*, London, Chapter 8 *passim*. For the travelling musicians, jugglers and ballad singers so much objected to by Thomas Whythorne, see pp. 94–106.

60 All these Essex cases are taken from Emmison, F. G. (1976) 'Tithes and Perambulations and Sabbath Breach in Elizabethan Essex', in Emmison, F. G. and Stevens, R. (eds) *Tribute to an Antiquary*, London, 198–209. Music, though we hear more of it on Sundays, since it was then an offence, was also an aid to work. Henry Best employed a piper all day to keep his sheep shearers happy. Best, H. (1857) *Rural Economy in Yorkshire in 1641*, Surtees Society 33, Durham, 97. I owe this reference to Bernard Capp.

61 Haigh, C. (1977) 'Puritan Evangelism in the reign of Elizabeth I', *English Historical Review* 92(362), 53.

62 Keeble, N. H. (ed.) (1974) *Autobiography of Richard Baxter,* London, 6.

63 Johnstone, H. (ed.) (1948) *Churchwardens' Presentments,* Sussex Records Society, Lewes, 50. I owe this reference to Bernard Capp.

64 Osborne, J. M. (ed.) (1962) *Autobiography of Thomas Whythorne,* written *c.* 1576, London, 193–4.

65 In Scotland, *Ane Compendius Buik of godly and spirituall songis, collectit out of sundrye partes of the Scripture, with sundrye uther Ballatis changeit out of prophaine sangis in godly sangis for avoyding of sins and harlotry . . .* discussed in Shire, H. M. (1969) *Song, Dance, and Poetry of the Court of Scotland and King James VI,* Cambridge, who describes it as one of the major cultural phenomena of the Reformation in Scotland. Mrs Shire draws a distinction between the courtly tradition of dancing to song and the vulgar tradition of dancing while you sing yourself. See also, above p. 10, for John Rhodes in (1588, reprinted in 1637) *The Countrie Man's Comfort . . .,* London.

66 Latham, R. (ed.) (1970) *Diary,* II, London, 8 May 1661. The uncle was Robert Pepys of Brampton, Huntingdonshire, the cousin Frank Perkin of Parson Drove, Cambridgeshire.

67 Scholes, P. (1934) *Puritans and Music in England and New England,* London, 154–5, 384–7. I am grateful to Dr Roger Pooley for calling my attention to Bunyan in this context.

68 Langdale, J. (nd) 'Some Account of the Birth, Education and Religious Exercises and Visitations of God to that faithful Servant and Minister of Jesus Christ, Josiah Langdale' (died 1723), Friends House Library, MS Box 10/10. See above, pp. 30–2.

69 Mulliner, J. (1667) *A testimony against Periwigs and Periwig-Making, and Playing an Instrument of Musick among Christians, or any others in the days of the Gospel,* London (reprinted 1872, Northampton).

70 Wilsford, J. (1677) *A general testimony to the everlasting truth of God, partly intended for the inhabitants of Nether-Broughton in the county of Leicester,* London, 5, my italics.

71 Goodman, K. W. G. (1978) 'Hammerman's Hill: The Land, People, and Industry of the Titterstone Clee Hill Area of Shrop-

shire, from the Sixteenth to the Eighteenth Centuries', I, University of Keele PhD, 68–9, 81–3, 110–12. I am grateful to Mrs Goodman for permission to quote her late husband's work.

72 'Survey of the Township of Eccleshall', 1697, nos. 4, 161, 57. 'Survey of the Parish of Eccleshall compiled by Bishop William Lloyd, 1693–8', 69, 61, 47, 75–6, 33, 51, 81–2; 'Survey of Eccleshall Poor, 1694'; and 'original list of heads of families, 1693'; transcripts by Tildesley, N. W. (1969), deposited in the Lichfield Joint Record Office with the original documents.

73 Lippincott, H. P. (ed.) (1974) Sir Nicholas Le Strange (1603–55) *'Merry Passages and Jeasts': A Manuscript Jest Book*, Salzburg Studies in English Literature: Elizabethan and Renaissance Studies 29 (117), 90. Harley, J. (1968) *Music in Purcell's London*, London, 46–9, assembles evidence of the work of poor, and often discordant, fiddlers, at feasts, fairs and weddings.

74 Horsfall-Turner, op. cit., III (1883), 194.

75 Marshall, J. D. (forthcoming) 'Social Structure and Wealth in Pre-Industrial England', *Economic History Review*.

76 'A Pleasant Dialogue between Honest John and Loving Kate', *PM*, I (10), 218, 225–8.

77 The French chapbooks used exactly the same system. Mandrou, R. (1975) *De la Culture Populaire aux 17ᶜ et 18ᶜ Siècles*, Paris, 118–21.

78 A tune could be pressed into service for many different occasions. Thus a book of carols, printed for Jonah Deacon in 1688, also makes use of 'My life and my death', 'Oh Mother Roger', and 'Caper and Jerk It' (Wood, 110A(5)).

79 Pearl, V. (1978) 'Puritans and Poor Relief: the London Workhouse, 1649–60', in Pennington, D. and Thomas, K. (eds) *Puritans and Revolutionaries: Essays in Seventeenth Century History presented to Christopher Hill*, Oxford, 212–13, 224, 226.

80 Tibbutt, H. G. (ed.) (1976) *The Minutes of the First Independent Church (Now Bunyan meeting) at Bedford, 1657–1766*, Bedfordshire Historical Record Society 55, 124 and subject index, 232. Transcript of Gamlingay Chapel Minute Book, May 1710 to October 1815, deposited at Gamlingay and with Mr Tibbutt, pp. 26, 278.

81 Thompson, art. cit., 659–67.

82 'The Life and Death of Sheffery ap Morgan, son of Shon ap

Morgan', *PM*, I (45), 977–1000; 'The Wonderful Adventures and Happy Success of Young Shon ap Morgan, the only son of Sheffery ap Morgan', *PM*, II (14), 277–320. 'The Welsh Traveller' *PM*, I (40); 'The Distressed Welshman', *PM*, I (30).

83 'Love's School', *PM*, II (15), 342–3. Welshmen and Scotsmen and their lovemaking are frequently mocked in the wooing dialogues.

84 Lippincott, op. cit., 45. Bernard Capp tells me that anti-Welsh jokes figure prominently in almancs from the late 1640s.

85 Goodman, thesis cit., I, 66–8, 77–8.

86 Mendelhall, T. C. (1953) *The Shewsbury Drapers and the Welsh Wool Trade in XVI and XVII Centuries*, Oxford, 44, n. 1, appendix B, 234. I am grateful to Angus MacInnes for this reference.

87 Bernard Capp tells me, however, that an earlier group of Irish jokes appeared by 1700; they appear in 'Bogg Witticisms: or Dear Joy's Common Places' (1700). I would like to thank Edmund de Waal very warmly for investigating *Punch* for me. It is virtually impossible to date the first printing of the burlesques on Welshmen from the *Short Title Catalogue* (Pollard, A. W. and Redgraves, G. R. (1926, revised 1976) *Short Title Catalogue*, 1475–1640, I; Wing, D. (1945–51, revised 1972) 1641–1700, II). Only two of the four appear at all. One of these, no. 60, is from the same date, 1685, as the version collected by Pepys but has a different publisher. The second, no. 1705A, only appears in the *STC* printed in 1700 for Norris. It is worth remembering that Shakespeare created the character of Fluellen as early as 1599. It seems very likely that the 'small merry' burlesques were also written at the end of the sixteenth century to coincide with immigration, but that no early copies survive.

88 Lippincott, op. cit., 160.

89 'The Birth, Life and Death of John Frank', *PM*, II (20), 481–2.

90 A good set of examples is to be found in 'Scogin's Jests', *Vulgaria*, IV (3). It includes groups of jokes about purges and their drastic effects, farts and turds. See, for instance, pp. 10–11, 13–14. This was in the collection of Captain Cox in the 1570s, so it, like Dame Alice Le Strang's childhood joke, takes us back to the sixteenth century.

91 'Pasquil's Jest', *Vulgaria*, IV (5), p. 3.'The Pleasant History of Tom Ladle' *PM*, I (58).

92 Anon (1659) *Strange and Terrible Newes from Cambridge, the True Relation of the Quakers bewitching Mary Phillips, etc.,* London.

93 Freud's discussion of his theories on excrement appeared in his (1905) *Three Essays on the Theory of Sexuality* (English translation, London, 1949). There is a bibliography and discussion of attitudes, language and behaviour towards elimination and its products by an architect, Kira, A. (1976) *The Bathroom*, Harmondsworth. Loudon, J. B. (1977), 'On Body Products', in *The Anthropology of the Body*, Association of Social Anthropologists, Monograph 15, London, 161–78, discusses anthropological observations and begins with the statement that 'the minutiae of this particular daily activity seem to be largely neglected by most anthropologists'. He does however quote a range of particular findings suggesting different reactions. They include a study of the Tallensi, who use faeces as manure, and appear to be fairly casual about the smell caused by depositing them just outside their homesteads. On the other hand, the Maenge, who also use them as manure, have feelings of revulsion for 'dirty substances'. Loudon draws attention to the inability of present-day anthropologists and vernacular architects working on house plans to provide labels for the privy. Historians have also been affected by the taboo. The exception is Richmond, C. (forthcoming) 'Dung'. He draws together a whole range of examples of the importance of dung from medieval and modern Europe and post-revolutionary China, where political awareness indicates that human excrement should become communal. I am much indebted to Dr Charmian Davie of the Psychology Department and Professor Ronald Frankenburg of the Sociology Department at Keele for thinking of references for me, and to Dr Richmond for lending me his paper.

94 Thirsk, J. (ed.) (1967) *Agrarian History of England and Wales*, IV, Cambridge, 27, 52, 197; and 'The Reverend Richard Baxter's Last Treatise' (1691), Thirsk, J. and Cooper, J. P. (eds) (1972), *Seventeenth Century Economic Documents*, Oxford 184.

95 At Castle-top Farm near Matlock in Derbyshire the outside privy still survives. There is space underneath to back a cart so that it can be easily emptied and the contents used on the fields.

VIII
Small godly books: popular religion

❦

The degree of importance that religion held in the lives of non-gentle parishioners in the sixteenth and seventeenth centuries will never be established. The beliefs of such people were not normally of interest, even to the ecclesiastical authorities, except in special circumstances, or in particularly idiosyncratic church courts. Genuine popular devotion of a humble kind leaves very little trace upon the records of any given time. The believer, especially the conforming believer, makes less impact than the dissentient. At no period is it possible to distinguish the conforming believer from the apathetic church-goer who merely wished to stay out of trouble.

It is possible, therefore, for the historian to start from the very probable thesis that the 'hold of any kind of organized religion upon the mass of the population was never more than partial', add the complaints of puritan reforming ministers about their flocks' performance of their uncongenial duties, support these with figures of the considerable minority who were presented for absenteeism in the church courts, and point the case further with the disrespectful remarks of a further minority, which was also presented in the church courts.[1] If it is set against this background, the importance of astrology and magic, possibly as an alternative to the 'practical' application of religion to everyday problems that was discouraged in the reformed Anglican church, then seems very great. Yet the negative picture that emerges is based on the silence of the majority of the witnesses.

An alternative picture, illustrating the religious convictions of the humble, also depends on the selection of examples which may be atypical. It runs from the demonstration of the bequests to the church lights, altar and fabric normally made by every parishioner who left a will before the Reformation, through the remarkably concrete fact that over half the Marian martyrs listed by Foxe whose social status is known were agricultural labourers.[2] It continues by showing that the rural laity were actively involved in the complaints against scandalous ministers and in the anti-Laudian petitions of the 1640s. Analysis of the dedicatory clauses disposing of the soul in wills shows that throughout the sixteenth and seventeenth centuries a minority of will-makers disposed of their most precious possession in idiosyncratic clauses that were not the normal ones used by the scribe who drew up the will. These idiosyncratic clauses probably therefore reflected the individual convictions of the testators. The records of the separatist churches under the Commonwealth and immediately after it show the very humble involved in religious debate. Examination of the social status of dissenters in their villages shows that dissenting opinions were not confined to prosperous yeomen only.[3] This picture of an involved group of non-gentle rural laity whose religious convictions were often sufficiently important to them for them to risk persecution after the Restoration is, of course, equally partial. It is based mainly, though not entirely, on the records of the separatist churches whose members made up 4 per cent of the adult population according to the Compton Census of 1676. It, like its alternative, is a picture that gives weight to a vocal minority of witnesses. One of the very rare pieces of evidence that survives on the attitude of the majority of conformists certainly does not suggest apathy. In 1684–5, there was a confirmation at Nafferton in the East Riding which coincided awkwardly with the great agricultural pressure of harvest. An eager twelve year old, who hoped for immediate spiritual blessings from the experience, wrote of the occasion:

Great Preparations were made for [the Bishop's] Reception, and not-withstanding it being Harvest-time, Abundance of all sorts of People, Men, Women and Children flock'd to our Town to see the Bishop, and those qualified to be confirmed: We had a little Time in Worship, and when it was over the Bishop went into the Quire to do his Office; a great Crowd there was of Children and Others; and as many as were bishop'd kneeled before the Altar, and the Bishop laid his Right Hand upon One, and his Left hand upon another, and said a short Prayer over them. . . . I being among the

Crowd of People, whilst the Bishop was doing his Office, waited an Opportunity that I might get under the Bishops Right hand.[4]

This pushing crowd of confirmation candidates crushing into the chancel shows that some conformists had beliefs that were important to them. But the truth on popular religious beliefs must necessarily comprehend both views. Parishioners are likely to have included on the one hand the frankly hostile, on the other the religiously committed, with in between the silent majority,[5] which included both the apathetic and the devout.

However, it is obvious that at most stages in the sixteenth and seventeenth centuries a segment of the rural population that might, like Foxe's labourers, be very humble, did take a lively interest in religion. How large, or small, a segment it was is an open question. However, from the opening of the Stationers' Register in 1557–8, it was a group worth publishing for. The sheer volume of religious print written in English is surprising, and seems, with ballads, at least to equal almanacs and prognostications in popularity. There was not, quite possibly, any conflict in the popular mind between the two. The second production from the press transported across the Atlantic with such loving care in 1639 was William Pierce's *Almanack*. It preceded the *Whole Book of Psalms* which appeared in 1640.[6] The devout settlers of Puritan New England can scarcely be accused of religious indifference, and, to them, there can have been no conflict.

No doubt deliberate Puritan propaganda was in part responsible for the religious works produced by the presses, but it is impossible to believe that it would have gone on being produced if it had failed to sell. And sell it most certainly did. In 1659 Andrew Jones's *Black Book of Conscience* was only in its tenth edition,[7] but by the time Pepys collected it, less than thirty years later, it had reached its forty-second edition.[8] It was so popular that it had to be reprinted, on an average more than once a year, for a whole new generation of readers.

In the first four years for which the licences by the Stationers' Company survive, apart from the religious ballads, the titles of books licensed included *Devout Prayers, Ring of Rest* and *Ring of Righteousness, Sermon of Repentance, Troubled Man's Medicine, Sick Man's Salve, Instruction of Questions for Children of the Lord's Supper, A Morning and Evening Prayer*, a book called *Have an Eye to your Conscience, How a Christian Man ought to behave himself in the Danger of Death*, and the *Entering of Christ into England*.[9] As these titles show, cheap religious publications were by no means a new line in late Stuart England. The earliest survivals of the *genre* I have yet found were printed almost exactly 100 years after the opening of the Stationers' Register, however.

By the time Samuel Pepys was collecting chapbooks, the trade-lists of the specialist publishers show that approximately a third of their output was made up of small godly books.[10] Pepys seems to have collected a representative sample both of different types of godly chapbooks, and also of the output of the different publishers involved in the trade. However, comparison of the titles collected by Pepys with the trade-lists of William Thackeray and of a group of lesser men in the trade shows that, perhaps predictably, he did not buy as high a proportion of the small godly books as of the small merry books (see above, pp. 132–5). He had his small religious books separately bound, and collected forty-six of them.[11] This was 24 per cent of his whole collection, excluding almanacs. This is very close to the French proportion of 26 per cent.[12] If Pepys had not been less attracted to the godly books, the dominance of cheap religious print would have appeared even greater, and presumably approached the proportion of 32 per cent of religious tracts on the publishers' trade-lists. Even as it was, religious chapbooks formed the most numerous single group as it did in France.[13] Indeed it looks as if the English trade concentrated even more on religious print than the French and the Welsh even more than the English.[14] This is a startling predominance, which does indicate that cheap religious tracts found a ready market, and suggests very strongly that popular interest in religion was not confined to a small minority of dissenters. Popular religion, like astrology, was an important phemomenon in the late seventeenth century, which must be reckoned with.

Religious books may have been best-sellers in England, as much as, or even more than, in France. Their contents were of course completely different.

The main publishers of chapbooks seem to have had separate trade-lists of godly chapbooks printed only in godly chapbooks, to tempt the pious to further purchase.[15] Thus, Clarke, Thackeray and Passinger printed a list of twenty-two titles on the back of their *Black Book of Conscience* in which *Death Triumphant, Doomsday at Hand*

and *The Sinner's Sobs* jostled *The Short and Sure Way to get Grace
and Salvation, The Plainman's Pathway to Heaven, The Christian's
Guide* and *A Book of Prayer and Graces*, as well as the temptingly
titled *Ready Way to Get Riches, or the Poor Man's Counsellor*. Their
advertisement skilfully mixed the holy and the profane by their
inducement to the prospective reader: 'Read them over carefully, and
practice them constantly, and rest assured thou wilt find comfort in
them to thy own Soul; and are but twopence a piece.'[16]

Joshua Deacon at the Angel in Giltspur Street likewise had a
separate trade-list for pious books, even decorated with a different
woodcut of his Angel,[17] but his normal trade-list (see above, p. 112),
advertising *Markham's Faithful Farrier, The Seven Champions of
Christendom* and *A Groatsworth of Wit for a Penny*, appeared rather
oddly at the end of *The Young-Man's Last Legacy: Left and Bequeathed on his Death Bed*,[18] together with his usual rather attractive
Angel garlanded with flowers. Only Back, at the Black Boy on
London Bridge, broke this convention of separate lists by printing a
list of twenty-three twopenny books,[19] perhaps his entire stock at
that time, in which *The Dying Man's Good Counsel* rubbed shoul-
ders with *The Art of Courtship*, and *Canterbury Tales, for the
Entertainment of Young Men and Maids* with *The Danger of
Dispair, Arising from a Guilty Conscience*.

Amongst the godly chapbooks, the twenty-two page version of
The Pilgrim's Progress published by Thomas Passinger in 1684 stood
alone amongst those Pepys collected in its attempt to convey a
religious message through the medium of allegory. The others all
debated or conveyed religious problems straight, unsugared by
story-telling. Indeed, over a quarter of them were self-confessed
sermons written by named divines, and the woodcut of a grave and
sober cleric in Geneva gown[20] was used frequently enough as a
frontispiece to suggest that such a picture immediately gave the
publication an air of credibility and authority to the reader, and acted
in the same way as an *imprimatur*. The whole group of godly chapbooks suggests that the long Puritan campaign still bore fruit in the
popular mind, even after the Restoration, in a tradition of lay de-
ference to 'painful ministers'. The only rogue chapbook suggesting
any alternative view was the *Dialogue between a Young Divine and
an Old Beggar . . . shewing . . . that it is not always the Accomplishment of Humane Learning that makes a Compleat Man*[21] in which a

The godly minister

minister who had spent eight years in incessant prayer desiring to attain the knowledge of God was eventually directed to gain it from a dirty beggar sitting at his church door, who proclaimed his own perfect acceptance of the divine will. In reply to the divine's anxious question, 'But what if the Lord of might should drown thee in the bottomless Pit?', the beggar replied,

> Why certainly, if he should, I have two Arms with which I would still embrace him. . . . One is true Humility. . . . The other is the Right-arm which is Love, by which I am united to his Divinity, and by this Love given to me from himself, I would hold him so fast, that he would be forced to go down to Hell with me, and it

were much more to be wished by me to be in Hell with God, than to be in Heaven without him.[22]

But such a note of confidence and of aspiration to the union with God which is the end of religion to the mystics was almost as rare as the suggestion that the illiterate might, as the chapbook put it 'by the help of Natural Genious . . . far out-vie those that are Scholastically Educated'. The divine's question, 'What if the Lord of might should drown thee in the bottomless Pit?', can never have been far from the thoughts of the public who read the *Penny Godlinesses*. Over half those Pepys collected were calls to repentance, death-bed testimonies, and meditations on death and on the Last Judgement.[23] Connection of sin and conversion were the object of them all. Fear was often deliberately evoked. The main inducement to conversion was not usually as snappily or crudely put as in the subtitle of *The Door of Salvation Opened: Or, A Voice from Heaven to Unregenate Sinners*,[24] which described itself as 'Plainly showing the Necessity of opening your hearts to Christ, or else he will open Hells mouth to devour you . . . preponderling Blessing and Cursing, Life and Death, Salvation if you open to Christ, Damnation if you refuse', but it was usually there. Condemnations of sin were sometimes catalogues of vices like *One of Mr Vincent's Last Sermons or A Suitable Warning to all Stubborn Sinners* which included rousing adjurations to each group like 'Come forth ye Adulterers, you who have neighed like full-fed Horses, after your Neighbours Wives, and have assembled by Troups into Harlots Houses'.[25]

They were also sometimes attacks on particular vices, amongst which drunkenness seems to predominate.[26] The harlot's door and the alehouse bench seem generally agreed to be the greatest external temptations.[27] Catalogues of sin led on to the call for repentance, usually linked to the ominous warning of the coming of death, and the reminder that time was short.

'As there is no return after this Life, to live upon the Earth' wrote the author of *Now or Never*',

so there will be no doing this work hereafter; Heaven is for a more glorious work, and Hell will be for the most horrible punishments: It is now that you must Sow, and hereafter that you must Reap: it is now that you must Work, and then that you must receive your

Wages. O therefore poor Soul . . . let me perswade you to be up and be doing.[28]

'Put yourself often into your Graves, and look from thence upon the World, and see what Judgement you have of it then' demanded another author, asking his reader to make the imaginative leap that would change his perspective and lead to his conversion.[29]

The chapbooks give the impression that Death was a figure who was very well-known by, and very close to, their readers. Here so many different elements come into play that it is difficult for the twentieth-century reader to sort them out. Death is one of the few taboo subjects in present-day society, an event that happens relatively rarely before old age, and even then is experienced in hospital. The coffin in the parlour is almost as unknown now as the knowledgeable neighbours who can lay out the corpse. In seventeenth-century England Death lived nearby and might visit any time.[30] The *Penny Godlinesses* reflect this knowledge among their readers and it is difficult, if not impossible, to determine when their authors are simply using the hard, physical facts of life as their readers lived it, and when Death, with its attendants Judgement and the threat of Hell, were being used to frighten, and to aid the work of conversion. The theme of the coming of Death was a string that was never still.

'Are you Parents or Governors of Families?' enquired the author of *Now or Never*.[31] 'You have work to do for God and for the Souls of them that God hath intrusted to you. Be diligent in Family Duties; remember that you and your Families are going to the Grave.'

'What, Christless, and ready to dye? that's impossible; Christless, and willing to dye? that's Irrational' proclaimed another of the group of chapbooks calling for repentance.[32] Seven of the forty-six godly chapbooks furthered the theme by purporting to be written on a deathbed. The role of the family as the smallest effective teaching unit for Christian doctrine was emphasized in the *Godlinesses*. *The Dying Man's Last Sermon, or The Father's last Blessing Left and Bequeathed as a Legacy to his Children, Immediately before his Death*,[33] was published by Wright, Clarke, Thackeray and Passinger.[34] In 1685 they brought out the companion to it, *The Mother's Blessing*,[35] which included 100 'Devout Admonitions' in rhyme left by the dying mother to her children. The idea was obviously one that sold well, for Deacon, Conyer and Brooksby all included last testaments in their lists. Deacon's contribution was *The Young Man's Last Legacy: Left and Bequeathed upon his Death-Bed to his dear Mother and Brethren, together with the rest of his Relations, Being His Kind and Comfortable Admonition to prepare for Death, that Iniquity may not prove their utter Ruine.*[36] The sins of adolescents and the young came in for special attention, for two more

An Hundred Devout Admonitions left by a Dying Mother to her Children.

Being moſt Excellent Directions for a Religious Chriſtians Converſation.

The mother's blessing

of these death-bed testimonies were aimed specifically at this age-group. Dying fathers, mothers and brothers could only be rivalled in emotional appeal, apparently, by dying ministers like Mr Brook, 'who was struck with Pangs of Death in his Pulpit, and, coming to himself again, wrote this last Sermon'.[37] A minister's words already carried great weight; the further authentication given them by the approach of death was obviously supposed irresistable.

Some of the chapbook material on death may have reflected the reality of seventeenth-century life, but some of it certainly was intended to frighten. A fifth of the godly chapbooks[38] were specifically on death and judgement. The themes of the Four Last Things had always, of course, been used to urge the faithful to repentance; the number of late medieval frescoes of the Last Judgement that survive in parish churches are adequate visual testimony of this. The inevitable coming of the universal tyrant was a favourite theme of medieval pulpit oratory, which can be traced back to the early twelfth century.[39] From this tradition, the *danse macabre* probably evolved, as did the pitiless funeral monuments of the fifteenth century emphasizing the physical decay and putrefaction of the corpse.[40] Doomsday was as familiar a theme as Death in medieval homilectics. The main themes of popular sermons may have changed less at the Reformation than is at first supposed,[41] although the anxieties felt by the devout in the face of a Death, used as an aid to conversion from the twelfth century onwards, may have grown more acute in the same measure as the doctrines of election and assurance spread.[42] The surviving chapbooks from the 1650s on may only indicate the spread of a theme in cheap print that had been familiar orally for five centuries, or, on the other hand, they may indicate its growing hold on the popular imagination. In the chapbooks, however, the images of Death and Judgement do seem to predominate, and to be stressed at the expense of other Christian imagery.[43] The titular *Heaven's Messengers*[44] were not New Testament figures, as the unwary reader might suppose. The title page bore a woodcut of Death blowing a trumpet with Father Time standing on it. There are nine woodcuts of Death, Judgement and the General Resurrection in the *Penny Godlinesses*, compared with two of the Incarnation, two very dubious ones of the Trinity and only one, astonishingly, of the Crucifixion. The skeletal Death appears even more often than the authority-conferring figure of the godly minister, who in turn, according to the

Young man's guide to heaven

publishers, seemed likely to be a much more evocative image for the readers than any episode from the life of Christ. This grim hero of the woodcuts, armed with arrows to slay young men and young women, a ribbon-banner bearing the words 'I kill you all' issuing from his skull, directed at father, mother and children alike, seems to have been portrayed sometimes in a reference that may well have been conscious to the pretty, lethal Cupid who was the hero of the art of compliment chapbooks. Courtship, with all else, ended with Death. Sometimes the end that Death should serve, the conversion of the reader, appeared to be forgotten in the near-adulation of this anti-Cupid, and anti-hero, as in the title of *Death Triumphant, or, The most Renowned, Mighty Puissant and Irresistable Champion and Conqueror Geneneral [sic] of the Whole World. DEATH.*[45]

The *danse macabre* does not seem to have lost its hold on the popular imagination. We may doubt whether the Puritans of New England were really more preoccupied with death than their English counterparts,[46] in the face of this cheap literature that was obviously so profitable a line to its publishers.

There is just enough contemporary reference within the generalized proclaimings of the coming of death and judgement to suggest that the plague and fire of the 1660s had themselves stimulated the eschatological chapbooks. Some of the chapbooks unblushingly proclaimed the simplest type of connection between morality and prosperity, as did the author of *Now or Never* – 'Success is God's ordinary reward of temporal diligence; and disease, poverty and shame are the usual punishments of sloth'[47] – although the majority, of course, preached an alternative version of 'whom the Lord loveth, He chasteneth'. Either way, fire and plague could be related to the judgement of God, and, in at least one chapbook, was explicitly so related. The call to repentance of *Christ's Voice to England* ran:

> Cast away thy lukewarmness, O England, now repent before it be too late, God hath a controversie with thee, he hath afflicted thee: but thou hast not returned, he hath burnt down thy stateliest City, and other places, the Pestilence hath destroyed many thousands in the midst of thee, and wilt thou not yet repent that he may heal thee? I say, Repent, O repent thee of thy former follies and vain thoughts of thy self, then will the Lord hear from Heaven, and turn away his fierce eyes. . . . The Sickness hath been very much in the City, and much in the Country, and why is it, but because our Sins do not abate?[48]

The grim skeletal sexton with the spade who dominated the wood-cuts in the *Godlinesses* may perhaps have done so as a reaction to plague. Obviously, the imagery of the Last Judgement was almost always linked with that of death. The popularity of the theme was illustrated by the pair *An Almanac, But for One Day, or The son of Man reckoning with Man upon an High Account Day*[49] and *An Almanack for Two Days, viz. the Day of Death and the Day of Judgement,*[50] which themselves played on the popularity of that basic practical 'necessity', the almanac, and, by this very pun, suggested the practical quotidian implications, of immediate importance to everyone, of their subjects. The law courts, which were presumably familiar, by hearsay at least, to the reader, set the scene for *The Great Assizes,*[51] and, at these, Christ as Judge presided. Indeed, the Christ of this group of chapbooks very frequently appeared only as the eschatological Christ of the Second Coming, the terrible Lord who condemns inpenitent sinners, and, almost as an afterthought, in one or two of the chapbooks at least, admits repentant sinners to his bliss.[52] The Christ of the New Testament, the events of His earthly life repeated there, and their implication for the contemporary believer, even the great drama of the Crucifixion on which the hope

A N

ALMANACK

But for one Day.

O R,

The S O N of M A N Reckoning with Man
upon an High Account-Day,

The
⎧ Laſt Day.   ⎫   The
⎨ Latter Day. ⎬
⎩ Lords Day.   ⎭

⎧ Day of Iudg-
⎨ ment.
⎩ Day of Doom

Licenſed and Entred according to Order

Printed for J. Clarke, W. Thackeray,
and T. Paſſinger.

The Resurrection

of salvation through His blood rested, received scanty attention in
the majority of the chapbooks. The sole exception to this was the
chapbook version of the life of Christ,[53] which in only twelve pages
rehearsed the principal events first in prose and then in a rhymed
version to be sung. It stressed His humble birth, the healing miracles,
the Crucifixion and the evidence for the Resurrection, all prefixed by

the only woodcuts showing the Adoration of the Magi and the Crucifixion to survive amongst Pepys' *Godlinesses*.

The main message, then, of over half the godly chapbooks was a call to repentance and to faith in the Christ who alone, at the last day, had the power to save. But this hope, and the figure on which it rested, remained alike nebulous compared with the fears of rejection by an awful Judge, which were all too well clarified.

The predominance of the negative in over half the godly chapbooks and the unabashed use of fear as a lever to conversion[54] makes the status of chronic religious anxiety frequently displayed by very humble lay men and women in the second half of the seventeenth century much more comprehensible.[55] The best-known example is, of course, John Bunyan. Anyone who has read his autobiography, *Grace Abounding to the Chief of Sinners* has travelled with him the weary road of fear of the seventeenth-century pilgrim who for years was unable to believe that he was saved. The majority of the religious chapbooks in circulation, on the evidence of the Pepys collection, would certainly have tended to accentuate, rather than alleviate, that kind of distress. The practical weakness of the doctrine of justification by faith unsupported by an emphasis on the validity of the sacraments,[56] independently of the believer's worthy reception of them, seems to be that it depends on the believer's own conviction that he possesses that faith. This is necessarily entirely subjective. For some psychological types, the sort of self-questioning the doctrine raises is almost intolerable, as it was for Bunyan.[57] The godly chapbooks were not always specific on justification by faith, but some of them were.

'You must be converted or condemned' thundered a writer in 1677.

> It is not enough that you have some love and liking to God's ways and people . . . this will not prove you sound Christians; Have your hearts been changed? Have you been soundly convinced of your sins? of your damnable and undone condition in yourselves? and your utter inability to lick yourselves whole again by your own duties?[58]

Most of the chapbooks simply urged the believer to faith in Christ. But their constant threatening must have encouraged anxiety. Sometimes the author admitted as much.

'Art thou in ignorance concerning thy Converted Estate, dost thou not know whether thou art in a state of Life or Death?' asked the writer of *Now or Never*. But his prescription seems likely only to lead to an extension of doubt, as it did for years with Bunyan. 'Be thou careful, then, and use the means that God hath appointed thee for assurance, search the Scriptures, for in them are the Words of Eternal Life. Examine yourselves whether you be in the faith, prove yourselves.'

A fifth of the godly chapbooks collected by Pepys[59] set out to allay the doubts and fears which seem to have been deliberately whipped up by the majority of them. This substantial minority group make very heartening reading after their distressing neighbours on the publishers' lists. They tended to rest more heavily on demonstrations of God's mercy and love illustrated from Christ's actions and sayings recorded in the New Testament than the rest, and Christ therefore appeared as a much less nebulous figure in them. One passion meditation on his blood-shedding had all the Gothic vividness of late medieval mystical meditative writing, and one of them also drew on sayings from St Bernard, St Ambrose, St Chrysostom and Gregory the Great on temptation. A couple of them[60] were powerful pleadings on the love of God, his compassion towards his people, and the felicity they might expect in adoration of him. They were quite untouched by the intent to convert through fear.

> Christ receives those he saves, though they come home in Rags; the beggarliness of the Prodigal did not hinder his Father from turning to him, and embracing of him, their emptiness of worth doth not stir up his hatred, but his pitty. Christ hath enough and to spare for them . . . he can put comeliness upon those who by sin are never so much deformed. . . . Consider his compassions are joyned with such a fulness, that there is nothing miserable sinners need, but out of this fulness, they may have abundance of supply; our Lord hath power, as well as pitty, why then should we not trust in him, and go to him at all times, since his power shows him so able, and his pitty so willing, to relieve and save

ran part of *The Day of Grace*.[61]

The Christian's Triumph was likewise strongly rooted in confidence in the Atonement.

A Reward it is, the very thought of which should fill us with amazing Rapture, and astonish us with Wonder, to think that the wise Creator (infinitely good and blessed in himself, to whose incomprehensible Existence all his Creatures cannot make the smallest addition,) shall take such care of men . . . as to reconcile him in the previous blood of his dear Son, and our ever blessed Saviour, to render him capable of Eternal Life . . . that mortality should put on immortality and shine like stars in the Firmament.[62]

This writer's confidence in the love of God and his astonishment at its nature took him into a meditation on the kingdom of God which has the enthusiasm of Thomas Traherne. His inducement to the conversion of the reader was not the fear of the flames of Hell, it was the vision of the glory of God in

A Kingdom above all kingdoms, shining with inexpressible brightness and glory, where in the enjoyment and fellowship (in Community) of Saints and Angels, of the Souls of just men made perfect, an enjoyment without any fear of even being deprived of that right transcendant Felicity, a Felicity that Eye hath not seen, nor Ear heard . . . all the Power and grand Applause [of earthly life] would shine but like a Glow-worm to the Sun.[63]

But meditations filled with confidences and adoration of the love and wisdom of God were rare indeed in the chapbooks. Most of the 'comforting' group confined themselves to trying to cope with the believers' scruples.

No man ought to draw such a sad conclusion in reference to himself, as that the season of Grace is quite expired. . . . When Sathan pesters you with thoughts that there is no help remaining, but that the acceptable time is all slipt away, rather hope to the contrary, for Sathan is a lyer, and because he is so busie about you, is a sign he is afraid to lose you

ran the soothing message of *The Day of Grace*. But not all writers of comforting chapbooks carry conviction, to the modern reader at least. Roger Hough's intention was to reassure, as his subtitle declared, 'assuring every true Believer of their Blessed Estate and Condition'.[64] God's people, he wrote 'shall never be forsaken of God', although they might, of course, from time to time be afflicted.

But he went on to consider how the believer could tell he belonged to God's people. It is difficult to believe that his proof, that the believer would have an assured confidence in God, would be of much use to the troubled. The reality of the problem and the potential market amongst sufferers from religious doubt and fear was attested to by a chapbook written as a meditation upon a recent suicide, addressed specifically to those tempted likewise.

> Despair is a suggestion of the Devil to insnare and overthrow unwary Souls . . . nor is it one of his weak Temptations . . . but such a one as shakes the whole frame of Man, and disorders the faculties of the Soul, raising a Civil War within . . . tormenting and torturing him to that degree, that carrys with it a kind of Hell upon Earth.

The sufferer is told to seek 'sound and able Advice', to meditate on the love and sufferings of Christ, and, above all, 'suffer neither doubting nor distrust to prevail against the received Truth; no, not of your unworthiness, nor Horror arising from the sense of Sin, by which you conceit yourself unfit for pardon, or past recovery'.

If it was worth issuing a twopenny chapbook[65] written for those tempted to doubt their acceptability to God to the point of suicide, the range of problems involved cannot have been very uncommon, and John Bunyan was certainly not an isolated figure in his generation.[66] The appropriately-titled *Poor Doubting Christian drawn unto Christ* was in its ninth impression by 1683,[67] so it certainly sold well. It was aimed very accurately at the type of worrier who was incapable of resting in any assurance of salvation. The author imagined the sinner fearing his repentance was inadequate:

> 'See my sins I do, but this is my misery, I cannot be burdened with them: I have a Heart that cannot break and mourn for dishonouring God, and offending him in so many waies', but I say,
> This hurts not neither, provided that they Heart be weary of itself, because it cannot be weary of Sin. The Lord showeth mercy because he will show mercy. . . .
> Thou sayest: 'These Sins can never be pardoned.'
> Is there anything too hard for the Lord? You wrong God exceedingly.

This robust and balanced little book assured the doubter, needing to, and incapable of believing in his justification through faith, of God's love and mercy as shown in Christ, and of his intention to give faith.

> Faith is the free Gift of God. It is God that must do it, who yet will not do it without us, being reasonable men and women in the power of willing. Again, the Lord affords us means; yet not to abuse them, and give him the slip. And here it is a good Saying; let the Lord do what he will, and let us do what we should. . . . The same Power that raised up Jesus from the Dead, must make us able to believe, or else all the Angels in Heaven and all the Ministers on Earth, and all help that man and means can give us, will do us no good. Now the meanes are divers kinds; As Hearing, and Prayer, and Sacraments which are the Conduits from which God Communicates Faith.[68]

The doubter who feels himself without faith must therefore wait patiently, continuing to ask God for that gift which it is undoubtedly His intention to bestow.

The last group of godly chapbooks were made up of instructional or catechismal manuals.[69] They all stressed the role of the family in religious education, and usually contained morning and evening prayers, sometimes for each day of the week, together with graces for before and after meat, and special times of stress. *The Poor Man's Help to Devotion*, attributed to Baxter, contained a week-long cycle of prayers, together with occasional prayers for poor men, debtors, malefactors, the sick, parents for their children and children for their parents, and so on. It would be extremely interesting to know how many families amongst the 'poor' at whom these books were aimed actually regularly practised family prayers in the morning and evening. The line must have sold reasonably, for Brooksby and Back each had an instructional series. Back issued a *School of Holiness* and a *School of Learning*,[70] both priced at 2*d*, as well as his *School of Piety*, which was in its fourth edition in 1687. *The School of Piety*, or *The Devout Christian's Duty*, contained an interesting section on the duties of parents bringing up children, the reciprocal duties of children, and the duties of masters to servants. Parents were to bring children up to 'Reading, as soon as they are capable, that they apply themselves to the study of good Books . . . when they are not at

School, or otherwise necessarily busied call upon them to read and repeat Scripture Proofs'.[71] Masters and mistresses were likewise to call upon their servants 'often to read and hear Sermons'. These suggestions might seem to belong to a Puritan utopia, but the example of Josiah Langdale of Nafferton, the servant-in-husbandry who passed his leisure time and his Sundays studying the Bible with his mate and walking to sermons, shows that it was by no means totally unrealistic. The importance of Bible reading was stressed everywhere in the godlinesses. The reader is reminded how privileged he is 'to have the Scriptures in a known tongue . . . the word is the key which unlocks the Treasures both of grace and glory'. The possession of the Bible is assumed in them: 'You have the Scriptures, in your houses, in your hands.' The instructional manuals sometimes contained lists of scriptural questions and of 'scriptural proofs' as well as a short form of the catechism. When they did so, the correct scriptural text was always cited. The lists look as though they were intended for rote-learning, as *The School of Piety* recommends, but they could also lead on to reading the relevant section of the Bible. William Weston's vivid description of the mass meeting of Puritans including 'rustics, women and idiots' searching the Bible for texts as they were cited in the 1580s[72] shows that formal Puritan exercises used this technique. If the instructional chapbooks were indeed used in homes, the critical literacy of the village group in Thriplow in Cambridgeshire who challenged the preacher on his text in the 1680s[73] would be accounted for. *The School of Piety*[74] and *The School of Godliness*,[75] which both set lists of scriptural questions 'very fit for all Children and Servants . . . and very useful for all people, and necessary to be had in every Family', both showed a strong Old Testament bias. *The School of Godliness* had seven pages of questions on the Old Testament compared with two on the New. *The School of Piety* set seventy-seven of its 'Hundred Divine Questions and Answers' on the Old Testament compared with twenty-three on the New. Again, the figure of Christ was a nebulous one. The other emphasis lacking was on the sacraments. Neither of these two chapbooks mentioned them. *The School of Holiness*[76] did at least mention 'the receiving of the Lord's Supper' as a duty, coupled, of course, with an admonition that such reception must be worthy. Even the instructional chapbooks therefore shared the theological bias of those specifically aimed at repentance and conversion.

The impression of religion handed out to the people in the twopenny chapbooks is a gloomy one. There was little proclamation of the love of God shown in Christ compared with emphasis on fear of death, judgement and the wrath of God. There is no means of knowing how far the chapbooks of the 1680s demonstrate changes in emphasis and thought brought about by the Commonwealth, and by fire and plague. If the type of thinking they demonstrated spread amongst the popular audience at which they were aimed, as Bunyan's and other spiritual autobiographies suggest, religious anxiety and fear must have been a major factor in popular belief, and should be reckoned with. Even amongst the perverted gospel of the chapbooks, however, there were one or two crumbs of much more positive doctrine to be found, and one or two indications that even at this level God was not worshipped solely in negative terms. Oddly enough, the fearsomely named *Almanac for Two Days, viz. The Day of Death and the Day of Judgement* was one of the publications that contained a lengthy consideration of the delight to the soul of union with God, mingled with its message of fear. The less common note of hope for this union must be borne in mind as another possible element of seventeenth-century popular belief along with scrupulosity, fear and dread of the Four Last Things. Armed with it, in the words of the chapbook, 'thy heart will leap within thee at Death's approach: it's a dark entry, but leads to a stately Pallace . . . thy own home, thy father's house'.[77]

NOTES AND REFERENCES

1 Thomas, K. (1973) *Religion and the Decline of Magic*, Harmondsworth, 189–96, 206, 764 and *passim*.
2 Dickens, A. G. (1964) *The English Reformation*, London, 266–7.
3 Spufford, M. (1974) *Contrasting Communities*, London, 232–7, 300–6, 320–34.
4 Langdale, J. (nd) 'Some Account of the Birth, Education and Religious Experiences and visitations of God to that faithfull Servant and Minister of Jesus Christ, Josiah Langdale', Friends House Library, Ms. Box 10/10.
5 Miss Judith Maltby of Wolfson College, Cambridge, is in the process of examining the signatories of county petitions in favour of the Prayer Book in the 1640s. This examination may at last

throw some light on the attitudes and background of just this silent majority.

6 Wroth, L. C. (1938) *The Colonial Printer*, Portland, Maine, 17.

7 LC, 2745(6).

8 *PG*, 5.

9 Arber, E. (1875) *A Transcript of the Register of the Company of Stationers of London: 1554–1640*, I, London, 76, 77, 93, 96, 97, 125, 153, 177, 178.

10 Thackeray's broadside trade-list covered 101 octavo chapbooks and forty-four quartos. Thirty-seven of the octavos and at least ten of the quartos were godly. Forty-two of 133 titles on lists put out by Brooksby, Deacon, Dennisson, Back, and Joshua and George Conyers were likewise godly. The overall proportion of godlies was 32 per cent in both cases. Mandrou found 26 per cent in the *bibliothèque bleue*. See above Tables II and III, pp. 134 and 136–7.

11 *PG*, 365. The volume has been paginated in pencil and the chapbooks also numbered one to forty-six. My references are to this pencilled numeration.

12 Mandrou, R. (1975) *De la Culture Populaire aux 17ᵉ et 18ᵉ Siècles*, Paris, 45, 87 *et seq.*

13 These really cheap religious pamphlets are not considered by Sommerville, C. J. (1977) *Popular Religion in Restoration England*, Gainesville, Fla., see above, n. 7 pp. 150–1. The only exceptions are the works of John Hart, *alias* Andrew Jones and William Jones (Sommerville, ibid., 45–7). All six of his titles listed by Sommerville were published by John Andrews of the White Lion near Pye Corner, see n. 15 below.

14 Jenkins, G. H. (1978) *Literature, Religion and Society in Wales, 1660–1730*, Cardiff, 35–36, 41, finds a striking 82 per cent of religious books amongst Welsh titles published in his period. Since the titles he considered included the more substantial publications, as well as the more ephemeral, no strict comparison is possible.

15 This was so in the 1650s also. John Andrews of the White Lion near Pye Corner had a trade-list of two 3*d* and seven 2*d* godly books in 1659. All but one of his tracts are preserved in the National Library of Scotland, LC, 2745. Four of them, 'The Dreadful Character of a Drunkard', 'Dying Man's Last Sermon',

'Black Book of Conscience' and 'Charitable Christian' were collected by Pepys in later editions. Even the woodcut of a divine, frequently used in Pepys's *Godlinesses* (see above p. 199), was a re-use from the 1650s.

16 'Black Book of Conscience', *PG*, 5, 112.

17 On the back of 'The Christian's Triumph over Temptation, Tribulation and Persecution', *PG*, 13, 270. For his normal sign see illustration above, p. 87.

18 *PG*, 15, 309.

19 On the back of 'School of Holiness', *PG*, 23, 508–9. This was his standard practice. The same list reappeared at the back of 'The Wicked Life and Death of Thomas Savage', *PG*, 37, 805–6, with 'The Gentlewoman's Delight in Cookery' and 'Crown Garland of Mirth' added to his twopenny titles, along with the savage 'godly' chapbook 'Now or Never'.

20 *PG*, 8, Compare LC, 2745, woodcut between items 6 and 7, which shows the same block being used in the 1650s.

21 *PG*, 33.

22 ibid., 700.

23 Twenty-six out of forty-six.

24 *PG*, 8, 145.

25 *PG*, 35, 744.

26 For instance, *PG*, 1, 'The Dreadful Character of a Drunkard; Or, the Odious and beastly sin of Drunkenness, Described and Condemned'.

27 'Now or Never', *PG*, 42, 913.

28 ibid., 911.

29 'A Christian Indeed; or Heaven's Assurance' (1677), *PG*, 22, 444.

30 Smith, R. M. (1978) 'Population and its Geography in England 1500–1730', in Dodgson, R. A. and Butlin, R. A. (eds) *An Historical Geography of England and Wales*, London 212–13, shows the worsening expectation of life at birth to be at its lowest in the 1680s.

31 *PG*, 42, 912.

32 'A Knock at the Door of Christless Ones, or some Considerations for Unchanged Persons' (1683), *PG*, 38, 813.

33 *PG*, 34, 711–34.

34 As was 'The Dying Christian's Pious Exhortation and Godly Connsel to his Wife, Children and Friends', *PG*, 7.

35 *PG*, 31 (1685), 647–70.

36 *PG*, 15 (1687), 295–310.

37 *PG*, 11, 199–222.

38 Nine out of forty-six.

39 Owst, G. R. (1933) *Literature and Pulpit in Medieval England*, Cambridge, 113, 527–35.

40 Stannard, D. E. (1977) *The Puritan Way of Death*, New York, 16 and 18, Figures 2 and 3; compare Puritan mourning rings and tombstones, 114 and 120, Figures 7 and 9.

41 Owst, op. cit., 98–102. He traces medieval antecedents in Latimer's preaching, and also shows that medieval influences evident in Bunyan's writing might have come to him through the pulpit. He uses Bloom, J. H. (1831) *Pulpit Oratory in the Time of James the First, Considered and Principally Illustrated by Original Examples AD 1620–1622*, London and Norwich; see also Beard, T. (1597) *Theatre of Divine Judgements*, London. I am grateful to Professor Collinson for this example of a Puritan's preaching in Huntingdonshire in the late sixteenth century. See Jenkins, op. cit., 134–44, for the stress on death and judgement in Welsh religious writing from 1660 onwards.

42 Stannard, ibid., 41–2, 72–5, 83–4.

43 Significantly, C. J. Sommerville finds that the works of John Hart whose chapbooks are the only godly ones to fall within the scope of his analysis are amongst those highest in emphasis on Satan, the threat of atheism, judgement, the after life and 'categories revealing anxiety', op. cit., 47.

44 *PG*, 21, 423.

45 *PG*, 19, 383–406. See illustration above, p. 140.

46 Stannard, op. cit., 85–9.

47 'Now or Never', *PG*, 42, 911.

48 'Christ's Voice to England calling for Repentance' (fifth edn, 1683), *PG*, 32, 677, 689.

49 *PG*, 14, 271–94.

50 ibid., 951–74.

51 *PG*, 17, 335–58. See particularly, *PG*, 14, 'An Almanack but for one Day', which lists under Contents the 'General Sessions', 'Judge', 'Jury', 'Prisoner', 'Sentence' and 'Executioner', p. 272.

52 See, for instance, 'Christ in the Clouds, Coming to Judgement, Or, The Dissolution of all Things', *PG*, 36, 759–82.

53 'The Golden Draps of Christian Comfort: Or, A safe Sanctuary for all True Penitent Sinners', *PG*, 25, 511–26. It is interesting that it contains no reference at all to the Last Supper and the institution of the Communion, or, indeed, to Christ's baptism.

54 If, that is, the chapbooks fairly represented the general level of preaching the laity encountered, and commonly-held religious ideas and beliefs, as seems likely.

55 Spufford, op. cit., 216, 231, 349.

56 I am grateful to Professor Collinson who read a draft of this chapter, and objected that the picture it gave does little justice to the main stream of Protestant casuistry. This is indeed true; the answer is that this religious literature for the uneducated also did little justice to the main stream of Protestant casuistry, any more than the 'small merry books' and 'histories' gave an accurate reflection of the development of literature. Many themes went undiscussed in it, amongst them the emphasis on the sacraments as an expression of God's covenant with the believer as an aid to the anxious which was found in manuals on reception from the 1630s onwards. Holifield, E. B. (1974) *The Covenant Sealed: The Development of Puritan Sacramental Theology in Old and New England, 1570–1720*, New Haven, Conn., 39–55, 126.

57 Monica Furlong in her biography of Bunyan, discusses this extensively.

58 'A Christian Indeed; Or Heaven's Assurance', *PG*, 22, 448.

59 Nine out of forty-six. I have included the life of Christ, 'Golden Drops of Christian Comfort', 25, amongst them.

60 'The Day of Grace, or Christ's Tears over Jerusalem' (1687), *PG*, 12, 223–46, and, outstandingly, 'The Christian's Triumph over Temptation, Tribulation and Persecution', *PG*, 13, 247–70.

61 *PG*, 12, 227–8.

62 *PG*, 13, 257.

63 *PG*, 13, 255, 257.

64 Hough, R. 'Saints Blessed for Ever, or God's People never forsaken', *PG*, 2, 25–48.

65 'Dangers of Despair' was priced on Back's trade-list, *PG*, 24, 509. The chapbooks would also, of course, have appealed to those hoping for further details of the death by drowning illustrated on the cover.

66 Bunyan was himself concerned with the case of John Child, who

had been an eminent member of the Bedford congregation, and hung himself in despair after conforming at the Restoration. Pooley, R. (1977) 'A Study of the Language and Milieu of John Bunyan', University of Cambridge PhD, 200–4. I am grateful to Dr Pooley for drawing my attention to this case. Henry Newcome in his (1852) *Autobiography*, Manchester, 86, wrote 'I remembered what Sir Ch. Adderley once said in way of reproach to some eminent startling minister, that he had made several to hang themselves'. The problem continued: Tibbutt, H. G. (ed.) (1976) *The Minutes of the First Independent Church (now Bunyan Meeting) at Bedford 1656–1766*, Bedfordshire Historical Record Society 55, 129, 161 and 188, contain notes of two eighteenth-century cases of people committing, or attempting to commit, suicide by cutting their throats, as well as the 'case of Sister Ann Groves, who labours under a melancholy disorder, or the power of temptation, by reason of which she absents herself from the Lord's Supper'.

67 *PG*, 30, 623–46.

68 *PG*, 30, 628, 631, 635–6.

69 Five out of forty-six. See Jenkins, op. cit., 39–42, 119–22, both on the emphasis amongst Welsh authors on the family as a teaching unit, and some examples of the purchase of books to aid in such teaching by yeomen.

70 Trade-list, *PG*, 28, 508–9.

71 *PG*, 43, 931–2.

72 Quoted by me, op. cit., 263.

73 ibid., 209.

74 *PG*, 43, 927–50.

75 *PG*, 16, 311–34.

76 *PG*, 23, 480.

77 'Almanac for Two Days', *PG*, 44, 963–4.

IX
Portraits of society: historical and chivalric novels

❦

The English were extremely fond of reading stories set in a vague and idealized version of the past. Indeed, they were even more addicted to their own past than were the French; thirty-four, or 14 per cent, of the chapbooks collected by Pepys had some sort of historical setting, compared to 9 per cent of the *bibliothèque bleue* (see above, p. 137). But the popularity of the past must not in any way be taken to suggest that the English readers of chapbooks were well informed about it. The historical past of the chapbooks was mythical and fantastic. If the reader of twopenny and threepenny publications did get any accurate information, it came from the almanacs, which appear to have been the practical guides, at least to contemporary politics.[1]

The chapbook world is one in which the Restoration and the Civil War might never have happened. Charles I does not appear, either as martyr or as villain. There is one reference to Cromwell. Oliver and Old Nick, his Holy Father, are the two judges in the burlesque trial of Sir John Barleycorn.[2] There is no kind of folk memory of the Wars of the Roses. The Reformation might never have happened either. There is a curious, muddled timelessness about references to the church. Priests, at the time of publication of the chapbooks in the 1680s, are often still saying Mass at Easter, and friars cheating old women of their food. The clergy who do appear and are satirized are local clergy anyway; like the priest who is too ignorant to know what day of the week it is, who takes up basket-making at the rate of a basket a day, partly to eke out his living, and partly to remind himself that after he has made six baskets he should stop and ring the church bells. Another priest sees pigs in his corn at sermon time and rushes out to shoo them out, leaving his people standing 'like fools'. There is the clergyman who gets so drunk he takes the moon for a cheese. Yet another parish priest keeps a concubine, and becomes the butt of bawdy jokes the miller justifies in full to the bishop. The archetypal figure of the lecherous medieval friar appears again.³ The Friar steals the hero's girl. But Jack, the hero, who invokes Venus, Cupid and Pan, has the gift of piping so that all must dance. When next he catches the Friar naked in bed with his girl, he plays them out of bed and out of town, where he ties them 'belly to belly' to a tree and inexorably plays on. The whole town comes to watch, dancing as it comes,

> Which when they came, did laugh amain,
> To see the Fryer and's lass half slain;
> 'Thou holy Fryer, they said, dost thou
>   love the flesh so well
> That this gay tree thou meanst to fell
> And kill this comely maid?'

The Friar complains to his superior, so Jack is brought before the Prior. That ecclesiastic very properly asks to hear the evidence, and gets more even than he bargains for. As Jack plays,

> A Nun that with a Fryer did lye
> Came skipping in immediately,
> Clad in a Fryer's cowl.

These stories are pre-Reformation anti-clerical satires surviving from the early sixteenth century, and still reprinting in the late seventeenth, rather than Puritan satires on the unreformed church.⁴

The only remotely topical bits about the church in the time of publication of these chapbooks of the 1680s are the jokes about the sexual habits of Quakers. The chapbook that tells the story of the Quaker's affair with his maid, which is both blasphemous and bawdy,⁵ is by no means alone in this genre. Quaker lovemaking was mocked in the same terms elsewhere. *Love's Masterpiece* contains, amongst other lovers' dialogues, a piece ending with the Quaker addressing his mistress, 'Let us retire, let us retire, I say, into the Cole-hole, there only the light within will shine'.⁶ And Quakers were always fair game, even for people in society who normally themselves were objects of mockery. Shon ap Morgan, one of the despised itinerant Welshmen who were common anti-heroes in the burlesques, stole four flitches of bacon from the local Quaker⁷ without local disapproval. 'He is such a fantastical Fellow, I do not care to have any dealings with him,' says one of the neighbours. So the despised Quakers appear, oddly, in the distorting mirror of the chapbooks, as the only contemporary figures in the seventeenth-century church worthy of remark, along with the stock pre-Reformation figures of the incontinent friar and the ignorant country priest. There is an odd and complete cleavage here between the content of the secular chapbooks and the content of the religious ones.

Stories about royal mistresses were popular. Both Fair Rosamond, mistress to Henry II and Jane Shore, mistress to Edward IV, were well-known. The chapbooks about them were simply excuses for a good story of adultery, high life, rich living and repentance in both cases, reinforced with a moral at the end.[8] Queen Elizabeth, oddly, did not exist as a personage in her own right in the chapbooks Pepys collected, except in *The Crown Garland*, although a woodcut of her was re-used as an illustration. She did, however, exist as an adjunct to Sir Francis Drake. One twenty-four page quarto threepenny 'double-book' in the collection stands out as a unique attempt at a description of actual, not mythological, historical events and their physical background.[9] It is an account of Drake's voyages to the West Indies, and his circumnavigation of the world. It is lightened by much detail of silver and golden loot, but also contains details of the ways that the Indians manufactured their canoes, their arrowheads and their huts, and even some descriptions of exotic birds, animals and temperatures. Penguins appear as

> Birds as big as Stuble-Geese, without Feathers, having matted down on their backs and beaks like a Crow: they cannot run fast, but swim exceedingly swift; they lay their eggs in the Ground, where they make holes with their Beaks like Conies.

In the Pacific, Drake's crews found 'crab-fish that lived on the Land, making holes in the Earth and running up Trees' along with 'Worms that shined in the night like Fire'. The 'globes of Ice' covering the seas in mid-June at a latitude of under 60° 'north' were described, too. This chapbook was alone in the collection amongst the 'histories' in its attempt at realism. It is doubtful, however, whether the descriptions of penguins and land-crabs could have been recognized as in any way realistic by the non-gentle reader, accustomed as he was to monstrous cows, mermaids and mythical beasts.

The one monarch who appeared as a personality in the chapbooks was Henry VIII. He was not there as the hero of the Reformation, nor as the villain of the Dissolution. He appears in a couple of *Merriments* as an unpredictable, jolly monarch given to wandering round the country in disguise. Disguised, he dines with the Abbot of Reading, who is unfortunate enough to say he would give £100 to have as good an appetite at table, and presently finds himself cast into the Tower on bread and water until the King appears to claim his £100 for amending the Abbot's appetite.[10] Disguised, he wanders round the City at night to make sure that the watch is doing a good job, and meets a cobbler of the Strand who sings him 'merry songs and catches' and broaches a new cask of beer for him. The incognito king invites the cobbler to visit him at Whitehall, where he should seek him under the name of Harry Tudor. They end up carousing together in the palace cellars and the cobbler gets a pension of forty marks a year.[11]

Henry II is the hero of another chapbook in the same vein,[12] which has links with the Robin Hood group. He gets lost whilst hunting in Sherwood Forest, and is put up for the night by a miller in a smokier hovel than he has ever been in before. The wife is proud of her entertainment:

> Fresh straw I will have
> Laid on your bed so brave
> Good brown hempen sheets
> Likewise quoth she.

The king is to share this bed with their own son Richard, but the latter has doubts about it.

> Nay first, quoth Richard
> good fellow, tell me true,
> hast thou no creepers
> within thy gay hose? . . .
> Art thou not lowsie
> nor scabby, quoth he
> If thou be'est,
> surely thou lyest not with me.

The king is not familiar with the problems of lice about his person, and takes some while to comprehend, but when he does so, the son is reassured, and the miller and his family feast the king on illegally taken venison pasty. The king is so delighted with his entertainment that, when his identity is revealed in the morning, he creates the miller a knight, and bids the whole family to feast at court. They attend this in their old clothes, the uncouth son produces a well-warmed black pudding from his breeches for the king's delectation,

The Pleafant Hiftory of the M I L L E R

# of M A N S F I E L D

in *Sherwood*, and *HENRY* the fecond

K I N G of E N G L A N D.

Shewing how the King was lodged in the Millers Houfe, and the mirth and Sports he had there.

Printed for J. Clarke, W. Thacke-ray, and T Paffinger.

and the family retires, covered with honours. The miller is created overseer of Sherwood Forest, and granted a pension of £300 a year. There is no distinction in this group extolling kingship between the personalities of Henry VIII and Henry II. The ideal king of the chapbooks is jovial, unpredictable, and brings miraculous good luck to poor men in the form of legendary wealth, much in the manner of Dick Whittington's cat, or Fortunatus's inexhaustible purse. The motif of the disguised king lavishing pardons and favours flourished from the thirteenth century to the seventeenth.[13]

The past that does exist in these stories is a kind of composite, fabricated past, a very long time ago, a past strongly related to the 'Once upon a time' of fairy stories. This impression of a composite past is partly created by the history of the stories told in chapbooks and is partly the deliberate intention of sixteenth-century authors creating bastard descendants of medieval chivalric romances because the genre was popular and sold well. The new 'realistic' novels of Deloney, written at the end of the sixteenth century, glorifying the trades of the clothiers, the shoemakers and the weavers, were also deliberately set in the remote historical past, as were the group, mainly of unidentifiable origin, that quite deliberately set out to enable the poorer reader of these seventeenth-century chapbooks to identify himself with the chivalric adventures of a feudal aristocracy of which he can never even have heard.

MEDIEVAL AND CHIVALRIC ROMANCES

The only version of the past that purported to be pre-medieval was presented by the cycle of stories in the *Seven Sages of Rome*,[14] which was originally Hebrew, derived from Indian through Arabic and Persian. It had reached Europe by the twelfth century. It was printed by Wynken de Worde as *The Seven Wise Masters* in about 1515. In this cycle, the amorous wife of the emperor Pontinus tries to get her stepson, Diocletian, executed for refusing her advances. Every night, she tells her husband the story of an over-mighty son dispossessing his father; every day the boy's seven tutors tell the emperor stories of perfidious women, to induce him to stay the execution. The tutors, despite the lofty claim of the chapbook preface that they represent the Liberal Arts, are astrologers and diviners, magicians like Friar Bacon, who examine the child's absorption of their teaching by putting olive leaves under his pillow, and read his future in the stars. The classical veneer is impossibly thin: the Emperor's second wife is the daughter of the King of Castille; sons and heirs to the kings of Egypt, France and Spain appear and disappear amongst the barons, knights and courtly adulteries of the *exempla*. The collection was very popular. It was reprinted or re-edited over a score of times under the Tudors and it reached a wide public. Cox, the mason of Coventry, had it in 1575 (see above, p. 145). Pepys had it[15] together with a seventeenth-century imitation, the *Seven Wise Mistresses*[16] in extended octavo. He also had a threepenny abbreviated version in twenty-four page quarto.[17]

The genuine chivalric romances rivalled the origins of the *Seven Sages* in antiquity. *Guy of Warwick* originated in a French source round about 1200,[18] and *Bevis of Hampton* in a thirteenth-century Anglo-Norman romance that probably drew on much earlier popular themes.[19] *Guy* was collected by Pepys in two versions. The first was one of the *Vulgaria*[20] excluded from consideration here on the grounds of its length. The second was a twenty-four page octavo.[21] The only clue the chapbooks contain to a deliberate adjustment of the content of longer and more expensive quartos aimed at the gentry, to shorter versions more suitable for a different social audience, is contained in this pair. Guy is a Saxon, 'our Renowned Heroe, England's Greatest Boast'. The longer version has an introductory piece of Roman and Saxon settlement history, and a lengthy genealogy of Guy, which makes him remotely descended from Cassivellaunus, King of the Belgae. He is the immediate heir of a nobleman from Northumberland, who lost his estates on the disappearance of the Heptarchy. Guy now serves the Earl of Warwick as his steward, despite his noble birth. The shorter version omits this lengthy genealogy and simply presents him as the son of the Earl of Warwick's steward. He is in fact rejected by the Earl's daughter, Phyllis, on the grounds 'you are but young and meanly born, and therefore you may not love where you please'. This rejection is the spur to Guy to perform tremendous feats of arms, and win the lady by strength and prowess, despite his birth. His feats of prowess take place in the Duchy of Normandy, the Empire, and fighting for Christendom to relieve the siege of Byzantium by the Turks. They are brought to a close when he returns to England and finds the 'bloody Danes' have invaded. His final adventure is the slaying of the

Danish champion, who is, of course, a giant. For into this historical hodge-podge of Saxons, Danes, the Empire and the Turkish menace are also thrown, as equally realistic, giants and dragons, lions and even a monstrous cow 10 ft long and 6 ft wide. Superhuman strength, brawn, and faithfulness to the lady who inspires his exploits are Guy's characteristics. He becomes the Earl's heir and Earl of Warwick in his turn, although, immediately after winning his lady in marriage, he repents of making his earthly happiness his goal, and leaves her to wander off as a pilgrim to the Holy Land. Even after his

The Famous History
of Guy Earle of *Warwick*.

By Samuel Rowlands.

London, Printed by J. Bell for Thomas Vere in the old Bayley. 1 59.

return to England after twenty years wandering and more noble deeds and slaughter, this time disguised, he still lives retired as a hermit in a cave. The reader's attention is held by enormous amounts of bloodshed in huge battles in which Guy always kills incredibly large numbers of men. It seems very likely that the longer version is written for a gentle audience for which Guy has to have birth and breeding, the other for the commonalty, for which he needed to win the lady, and achieve social rank without any advantages of birth and breeding, by his own tremendous efforts.

There were other early medieval romances in the collection made by Samuel Pepys, shamelessly adapted. The twenty-four page version of King Arthur selling at 3d[22] starts off solidly enough, with an Arthur ruling over a British remnant against the Saxons. It takes airy flight halfway through, however, and ends up, by way of the reduction of the kingdom of Denmark and of the town of Marseilles, with Arthur's flag flying over the walls of Jerusalem in the first Christian conquest of the city.

There was no nonsensical notion of England's champion, St George, beloved of mummers,[23] coming of the common-stock. He, not unlike Guy, was son of a 'Noble Peer of England's Realm', Lord Albert of Coventry, who was married to the king's only daughter. George 'never failed of carrying off the Prize at Tilts and Tournaments, quell'd Monsters, overcame Gyants, and slaughtered Beasts'. To this career of chivalric arms, the killing of the 'horrid Aegyptian Dragon' who, fussily, would eat nothing but virgins, was only a climax. His marriage to the Egyptian princess he rescued was the only suitable end, except of course that they

> many years of joy did see
> And led their lives in Coventry.

The inextricable involvement of oral tradition that encouraged the telling of familiar tales in print, which in turn fed back printed words to shape the oral tradition, is nowhere more closely illustrated than by the chapbook version of *St George* collected by Pepys.[24] This was one of the chapbooks loved by the young unreformed Bunyan in the 1640s, who in his reformed days was obliged to drop the saint's title and to refer to the story as *George on Horseback* (see above, p. 7). The brief version of the story given in *St George* was, Chambers thought, culled from the longer version[25] in Richard Johnson's *Seven*

THE
Life and Death
OF THE
Famous CHAMPION
OF
ENGLAND,
St. GEORGE.

Pinted by J. M. for J. Clrke, W. Thacker and T. Passnger.

Champions of Christendom written in 1596–7, and still in print in three lengthy parts in the 1680s.[26] Critics testily dismiss Johnson as a 'writer for the illiterate'.[27] If the chapbook version of *St George* was indeed drawn from him, he seems to have made a tremendous impact precisely on the illiterate, or rather, the semi-literate. The texts which survive of the Mummers' Play use the story told in the chapbook, and in the seventeenth-century ballad of St George which was printed with it by the Ballad Partners.[28] So the words of the chapbook fed into the oral tradition, and were reiterated in the Mummers' Play, and thence collected again, in exactly the same fashion as the printed broadside ballads fed into the ballad tradition. Here is potent evidence of the wide influence of the seventeenth- and eighteenth-century chapbooks on the rural public, which yearly re-enacted the fertility rituals and the death and rebirth of its hero champion over wide areas of England as late as the nineteenth century.

The picture is yet more complex, however. Johnson, when he wrote such a successful novel, was writing an elaboration of the story that had commonly and regularly been acted within living memory in the 1590s.[29] But the story that he may have heard or seen played as a boy in the 1570s had already been heavily influenced at an earlier stage by the written word.

Twenty-eight townships in western Cambridgeshire clubbed together to put on the play of the 'holy martyr, St George' on Sunday 20 July 1511. This was the day of the virgin St Margaret, who had become associated with St George's virgin princess, and may have been pre-figured by the 'Lady' of the wooing plays, whose fertility had, eventually, to be assured. The expenditure involved in this pageant was heavy; a dragon was furnished, tormentors' axes were painted, a property-maker was paid six days' board, as well as horse-pasture, minstrels and waits were hired to come from Cambridge for three days at a lump sum of 5s 11d, as well as bread, and ale furnished for the players themselves. The largest item of expenses was 22s 2d for properties and a play-book.[30] There were two further payments relating to the play-book, second only in size to the payments to waits, and on bread and ale to the players. Both were to John Hobard, priest, 'towards costs . . . of his labor for berying the play booke'.[31] It sounds remarkably as if John Hobard may have taught the actors their parts, out of the written text that had been bought at such expense, and acted as promptor. So even in 1511, the

The mummers of St George

oral tradition was being shaped by the written or the printed word. The story which Richard Johnson heard, and re-wrote, elaborated and lengthened and re-shaped in his turn, had already been formed by written texts, although their content is lost to view beneath derivation from some of his own words. The link between the chapbook version of St George and the Mummers' Plays is made explicit, in Pepys's version, by the last woodcut in the chapbook, which shows a group of mummers led by players of a flute and a tabor.[32]

Robin Hood was yet another hero with a very respectable medieval pedigree, that runs at least back to the fourteenth century, although there is lively disagreement about whether he originated as a hero for peasant audiences then or for a gentle audience which disliked the forest laws and shrieval administration of the thirteenth century.[33] By the end of the fifteenth century he had become a hero of some Mummers' Plays,[34] and in the sixteenth century presided widely in England as King of the May.[35] The problem of the nature of the original audience is therefore irrelevant.

By the sixteenth century, Robin Hood, whether portrayed as an aristocrat or not, was a folk hero. Wynkyn de Worde printed a 'lyttle geste' of Robin Hood as a quarto thirty-two leaves long. In 1575, Robin Hood and the related outlaws 'Adam Bell, Clim of the Clough and William of Cloudesley', who also went into print early in the sixteenth century, were two of the three 'historical' books possessed by the mason Cox of Coventry that were not chivalric.[36] There was already a market for Robin Hood in book form in the sixteenth century and, in this form, he reached non-gentle readers. As was to be expected from this, Robin Hood appeared in more than one guise. Pepys had Martin Parker's *True Tale of Robin Hood* of 1632, as a small merry book, as well as a cycle of twelve Robin Hood stories in a quarto double -book selling at 3*d*.[37] In both of them the hero was the noble Robin, Earl of Huntingdon, outlawed in one case by Richard I, in the other by Henry VIII. In Parker's Robin Hood, addressed to 'gentlemen and yeomen bold', the hero was noted for his hospitality and the size of his train before his outlawry; his chief enmity was to the clergy, above all to the Abbot of St Mary's, but also to local monks and friars, whom he gelded, 'for such as they the Country fill'd with Bastards in those days'. Yet he was not above plundering the royal revenues. There was no doubt where his social sympathies lay:

> poor men might safely pass by him,
> and some that way would chuse,
> for well they knew that to help them
> he evermore did use
> But when he knew a Miser rich
> that did the poor oppress,
> To feel his Coyn his hands did itch,
> He'd have it, more or less.

Even in the seventeenth-century chapbooks, Robin is an ambivalent figure, however; he gives nothing to the Beggar but the offer of a fight, and when he finds himself losing, he draws his sword on his poor opponent, who is armed only with a quarter staff.

The less well-known medieval outlaws of the forest, the yeomen[38] Adam Bell, Clim of the Clough and William of Cloudesley, also in the collection of Cox of Coventry, lived on into the seventeenth century. Their interest was not, even partially, in social justice. The adventure retailed in the Pepys collection[39] is the rescue of William, who was unwise enough to go and spend the night, despite his outlawry, with his wife in Carlisle, where he was caught. Adam and Clim free him from the very foot of the gallows in Carlisle market place, kill sheriff, justice and mayor, and get him away in a tremendous street battle. They very wisely win pardons from the king, before he hears of the death of his officers. That un-named monarch is so impressed by the prowess they show with their long-bows, particularly William's feat of splitting the apple on his seven-year-old son's head at six-score paces, that he makes William chief Rider over the 'north country', and 'a Gentleman of cloathing and of fee'. His wife becomes the Queen's gentlewoman to govern her nursery, and the other two outlaws are made yeomen of the king's chamber. The tale, in which the poachers of the king's venison become the wardens of it, gaining considerable social standing in the process, and the monarch unpredictably, and miraculously, produces pensions and rewards, is close in theme to the motif of *The King and the Miller* (see above, pp. 222–7).

THE NEO-CHIVALRIC ROMANCES

So far, all the heroes[40] of the chivalric chapbooks that have been surveyed are genuine medieval figures, now truncated and rewritten for an audience completely different from and much wider than the original aristocratic one. In the late sixteenth century, these genuine chivalric tales were reinforced, firstly, by a whole wave of translations which were mainly from Spanish. These were followed by imitations. It has been well said 'the translated romances of this period are, briefly speaking, of the type that drove the good knight of La Mancha mad'.[41] Anthony Munday brought out the first volume of *Amadis of Gaule*,[42] and *Palladin of England* in 1588. Munday was a draper's son apprenticed to the stationer and printer John Allde.[43] He was therefore in close touch with the market, and may well have been producing material for his former master's presses, as Thomas Gent did later. The books of the *Palmerin* cycle, which included a *Palmerin of England*, appeared between 1581 and 1594.[44] *Don Bellianis of Greece* appeared in 1598.[45] These translations must have proved hugely successful to spur Richard Johnson to write his *Seven Champions of Christendom* in 1596–7, the *Pleasant History of Tom à Lincoln, the Red-Rose Knight* in 1599, and the *History of Thom-Thumb . . . surnamed King Arthur's Dwarfe* in 1621.[46] Emmanuel Forde had made the same assessment of the market, and was at the same time producing his series, *Parismus, Prince of Bohemia* in 1598, *Ornatus and Artesia* in 1607, and the *Famous History of Montelyon, Knight of the Oracle* in 1633.[47] Marxists are 'baffled and challenged' by the appeal this romantic chivalric literature had in economically advanced mercantile England, as opposed to 'feudal' Spain.[48] However, the mason Cox of Coventry had had no less than thirteen separately titled chivalric tales of knighthood amongst his fifty-two books. From the printing history of these books in the seventeenth century,[49] Munday, Johnson and Forde were right in their judgement of the popularity of the chivalric mode.

The addiction the rural schoolboy Bunyan (see above, pp. 7–8), and the London and Lichfield schoolboys Kirkman (see above, pp. 72–4) and Johnson (see above, p. 75) all developed to the romantic tales helps to illuminate one, probably potent, section of the market. Beaumont and Fletcher put an absurd episode from Palmerin into the mouth of an ignorant grocer's apprentice, who was as inflamed by the romances as the schoolboy Kirkman was later to be in real life. At least eight other Elizabethan and Jacobean plays used the Palmerin romances, often as the favourite reading of women to whom the romanticized love of the chivalric works appealed.[50] The chivalric romances must have been pure escapism to the sober townsmen who read them, and the verbose equivalent of comics portraying heroics, bloodletting and violence to the schoolboys who dreamed themselves, in the manner of the heroes of the romances, unknown sons of 'Kings and great Personages'.

The chivalric romances were reprinted again and again in the seventeenth century. Tias, the ballad and chapbook publisher, was printing them in 1664, and they figured as chapbooks in the 'history' section of the Thackeray trade-list of 1689. Most of them were collected by Samuel Pepys in the 1680s, in his tellingly-titled *Vulgaria*.[51] However, most of them were too long to sell at 6d or less, and so they are not considered here.

Don Flores of Greece,[52] which was just over sixty pages long, and may have sold at about 6d, was one of the prolific tribe begotten by *Amadis of Gaul*. One of the sons of Amadis is the 'Emperor Esplandran' of Constantinople. The story concerns the wanderings in search of a knighthood of his second son, Amadis's grandson, Don Flores, who is to be compared with Arthur. He is eventually knighted by the Emperor of Rome, after keeping vigil by his arms all night and hearing Mass. One of the many disjointed themes of the story is a Turkish plot to invade Amadis's Great Britain, where 'within this little time knighthood is rusted among them . . . there is not any more talke of wandering knights, but all like carpet Knights . . . study only to sit by the fire and court fair Ladies'. The dedicatory epistle is to gentlemen, to encourage them 'to put themselves forth in Acts of Chivalry, rather than to courting Ladies, and being Effeminate from want of manly exercises'. Everything is hopelessly overstated. On a hunting expedition, the young squires wander into a forest, which is 'very full of Harts, Hindes, Does, Wolves, Bears, Lions, and other kind of Beasts, giving sufficient cause of recreation'.

However, *Don Flores* is relatively sensible compared with the Thackeray version of Johnson's *Tom-à-Lincoln, or the Red-Rose Knight*.[53] Tom-à-Lincoln is the bastard son of King Arthur, who falls in love with 'the fair Angelica, the Earl of London's daughter'. He installs the lady in a convent in Lincoln, founded by himself, so that he can visit her freely, while she spends 'the remain of her life in the service of Diana' as a professed nun. Her child, the fruit of this affair,

The moſt Pleaſant

HISTORY

OF

TOMALINCOLN

That Ever Renowned Souldier,

THE

Red-Roſe Knight.

Printed by *H. R.* for *W. Thackery* at the Angel in *Duck Lane*, 1682.

The neo-chivalric knight

begins his adventures very young. He is carried off by the midwife 'wrapped in a Mantle of green silk, tying a purse of Gold about his neck' and is laid at the door of a shepherd's house near the city, in the hope that the old man will foster him as his own. Johnson seems to have had as few scruples about borrowing from Robert Greene as Shakespeare himself.[54]

Johnson's *Red-Rose Knight* is, in turn, a marvel of invention and literary skill compared with the twenty-two page quarto double-book printed by Thackeray in 1677, the *History of the Golden Eagle*[55] by 'Philaquila'. This is not, as its title would suggest, one of the family of animal fabliaux ultimately descending from Aesop, but the story of the adventures of the three sons of the King of Aragon, who set out to seek for the miraculous Golden Eagle belonging to 'Agrippina, [the] most famous and invincible Queen of Green Ivy-land', which would restore their dying father to health. The two eldest turn out to be poltroons, in the face of all the monstrous opponents the author, who is not renowned for his imagination, as the title of the lady's kingdom shows, can lump together in one breath. The eldest relates:

> This Eagle is a bird kept . . . in a great City walled around with Brass, Pallizado'd with Iron, guarded with Lyons and Dragons and commanded by Gyants, and we must before we come to this City, Encounter with several Knights which attend purposely for such attemptors as we must be,

and the second replies:

> Oh, I am more than half dead already with the relation, talk no more of it. What, Dragons and Bears, Lyons and Gyants, Brazen walls and Iron Pallizadoes. Oh how I am thundred to death! Attempt it who will, for my part I will stay here rather than be eaten with Bears and Lyons and Dragons, and – oh Horrible Gyants, not I.

The youngest is made of sterner stuff. Eventually he reaches Green Ivy-land, after encountering damsels in distress, an enchanted castle, and a magic steed. There he overthrows.

> many Knights which waited there on purpose to encounter any that should approach: but he with his good Sword and Steed made

flight of them, then he approached to the Brazen Walls, where he was welcomed with the roaring of Lyons and Dragons, but as he brandished his Sword they fell into a dead sleep, than Innocentine passed freely, not long after he came to a Fort which was guarded by Gyants, who when they perceived his approach, presently came roaring at him with great violence, but he, no sooner brandished his sword but they fell all asleep; at length, having many more difficulties, which are now too tedious to relate, he came to the place where the Queen and the Eagle was.

Patently the cheap end of the chivalric market would take any threadbare absurdity. In the circumstances, the little duodecimo version of *Don Quixote*,[56] printed for Conyers in 1686, must have been as refreshingly funny to the newly-literate in the 1680s as when Cervantes first wrote it. Moreover, this chapbook must have made a special appeal to the humbly-born, who were perhaps familiar with that other literary figure, the Amazonian Long Meg who travelled to London on the Lancashire carrier's cart. They would certainly be familiar with their local inns and the figures of the carriers who used them.

Night coming on [Don Quixote] . . . came within view of an Inn, which he fancied to be a Famous Castle adorned with Battlements of Brass, Turrets of Silver, and the like: in the Door of which Inn stood two Wenches, brought thither by the Carrier, whom he supposed to be Inchanted Ladies.

Don Quixote spends the night keeping vigil over his arms by the water-cistern, and the host hastily dubs him knight the next morning, to speed his departure after he has attacked carriers watering their beasts, under the illusion that they are hostile knights. The ceremony is carried out, 'mumbling over him out of the Book he kept his Account of Straw and Oats in . . . he caused the Wenches, a Butcher's and a Miller's Daughter, to buckle on his Belt and put on his Spurs'. In this chapbook company, Cervantes reads as if he had written with a very different audience in mind from his original one. He might have been writing on purpose for a rustic audience that was familiar with the giants, dragons and heroes of the romances but also lapped up both slapstick and satire.

When Cox of Coventry was collecting in the 1570s, there were no books available to him that attempted to reflect his own urban or trade interests or specialities. All this changed when the works of Thomas Deloney appeared between 1597 and 1600.[57] Deloney had himself been a weaver, and both *Thomas of Reading* and *Jack of Newbury* deliberately exalted the clothiers' trade. *The Gentle Craft* extolled shoe-making. Pepys had long quarto and small merry versions of both *Jack of Newbury* and *The Gentle Craft*, and a medium-length quarto of *Thomas of Reading*. Pepys also had a verse glorification of the weaver's trade, *The Triumphant Weaver*, tracing the history of the art from the decoration of the Ark of the Covenant onwards.[58]

> The Tabernacle was erected, then
> The Curtains of fine twinned Linen were,
> And Blew, Purple and Scarlet Silk was there;
> All which must needs be Weavers work, ...
> More backward yet, when Noah did plant the Vine
> And became drunk by drinking of the Wine
> When his two modest Sons did make no stay
> To take a Garment, and going backwards do
> Cover his nakedness; and who can show
> That this Garment was Leather? Rather I
> Suppose it Cloath, and Weavings Antiquity
> A Thousand years more ancient than *Noah's Flood*.

The author traces the history of his craft from bibilical times onwards, and then goes on to make claims for its fundamental importance to the economy.

> The Merchant that on all the World doeth trade
> By whom our Nation is so famous made,
> Weavers work is the chief Commoditie
> That he transporteth hence . . . .
> Is not linnen cloath, brought hither, found
> Likewise to be a great Commoditie,
> Gainful, and needful, unto each degree?
> So were silk-stuffs, but we being skilful grown
> To make them here, that Trade's well-nigh o'erthrown.

He lists the other trades, mercers, suppliers of silk, haberdashers, upholsterers, tailors and the various cloth workers besides the weavers, who were involved in the production of the finished cloth, right down to the new luxury processes, to gold and silver wire drawers, and those who spin them into silk. The claim the chapbook makes is for respect for the trade, both on the grounds of its antiquity, and its current importance in the economy. This chapbook is unique as a straight-forward trade-description, just as the description of Drake's voyages is unique as a piece of historical description.

Deloney's novels were, on the other hand, stories with trade heroes. *Thomas of Reading* has six western clothiers from Reading, Gloucester, Worcester, Exeter, Salisbury and Southampton as heroes. They regularly travel the roads known to the chapmen as the 'Middle West Road' and the 'West Road' together, and meet at Basingstoke on their way up to London, where they encounter the three northern heroes, clothiers from Kendal, Manchester and Halifax. These men are estimable simply because 'every one of them kept a great number of Servants at work, Spinners, Carders, Weavers, Fullers, Dyers, Sheeremen, and Rowers' and provided so much work that there were few or no beggars in their areas. The children of the poor would be 'able to get their own bread' by six or seven years old.

This story is transposed back in time out of the period when English cloth exports were booming, from the 1460s on, back to the reign of Henry I. That monarch's attention is drawn to the importance of his clothier subjects when, on a journey westwards to Wales, he is first held up for an hour by a procession of 200 carts loaded with cloth belonging to Cole of Reading, and next by the wains of Sutton of Salisbury. He is so impressed that he asks the clothiers, before setting off on the French campaign of 1107, what boons they would like of him. They reply, standardized measure, good money and the death penalty for stealing cloth from its drying place on the tenterhooks outside Halifax. So the clothiers came by the yard measure, of Henry I's arm, not that of Edward I, 'slit' money since there was no time to reform the coinage and so all money was made bad, and the death penalty that they asked for.

The story is a loosely-structured one. Much of it takes place on the routes into London and in the inns at which the clothiers always stayed on all their journeys. Deloney obviously knew his English road system, and the importance the inns had not only as staging posts, but for all sorts of other trade transactions.

Within the loose framework provided by the clothiers' regular journeys and meetings, are woven both vivid descriptions of individual characters, and a set of sub-plots. After the western and northern clothiers had met at London, and made their sales to the waiting merchants at Blackwater Hall, they habitually went to dine at Bosoms Inn,

> which was so called of his name that kept it, who being a foul sloven, went alwayes with his nose in his bosome, one hand in his pocket, the other on his staff, figuring forth a description of cold winter: for he always wore two coats, two caps, two or three pair of stockings, and a high pair of shooes: over the which he drew on a great pare of lined slippers, and yet would he oft complain of the cold.

One of the sub-plots concerns the affair Cuthbert of Kendal had with the frigid old innkeeper's wily young wife, 'for no meat pleased [Cuthbert] so well as mutton, such as was laced in a red petticoat'.

Another sub-plot tells how the banished Earl of Shrewsbury's daughter is driven to offer herself up as a servant at a hiring fair near Gloucester, although she cannot 'brew nor bake nor make butter nor cheese nor reap corne, nor even spin and card'. Her only accomplishment, she tells the other girls at the fair, are to be able to 'read and write and sew, some skill have I in my needle, and a little on my Lute'. 'Good Lord,' quoth they, 'are you bookish? We did never hear of a Maid before that could read and write.' One of them immediately produces a love letter for her to read aloud, but despite her utility in this field, they are not encouraging about her prospects of obtaining a place. Nevertheless, the wife of Grey of Gloucester hires her. In her menial position, she, improbably, attracts noble suitors. Nevertheless, she becomes a nun in Gloucester Abbey, and her devotion to her heavenly bridegroom is oddly strongly emphasized for a piece written at this date.

> Do you think, if I had the offer and choice of the mightiest Princes of Christendom, that I could match myself better than to my Lord Jesus? No, no he is my husband, to whom I yield myself body and soul, giving Him my heart, my love and my most fervent affection.

A procession in which this postulant nun is to offer herself at the doors of Gloucester Abbey is vividly described in terms of the white velvet and jewels worn by the 'bride', the magnificence of the king and the attendant nobility who form the bridal escort, and the romantic nature of the self-immolation of the virgin heroine in a way that must inevitably appeal to feminine readers.

The apocryphal visit to London of the wives of Simon of Southampton and Sutton of Salisbury, their breathless round of sightseeing, and their return to nag their husbands into providing clothes as fashionable and rich as those of the London merchants' wives, is used to explain why, ever since, the wives of Southampton, Salisbury, Gloucester, Worcester and Reading are as finely dressed as any Londoners' wives.

The high point of the drama is the murder of Thomas Cole of Reading by the innkeeper and his wife of Colebrook, where he always stayed on his return from London, with the profits of his visit concealed about his person.

The sub-plots do not link. The constant interest of the novel is in the wealth of the clothiers, their importance in the kingdom's trade, their ability to set others to work, and their style of living, including their works of charity for the poor.

The same themes are underlined in the story of *Jack of Newbury*, which is set in Henry VIII's reign. He is an apprentice to a broadcloth weaver in Newbury, and is noted for his generosity. When his master dies, the widow puts him in charge of the business and eventually tricks him into marriage, despite her other suitors. The tale of their bedding, wedding and struggle for mastery over each other provides the sexual interest. But the emphasis is on the prosperity and employment offered by the trade. This is demonstrated three times by Jack, once when, after the death of his first wife, he courts a new bride, and shows her father

In one Room two hundred Looms all going.
Two hundred Boys making Quills.
A hundred Women Carding.
Two hundred Maids in another Room spinning.
One hundred and fifty Boys picking of Wool
Fifty Shiermen.
Eight Rowers,

Fourty Dyers in the Dy-house.
Twenty men in the Fulling Mill,
Ten fat Oxen he spent every week in his
house, besides Butter, Cheese, Fish, etc.,

Butcher, ⎫
Baker, ⎬ for his own house
Brewer ⎭

Five Cooks.
Six Scullion-Boys.
Divers Turn-spits, etc.[59]

Jack's house measures up to the number of his servants and the number of his employees. He has a 'fair and large Parlour wainscotted round about . . . with fifteen fair pictures hanging, covered with curtains of green silk fringed with gold'. Each was of a real or apocryphal king or emperor, kneeling before his own father, who was in each case a man of poor birth. Here in Jack's parlour were pictures of a shepherd, a potter, a cobbler, a carter, a bookbinder, a ropemaker, a gardener, a cloth weaver, a blacksmith, a shoemaker, a mariner, a tailor, a ploughman and even a 'common Strumpet's' son, all of whom had made good with a vengeance. Jack annually showed these pictures to his work-people, with the recommendation:

> There is none of you so poorly born, but that men of baser birth have come to great honours: the idle hand shall ever go in a ragged garment, and the slothful live in reproach: but such as do lead a virtuous life . . . shall of the best be esteemed, and spend their days in credit.[60]

Here is the capitalist ethic very straightforwardly stated, in a society in which upward social movement appeared possible to all.

The second occasion to demonstrate the power of the clothiers came about for Jack when the King of the Scots invaded England, in the campaign that ended at Flodden, when Henry VIII was fighting the French abroad. Queen Katherine raised the militia, and Jack was asked to raise six footmen. He in fact raised fifty mounted men, and a hundred footmen, all, of course, clad in good broadcloth coats. This conspicuous private army roused murmurings amongst some of the envious gentry, but gained the high approbation of the Queen when she came to inspect her levies. She summoned Jack and his men and, as they knelt, commanded them to 'Rise, gentlemen'. This called forth from Jack a key speech expressing his pride in his trade, and a comparison of himself with the country gentry. He also expressed the pride of the audience at which Deloney was aiming.

> Most Gracious Queen, quoth he, Gentleman I am none, nor the Son of a Gentleman, but a poor Cloathier, whose Lands are his Looms, having no other Rents but what I get from the backs of little sheep, nor can I claim any other cognisance but a wooden shuttle.

Jack's third opportunity to impress the Crown with the strength and needs of the clothing trade came on a royal progress into Berkshire at, according to Deloney, a time of recession of the trade because of the foreign wars. Jack, with thirty men, acted out a parable of the defence of the kingdom of the Ants against the idle Butterflies. He then entertained the king and queen to a sumptuous banquet, and offered the king a costly gift of a gilt beehive with gold bees, as a figure of his industrious servants of the commonwealth. The entertainment concluded with a royal tour, first of the weaving shed, with its hundred looms employing 200 men, next of the spinning and carding women, singing over their work, then of the fulling mills and dyehouse. Finally they met the ninety-six children of the poor who picked the wool, and so made a living.

> His Majesty perceiving what a great number of people were by this one man set on work, both admired and commended him: saying further, that as no Trade in all the Land was so much to be cherished and maintained as this, which, quoth he, may well be called, the life of the poor.

Jack is offered a knighthood, but declines it, proudly saying,

> I beseech your Grace let me live like a poor Clothier amongst my people, in whose maintenance I take more felicity, than in all the vain titles of Gentility: for these are the labouring Ants whom I seek to defend, and these be the Bees which I keep.

The quasi-royal clothier is left to the maintenance of his little commonwealth of contented and busy work-people. A more whole-hearted glorification of the cloth-trade can scarcely be devised.

Interestingly, the twenty-four page small merry version cuts the references to the jealousy of the county gentry, and the offer of knighthood, along with the rich gifts Jack makes to the king, and the marvellously romanticized clothing of his work-people. Instead, Jack's liberality to the poor, which is apparent in the longer version, has proportionately a much more predominant place in the shorter one. He remits his second wife's dowry, which her parents have only raised by selling all their milk kine, and also remits the debts of a creditor, for whom he provides a shop and stock. Here the humblest reader is encouraged to find in the rich clothier a source of help and charity. Jack is lavish with his charity just as the 'worthy yeomen' of the west, and their northern clothier friends, placed earlier by Deloney in time, performed a number of mixed medieval and sixteenth-century good works, founding, between them, a monastery and a free school, giving loans to poor weavers, and marrying and providing a stock in trade for poor couples.[61]

Deloney's third best-seller, *The History of the Gentle Craft*,[62] was written in quite a different vein from the pseudo-realism of his novels on the clothiers. It was written to appeal to shoemakers, but did so by telling the stories of St Hugh and his love, the virgin St Winifred who was martyred in an early persecution, and Crispin and Crispianus, the sons of the 'Queen Logria' of Kent, who was sought by the wicked 'Roman' tyrant, the Emperor Maximus. All these saintly figures, who moved with wooden jerks through the creakiest of fake medieval pasts, were given hospitality or help in moments of distress by shoemakers. Crispin and Crispianus actually served out their apprenticeship. Thus any shoemaker reader, whether apprentice, journeyman or master, was enabled to identify himself with the pseudo-Roman and medieval past of persecution, and with princes and princesses. *The Gentle Craft*, therefore, came nearer in intent to the last group of the 'historical' novels, those which quite deliberately set out to give the humbler, and perhaps newly literate, reader a means of identifying himself with the heroes even of the genuine medieval chivalric aristocratic romances.

POOR BOY AND GIRL MAKE GOOD

A group of the stories had poverty-stricken heroes or even heroines, who succeeded in life, sometimes somewhat after the fashion of their chivalric forebears. These were patently written for the non-gentle reader. It was the only group, with the exception of the equally non-gentle burlesques, written specifically for the just-literate. It is also, therefore, the only group that can tell us anything, through its printing history, of the earliest dates at which the existence of a humble literate audience who might spend 2*d* on a story in which it found itself reflected, was noticed and provided for by the trade.

Long Meg of Westminster[63] was the first of these of known date. It was first printed in 1582,[64] just at the appropriate time to coincide with the improvement in schooling and literacy of the 1580s and 1590s (see above, p. 19ff). Meg is a Lancashire lass who comes to London on the carrier's cart aged eighteen, with two other girls, in search of a place in service. She is a strapping wench, who beats up the carrier when he tries to overcharge the girls, and also uses her fists to set right other injustices. She is an Amazon, and acts as chucker out, when necessary, at the inn in Westminster where she is hired as a servant. She meets there, amongst other people, Sir Thomas More. She ruffles round London at night dressed in men's clothes with a sword and buckler, but is not thought of, or not presented as, a feminine threat to a male audience, but on the contrary is universally beloved even by those she beats in fair fight. She protects the poor, like herself. When she overcomes two footpads, she makes them swear not to prey on 'poor and impotent men, women, children or Packmen or Carriers, for their Goods and Money is none of their own', but she tells them that they may rob 'rich farmers' with impunity. When the timid ostler serving with her is pressed, she takes the press money in his place and goes to Boulogne to fight. She is serving there as a laundress when the place is besieged by the Dauphin of France, and leads her troup of laundresses to beat off a night attack when the sentries fail to wake up. For this she gets a pension for life. Despite her brawn and pugnacity, she keeps the rules of her society, and remains a sympathetic heroine for male readers, for she marries a soldier and proves an ideal submissive wife to him. She refuses to pick up the cudgel he offers her to return his blows. ' "Whatever I have done to others", she said, "It behoveth me to be Obedient to you, and never shall it be said, though I Cudgel a Knave that wrongs me, that Long Meg shall be her Husband's Master".'

The chapbook leaves her, very suitably, mistress of an inn in Islington, which she runs on strict principles. These include free meals for the hungry. Suddenly, in her presence,[65] the reader is in a new world of girls seeking service, carriers' carts from Lancashire, and the seamy side of life in inns, which owes nothing at all to a second-hand world of medieval aristocratic society.

In general, though, the chapbook world remains dominated by wealth, rank and blood. However, matters can be adjusted for the present audience by magic, and by marriage. The poorest of all, the orphaned country vagrant boy, Richard Whittington, is delivered by the magic virtues of his cat.[66] The poor man can 'discover' a lineage and find he is of gentle birth after all. *The Blind Beggar of Bethnal Green*,[67] who was one of the heroes, was blinded in the 'French wars' of uncertain date, and repudiated by his Essex, gentle, kinsfolk. He chose to beg, and only revealed his lineage when a knight fell in love with his daughter, who was a serving-maid at an inn. The father made enough by begging to have 'catskins of gold pieces' hidden under his bed, and was so able to pay her dower. He revealed at the wedding, to which he wore silk and gold embroidery, that his daughter's descent was as good as her knight's.

Tommy Potts's solution was even more magical.[68] Rosamund, heir of the Lord Arundel, refused to marry Lord Phoenix on the grounds

> I have a Lover true of mine own
> A serving man of low degree
> One Tommy Potts is his name
> My first love and last that ever shall be.

Lord Phoenix is indignant, on the reasonable grounds that

> I am able to spend £40 a week
> He is not able to spend pounds three.

Tommy Potts's master, Lord Jockeys, is all in favour of this romantic idyll, surprisingly enough, and offers to lend Tommy forty lances and half his own estates to secure the lady. Tommy is not an agricultural servant, but a retainer left over from a medieval world of livery and maintenance. But Tommy refuses to do anything as unsporting as that, and beats Lord Phoenix in single mounted combat. So Lord Phoenix says resignedly:

> It was never likely better to prove
> With me, or any Nobleman else
> That would hinder a poor man of his Love.

The Lady Rosamund ends up singing

> I have a lover true of mine own
> A serving man of low degree
> From Tom Potts I'll change his name
> The young Lord Arundel he shall be.

So all ends well, and Tommy Potts is duly elevated to the peerage.

The Famous History of Aurelius[69] must fulfil every apprentice's dream (see above, p. 55). *Tom Thumb*[70] on the other hand, is specially written not for apprentices, but to appeal to a rural audience.

> His father was a Plough-man plain
> His mother milk'd the Cow

and his minute adventures began by being rural. He fell into a furrow at seeding time, was swallowed by that self-same cow when tethered for safety to a thistle, and so on. His adventures, too, were readapted to the high chivalric mode, and so he ended up as the smallest knight at Arthur's court. There, for a boon, he was granted as much silver coin as he could carry away, and so proudly brought his mother home a threepenny piece.

Possibly the most interesting 'poor boy makes good' story is *The Pleasant History of Thomas Hickathrift*[71] because it so apparently accurately reflects the aspirations of the rural poor. It is one of the few glimpses of the real world in the fantasies of this literature. Tom Hickathrift is enormous, and very strong. He is the son of the widow of a day-labourer who lived 'in the reign before William the Conquorer', which is equivalent to saying 'Once upon a time, a very long time ago'. The Saxon past is always cited when real remoteness is required. The Hickathrifts live in the marsh of Ely in Cambridgeshire. Thomas's father 'put his son to good learning, but he would take none, for he was none of the wisest sort' – in fact he was 'soft', that is, a simpleton. Tom went into service with a brewer to cart the beer, and normally worked the route between Lynn and Wisbech. There he fell in with a Giant who terrorized the countryside and eventually killed him in a great and gory battle. By the common consent of the county, Tom was given the site of the Giant's cave, which was 'full of silver and gold'. And the use that he made of

THE
𝔓leasant 𝔥istory
OF
Thomas Hic-ka-thrift.

Printed by J. M. for W. Thackeray, and
T. Passinger.

this magically acquired fortune reflects the aspirations of the poor, who did not dream of changing their social order.

> Tom pulled down the cave, and built him a . . . House where the Cave stood, all the Ground that the Gyant kept by force and strength, some he gave to the Poor [to be] their Common, and the rest he made pastures of, and divided the most part . . . to maintain him and his old Mother . . . and Tom's fame was spread both far and near throughout the country, and then it was no longer Tom but Mr Hickathrift, so that he was the chiefest Man amongst them. . . . Tom he kept Men and Maids and lived most bravely, and he made him a Park to keep Deer in and by his House . . . he built a famous church.[72]

In fact he behaved as a country gentleman, and, presumably, as the reader would do if he could. There is no social protest here; all the poor boy wants is to become the country gentleman he has already seen so often riding by. The unknown author's imagination fails him here. The real world of the country gentry, the world of quarter sessions and county politics, is closed to him. So Tom, unable to ape this, ends by becoming bored. He rides round the countryside fighting tinkers and highwaymen, and kicking footballs so far they could never be found again.

This, then, is the 'historical' past to which the readers of chapbooks were admitted; a second-hand chivalric past, full of battles and adventures, signs and wonders. It had plenty to feed the imagination, and patently did feed John Bunyan's imagination, but it conveyed almost nothing of the real historical past and had above all no relevance to the urban classes, or to the countrymen who read it.

The whole point of this literature is that it is useless. It is truly a pass-time, as the advertisements recommended, and truly a relaxation, and it does not serve any other ends polemic or political. The exception is religion, for the religious chapbooks were of major importance in forming the attitudes and sensibilities of generations of the uneducated. Otherwise, the chapbooks are crude, unsubtle, earthy, uncompassionate, but full of movement and violence, sex, vivid imagery and better or worse jokes. It is perhaps helpful to us to realize the fantasy world, and indeed the mental jumble in which most people must have lived, to which the chapbooks are the key. In the popular mind, there were really likely to be giants in the fens, and dragons in Northumberland, astrology and divination were reliable 'scientific' guides to action, and the landscape was peopled with knights riding about performing vast slaughters to whose company the aspiring day-labourer's son might, if he was lucky, be admitted by some combination of luck, vast strength, magic or marriage. A stupid ineducable fellow might kill a giant, find a hoard of silver or gold, and build a great house, surrounded by a deer park, in which he could play the country gentleman. Or perhaps, even if he failed in all these, he might yet kick a football out of sight. Even Honest John and Loving Kate, that realistic and modest couple, might be lucky enough to get a stock of malt to set up their own alehouse. This literature, which was important enough to have its own printers, its own distributors plodding up and down the country, and its own advertising, seems to me to have been truthfully described in that advertising as the pastime and the relaxation it was. 'Good Reader, let they Patience brook, but to read over this small Book; which will thee satisfy a while, and surely force from thee a Smile.'[73] Another author recommended his book as 'very delightful to Read for to make laughter in long winter nights, but more pleasant in Summer days'.[74] These were the unpretentious aims of the authors and publishers of the popular print Pepys collected in the 1680s, and it seems very likely that it got the market right.

NOTES AND REFERENCES

1 Capp, B. (1979) *Astrology and the Popular Press 1500–1800*, London and Boston, 72–101.

2 *PM*, I (4), 73–95. I am excluding the books of garlands from this survey of the chapbook version of history. The ballads were very different in content from the chapbooks, and were frequently tied to specific events. Deloney's 'Garland of Delight' (*PM*, III (1)) contains a whole variety of songs written round, for instance, the deaths of King John and Edward II. There is even one on the Peasants' Revolt. Since ballads have been so thoroughly studied by literature specialists, it seemed better to exclude their content here.

3 'The Friar and the Boy', *PM*, II (23), 537–60.

4 The pre-Reformation atmosphere of the secular chapbooks is partially, but not entirely, accounted for by their printing his-

tory. 'The Friar and the Boy' was printed by Wynkyn de Worde about 1500, but 'The Sackfull of News' was first registered by the Stationers' Company in 1557–8. These are the two chapbooks in which most of the jests about ignorant and greedy churchmen that were reprinted in the 1680s are found. Furnivall, F. J. (ed.) (1871) *Captain Cox, His Ballads and Books*, London, lxvi and lxxiii-v. Where the theology of the secular chapbooks is updated, as it is in Martin Parker's version of 'Robin Hood', *PM*, II (36), 869, a very odd effect is obtained:

> with wealth that he by Roguery got
> eight Almshouses he built,
> thinking thereby to punge [sic] the blot
> of blood which he had spilt;
> such was their blind Devotion then
> depending on their works.
> Which if 'twere true, the Christian men
> inferior were to Turks.

5 'The Secret Sinners', *PM*, I (51), 1105–19, reprinted in part in Thompson, R. (1976) *Samuel Pepys's Penny Merriments*, London, 147–52.

6 *PM*, II (18), 437.

7 *PM*, II (14), 308–9.

8 *PM*, I (2 and 11).

9 *Vulgaria*, III (11). This history is unique only amongst the books in Pepys's collection, but such factual works were also highly unusual on the booksellers' lists of chapbooks at similar prices. There were plenty of genuine histories on the market, but they were normally priced at 1s and upwards. Clavel lists, for instance, 'A Short Relation of the River Nile' at 1s, the 'Memoires of Henry, Duke of Guise' at 5s and 'A Relation of the Siege of Canada' at 1s, in his large octavo histories printed before the end of the Michaelmas Term 1672. Foxton, D. F. (ed.) (reprinted 1965) Robert Clavel, *The General Catalogue of Books printed in England since the Dreadful Fire of London, 1666*, Part 3, English Bibliographical Sources, Series 2, Farnborough, 33.

10 *PM*, I (37).

11 *PM*, I (38). A similar chapbook that was in Captain Cox's library in 1575, 'The King and the Tanner', was still being printed in the

1680s, when it appeared in Thackeray's broadside trade-list, but Pepys did not have it. The monarch originally referred to in this story was Edward IV, but the first edition was printed in 1596. Clawson, W. H. (1909) *Gest of Robin Hood*, Toronto, 103, n. 2.

12 *PM*, II (7). This story is not extant in an edition earlier than the seventeenth century, and Clawson (op. cit., 111, n. 1) thinks it unlikely that it was earlier.

13 ibid., 111–12.

14 *PM*, 111(5), 451–626. Brunner, K. (ed.) (1933) *Seven Sages of Rome*, London, Early English Text Society 191. Commented on by Schlauch, M. (1956) *English Medieval Literature*, Warsaw, 253 and (1963) *Antecedents of the English Novel 1400–1600*, Warsaw and London, 60, n.22; and by Baker, E. A. (1924 and 1929) *History of the English Novel*, London, I, 287 and II, 53. The fullest account is in Hibbard, L. A. (1924) *Medieval Romance in England*, New York, 174–83.

15 *PM*, III (5).

16 *PM*, III (6), 627–807. It was also an extended octavo.

17 'Wisdoms Cabinet Opened: Or the Famous history of the Seven Wise Masters of Rome', *Vulgaria*, III (6), priced at 3d on the trade-list, *PM*, I, 95.

18 Zupitza, J. (ed.) (1875–6) *Guy of Warwick*, Early English Text Society 25 and 26. Hibbard, op. cit., London, 127–39. The oldest surviving version is in the Auchinleck Ms. Mills, M. and Huws, D. (eds) (1974) *Fragments of an Early Fourteenth-Century Guy of Warwick*, Oxford, Medium Aevum Monographs, New Series IV, discusses a manuscript that was in the possession of a knight of Somerset in the 1470s. It was so little regarded by him, however, that it was cut up, and used as binding strips for books of law and of medical recipes.

19 See above, pp. 7–8 and Hibbard, op. cit., 115–26.

20 *Vulgaria*, III (9).

21 *PM*, I (44).

22 *Vulgaria*, III (8).

23 I am grateful to Vic Gammon of Sussex University for drawing this connection to my notice.

24 'Life and Death of the Famous Champion of England, St George' (nd) *PM*, II (6). This is the same chapbook with ballad appended that was discussed by Chambers, E. K. (1933) *The English Folk*

Play, Oxford, 179–82, although Pepys's copy was sold by Clarke, Thackeray and Passinger, not by Thackeray alone.

25 This was Chambers's opinion. It may be right; the earliest version of St George in the *Short Title Catalogue* (Pollard, A. W. and Redgraves, G. R. (1926, revised 1976) *Short Title Catalogue, 1475–1640*, II, and Wing, D. (1945–51, revised 1972), *1641–1700*, I) is G. de Malynes (1601) 'St George for England, Allegorically Described', octavo. This is sufficiently soon after the appearance of Johnson's 'Seven Champions' to make it the likely link between that and the short chapbook version of 'St George' of the 1680s.

26 Pepys had all three parts, catalogued as items 1 and 1(b) in *Vulgaria*, II. They were all too long to be considered in this analysis. The first and second parts were both published by Scott, Bassett, Chiswell, Wotton and Conyers (1687), the third by Harris.

27 Baker, op. cit., II, 197. Dean-Smith, M. (1954) *A Note on Richard Johnson's Famous History of the Seven Champions*, English Folk Dance and Song Society, vii, 180–1, disagrees with both Chambers and Baker.

28 Chambers, op. cit., 24–6, 170–81. Brody, A. (1969) *The English Mummers and their Plays*, London, discusses the many additional folk-plays that have come to light since Chambers wrote, pp. 103–6, and considers he was wrong to have suggested that Johnson's 'Seven Champions' was the main source from which the texts were drawn, and also wrong to suggest that the words, rather than the essential actions, were in any way fundamental to the story. Brody limits the influence of the chapbooks to the introductory speech given by St George, which is roughly standardized. Brody, pp. 48–9, 124–6. In this he is following Helm, A. (1965) 'In Comes I, St George', *Folklore 76* (Summer), 121–4, who considers that only the introductory speech in the traditional plays comes from Johnson, but that the spread of chapbooks later led to chapbook versions of the play being given by the mummers as the traditional versions were lost, with stultifying effect.

29 Johnson was born in 1573. Plays were still being acted even in Puritan Essex as late as 1581 (Emmison, F. G. (1976) 'Tithes and Perambulations in Elizabethan Essex', in *Tribute to an Antiquary*, London, 205). Mepham, W. A. (1945) 'Medieval Drama in

Essex', *Essex Review* 54, 52–8, 107–12 and 139–42 shows that the last play supported by the town went on in Chelmsford in 1576, but that professional companies went on performing there often at markets and fairs, right up to 1635 ((1948) 'Chelmsford Plays of the Sixteenth Century', ibid. 57, 148–52, 171–8). Norwich lost its St George, although it retained its dragon, as early as 1552 (Burke, P. (1978) *Popular Culture in Early Modern Europe*, London, 216). Chambers, op. cit., 187–90, has references to plays being performed between 1588 and 1592 in Lancashire, 1597 in Suffolk and continuing, though with more slender references in the seventeenth century, right through to 1652–3.

30 Bassingbourn Churchwardens Accounts, Cambridge Record Office P.11/51.

31 The contents of this 'play-book' are a complete mystery. There is no 'St George' in the *Short Title Catalogue* (op. cit.) before 1601. See above, p. 150, n. 7. Play-books were used elsewhere. At Dunmow, in Essex, in 1528–9, the accounts noted 'gathered of the wyves for ye making of the (?) playbooks, iijs iijd' (Mepham, W. A. (1946) 'Medieval Drama in Essex: Dunmow', *Essex Review* 55, 59). In 1574, the value of the remaining play-books in Chelmsford was as high as £4 ((1948) 'Chelmsford Plays of the Sixteenth Century', ibid. 57, 173).

32 *PM*, II (6), 128.

33 Hilton, R. H. (1958) 'The Origins of Robin Hood', Keen, M. (1961) 'Robin Hood-Peasant or Gentleman', and Holt, J. C. (1960) 'The Origins and Audience of the Ballads of Robin Hood', all originally published in *Part and Present*, reprinted in Hilton, R. H. (ed.) (1976) *Peasants, Knights and Heretics*, Cambridge.

34 Chambers, op. cit., 11, 89, 156, 161.

35 Burke, op. cit., 180–1.

36 The other was the 'King and the Tanner', Furnival, op. cit., xii–xv, li 'Adam Bell' was possibly printed by de Worde, but was certainly printed by 1557–8, p. lv.

37 *Vulgaria*, III (15).

38 When the story was written, they would have been yeomen in the original sense, members of the household hierarchy, ascending from yeomen through squire to knight. (See Holt, art cit., 100–1.) For the seventeenth-century reader, the heroes will have been yeomen farmers, not men with 40s freeholds, but men who

farmed substantially more land, held by whatever tenure, then the standard 15 or 30 acre holding, and were worth substantially more at their deaths than the husbandmen further down the farming scale.

39 *Vulgaria*, III (16). This is again, a quarto double-book priced at 3*d*.

40 With the possible exception of *St George* in the form in which he survives.

41 By Margaret Schlauch, who surveys the whole movement and splendidly conveys the content of the neo-chivalric romances in (1963) op. cit., 164–74.

42 Who may have had a respectable fourteenth-century Catalonian origin. Baker, op. cit., I, 250–3.

43 See Lee, S. (ed.) (1894) *Dictionary of National Biography*, London, 290–7.

44 The first of which may have been written by a carpenter's daughter of Burgos (Baker, op. cit., 253–4).

45 Schlauch (1963) op. cit., 167, n. 5. In the late seventeenth century, Francis Kirkman, who had been such a devourer of chivalric tales as a boy, wrote Parts II and III for it. See above, pp. 72–3, and Patchell, M. (1947) *The Palmerin Romances in Elizabethan Prose Fiction*, Columbia, 15.

46 Baker, op. cit., 197–8.

47 ibid., 123–4.

48 Schlauch (1963) op. cit., 165–6. R. S. Crane discusses the popularity of the medieval romances in (1915) 'The Vogue of *Guy of Warwick* . . .', Modern Language Association of America 30, NS 23, Baltimore, Md., 131–6, and concludes that not only the majority of the reading public (by which he means the gentry) was conservative in its reading tastes, but also that its conservatism was fostered by the equally conservative tastes of the early printers. He also emphasizes the importance that the national hero, from Guy to Arthur, plays in the stories, and suggests this fed the streak of national identity and pride.

49 Mish, C. C. (1953) 'Best Sellers in Seventeenth Century Fiction', *Papers of the Bibliographical Society of America* 47, 356–73.

50 Patchell, op. cit., Introduction, and 21–2, including n. 71.

51 Pepys did not have 'Amadis of Gaul' or 'Palladin of England'. He

did have 'Palmerin', *Vulgaria*, I (1) and 'Don Belianis of Greece' in two parts, *Vulgaria*, I (2) (priced at 3s, bound in 1674). He also had 'The Seven Champions' in three parts, *Vulgaria*, II (1 and 1a) (the first two parts were priced at 3s in 1674), 'Parismus, Prince of Bohemia' in two parts, *Vulgaria*, II (3) (priced at 3s together in 1674), 'Ornatus and Artesia', *Vulgaria*, III (4), and 'Montelyon, Knight of the Oracle', *Vulgaria*, III (2) (priced at 1s in 1674). These are all discussed above. He also had, as longer histories which are not discussed above, nor anywhere else in this text, 'The Destruction of Troy' in three parts, *Vulgaria*, I (4) (priced at 3s bound in 1674), 'Valentine and Orson', *Vulgaria*, II (2) (priced at 1s 6d 'stitcht' in 1674), a long version of 'Fortunatus', *Vulgaria*, III (3), a long version of 'Faustus', *Vulgaria*, III (14), and a long version of 'Guy of Warwick', *Vulgaria*, III (9); the last was published for Brooksby. Brewster's 'Guy' was priced at 10d 'stitcht' in 1674. Pepys also had a pair from the Reynard cycle, 'Reynard the Fox', *Vulgaria*, IV (8) (priced at 10d 'stitcht' in 1674), and 'Shifts of Reynardine, son of Reynard', *Vulgaria*, IV (9). There was also a long version of the 'Honour of the Merchant Taylors', *Vulgaria*, IV (13), and 'A Post with a Packet of Letters', *Vulgaria*, IV (17). These are the twenty-two items omitted from this survey on the grounds of their length and prices. The prices given here are taken from Foxton, D. F. (ed.) (1965) Robert Clavel, *The General Catalogue of Books printed in England since the Dreadful Fire of London, 1666*, English Bibliographical Sources, Series 2, Farnborough: Part 3, 'To the end of Michaelmas Term, 1672'; and Part 4, 'To the end of Trinity Term, 1674'. It is worth noticing that Pepys's choice of the longer items in the *Vulgaria*, was highly idiosyncratic, as a study of the section of Clavel's lists devoted to 'History in Quarto', ibid., Part 3, 31–2 and Part 4, 34–5, shows. He chose only the romances from what was available, and resolutely avoided the histories which purported to be factual accounts.

52 *Vulgaria*, I (3).
53 *Vulgaria*, III (18), first published in 1599. Baker waxes very hot in his discussion of it. 'The book is trash, and an egregius example of what delighted the mob in the early 17th century,' Baker, op. cit., II, 197.
54 Greene's 'Pandosto', which was later retitled 'Dorastus and Faw-

nia', from which Shakespeare took *The Winter's Tale*, first appeared in 1588.

55 *Vulgaria*, IV (11).

56 *PM*, II (29), 687–710.

57 Deloney is discussed at length by Baker, op. cit., II, 170–92 and Schlauch (1963) op. cit., 237–45. His works were edited by F. O. Mann in 1912.

58 *Vulgaria*, III (19), *PM*, II (50), *Vulgaria*, IV (12), *PM*, I (36), *Vulgaria*, III (17), and *Vulgaria*, IV (14).

59 *PM*, II (50), 14–15.

60 *Vulgaria*, III (19), Chapter V.

61 'Pleasant History of Thomas of Reading, or, the Six Worthy Yeomen of the West', *Vulgaria*, III (17), last chapter.

62 *Vulgaria*, IV (12) and *PM*, I (36).

63 *PM*, II (26).

64 Pollard and Redgrave, II, op. cit. (second edn 1976), no. 17, 782.

65 Long Meg was incorporated by Deloney into 'The Gentle Craft' in 1597–8. She is discussed by Schlauch (1963) op. cit., 117–19 and 243, and by Q. D. Leavis in the Deloney version, in (1939) *Fiction and the Reading Public*, London, 92–3. It is perhaps not possible to share Mrs Leavis's admiration for Deloney's 'Chaucerain clarity and freshness and his innocence of any literary artifice' since his more libertine Meg becomes a common camp whore in France and pursues her career of prostitution until old age puts a stop to her labours.

66 *PM*, II (31) and also the double-book, quarto version priced at 3*d Vulgaria*, III (12).

67 *PM*, I (15). Day, J. (first acted 1659) *The Blind Beggar of Bethnal Green*, Cambridge Bibliography of English Literature 1, 535.

68 'The Lover's Quarrel or Cupid's Triumph, being The Pleasant History of Fair Rosamund of Scotland', *PM*, I (9). This is entered on the Thackeray trade-list of 1689 simply as 'Tom Potts'.

69 *PM*, I (14).

70 *PM*, II (22).

71 *PM*, I (3).

72 ibid., 65.

73 *PM*, I (27), 585.

74 *PM*, I (5), 97.

X
Conclusion

§

My chief interest in this essay has been to establish the nature of the
world of imagination, fiction and fantasy opened to the unlettered
reader of the seventeenth century, who had 2*d* or 3*d* to spend. During
the 1680s Samuel Pepys assiduously acquired a very large proportion
of the output of each of the main publishers in the field. His collection therefore seems to give a good cross-section of these stories,
which were peddled round the country at prices up to 6*d*. But Pepys
was a very methodical and thorough collector with considerable
purchasing power. When I stress the richness and variety of his
collection, I must not be supposed to assume that the humble reader
would ever be able to buy many such works and so have many such
imaginative worlds at his disposal. The whole question of readership
is maddeningly obscure. If the substantial yeoman Robert Loder
only spent 2*d* on an almanac in 1613, and 17*d* on books in 1614,[1] it
is unreasonable to assume that equally prosperous, let alone less
prosperous, readers managed to save up many more 2*d*s and 3*d*s to
dip a wide selection of small books out of the chapmen's bags in the
post-Commonwealth period, even though the trade was certainly
expanding, as were the numbers of chapmen in the distributors'
network. Despite this caveat, though, the contents of this cross-
section of 'Small Godly Books, Small Merry Books and Pleasant
Histories' enable us to begin to perceive a little better some of the as-
sumptions of the society that supported its producers and distributors.

One of the most interesting and striking characteristics of this
literature for the unlearned was its continuity.

Bevis of Hampton, which originated in an Anglo-Norman
romance of the thirteenth century, itself probably drew on popular
themes coming ultimately from the revenge feuds of the Vikings, and
others even earlier.[2] The *Seven Sages of Rome*, with its groups of
stories told within the framework of a story of a mythical Roman

emperor and his amorous wife who wishes to seduce her stepson, had reached Europe from the Orient and was already old when Chaucer used the device.[3] *The Friar and the Boy* was printed by Wynkyn de Worde, Caxton's successor. These were all in the collection of books of the mason Cox, who was the proud leader of the Coventry men performing their traditional play before the visiting Queen Elizabeth in 1575.[4] Cox of Coventry was probably as ignorant of the origins of his reading matter as was John Bunyan, who, in turn, revelled in the adventures of Bevis, and drew on them for the source of his own fiction. Purchasers like this were totally unaware that they were emotionally sharing in an artificial world of adventure created originally in some cases for bored and sexually starved younger members of the courtly aristocracy of the twelfth century, or in others in recent productions, written perhaps by an apprentice in the printing trade specializing in chapbooks. My reader would be as ignorant of such matters as was his lineal descendant, John Clare, at the beginning of the nineteenth century, who firmly believed that, in the chapbooks containing, in some cases, the very same stories, he was heir to 'the chief learning and literature of the country'.

Bevis, the *Seven Sages* and *The Friar and the Boy* were all collected as chapbooks by Samuel Pepys, and were obtainable by any customer of the chapmen who had 3*d* to spend. The longest roots of the familiar tales may have reached deep into the middle ages, but their tallest branches reached almost as impressively 300 years forward into the nineteenth century. *Amadis de Gaul*, probably of fourteenth-century Catalonian origin, translated in 1588, printed by Charles Tias to sell at 6*d* in 1664, figures, with Southey rather oddly as the author, in an edition issued in 1803, in a bibliography of fiction available to the working man between 1830 and 1850.[5] So did the comparative newcomer, *Jack of Newbury*, written by Deloney in 1597, printed by Tias in 1664 to sell at 2*d*, collected by Samuel Pepys in the 1680s, and still available to the nineteenth-century artisan. Thomas Frost, reflecting on the reading matter available to the working-classes before the 1830s when 'the majority wanted only to be amused', described the 'prominent favourites' as 'The wonderful lives and adventures of Friar Bacon and Dr Faustus . . . the venerable history of the Seven Champions of Christendom, some selections from the Arabian Nights and an abridgement of the Memoirs of Baron Trenck'.

'These stories', he wrote sadly, 'formed the staple reading of the masses.'[6] He did not know, of course, that three at least of them had filled that function for several centuries. This historical dimension backwards to the late thirteenth century, and forwards to the mid-nineteenth century, is necessarily lost in a study of the tremendously rich and divergent content of only some of the varieties of cheap print available in a single decade of the seventeenth century.

We may be more knowledgeable in some ways than our ancestors, our sense of the probable may be different, so that space fiction and its heroes have at last ousted the chivalric, and the visual effect of the nudes in the tabloids may have supplemented the bawdy joke. We may well be embarrassed by different things and may be individually more compassionate. But the chapbooks Samuel Pepys collected had already formed the expectations and replenished the tale-telling of several generations. They continued to do so, reprinting over and over again, until well into the nineteenth century. Their importance in the lives of less educated people should not be under-estimated.

NOTE AND REFERENCES

1 Fussell, G. E. (ed.) (1936) *Robert Loder's Farm Accounts, 1610–20*, London, Royal Historical Society, Camden Third Series 53, 71, 89.

2 Köbling, E. (ed.) (1885–94) *Bevis of Hampton*, Early English Text Society, 46, 48, 65. Schlauch, M. (1956) *English Medieval Literature and its Social Foundations*, Warsaw, 178.

3 Brunner, K. (ed.) (1933) *Seven Sages of Rome*, Early English Text Society, London, 191. Schlauch, op. cit., 253.

4 Furnivall, F. J. (ed.) (1871) *Captain Cox, His Ballads and Books; or Robert Lanehan's Letter*, London, xii-xiv, and lxxii-iv for 'The Fryar and The Boy'.

5 James, L. (1963) *Fiction for the Working Man, 1830–1850*, Harmondsworth. Nothing brings home more clearly the amazing continuity of this literature than the comparison of William Thackeray's trade-list of 1689 (Appendix) with the Dicey and Marshall catalogues for 1744, and the Cheney list for 1808–20, printed in Neuburg, V. (1972) *Chapbooks: a bibliography*, London, 75–81. 'Valentine and Orson', 'Jane Shore', 'Honest John and Loving Kate' and 'Mother Bunch' were standard fare for the

poor, and, I suggest above, p. 75, for upper-class schoolboys, from sixteenth to the nineteenth centuries. The continuity of one particular title was traced in great detail by Ronald Crane in (1915) 'The Vogue of *Guy of Warwick* from the close of the Middle Ages to the Romantic Revival', Modern Language Association of America 30, 125–94. The same continuity over centuries was found in the contents of the Spanish chapbooks. The ballads of the 1570s celebrating Lepanto, and catechisms authorized in the seventeenth century, were still printing this century, along, of course, with newcomers summarizing North America films. Wilson E. M. (1967) *Some Aspects of Spanish Literary History*, Oxford, 12–19. A completely different aspect of the continuity of popular culture, this time of form, was shown in the creation of new topical ballads. Hawkers in Cambridge marketplace in 1910 during the Crippin trial could be heard shouting, 'Here you are! The latest songs! All about the Dirty Doctor!' Williams, L. A. (1935). *English Folk Song and Dance.*

6 Frost, T. (1880) *Forty Years' Recollections: Literary and Political*, London, 78–9. Compare the similar lists given above for Irish cottagers in the early nineteenth century, p. 74. I owe the quotation from Frost to David Vincent.

Appendix

❧

The chapbook section of the trade-list of WILLIAM THACKERAY at the
Angel in Duck Lane, near West Smithfield, dated by Blagden to 1689,
annotated with references to the items on it collected by Samuel
Pepys, Pepys Library, Magdalene College, Cambridge.

Small godly books

'Englands Golden Watchbell'
'Mothers Blessing', *PG*, 31, 647 Clarke, Thackeray and Passinger
(1685)
'England's Alarm'
'Gabriel Harding', *PG*, 45, 975 Thackeray, Passinger (nd)
'Touchstone of a Christian'
'Great Brittain's Warning-piece'
'Godly Man's Gain'
'Serious Call', *PG*, 29, 599 Thackeray (1684)
'Short and sure way'
'Roger's exhortation'
'Black Book of Conscience', *PG*, 5, 89 Clarke, Thackeray and
Passinger (forty-second edn nd)
'Plain Man's Path-way'
'Almanack for a Day', *PG*, 14, 271 Clarke, Thackeray and
Passinger (nd)
'Death Triumphant', *PG*, 19, 383 Clarke, Thackeray and Passinger
(sixth edn nd)
'Ready way to everlasting Life'
'Character of a Drunkard', *PG*, 1, 1 Clarke, Thackeray and Passinger
(1686)
'England's faithfull Physician'

'Christ's voice to England', *PG*, 32, 671 Wright, Clarke, Thackeray and Passinger (fifth edn 1683)

'Christ in the Clouds', *PG*, 18, 367 Wright, Clarke, Thackeray and Passinger (1682)

'Way to get Riches'

'Sin of Pride'

'God's terrible voice'

'Andrew's Golden Chain'

'Christians Race from the Cradle to the Grave'

'Christs coming to Judgment', *PG*, 36, 759; 'Christ in the Clouds, coming to Judgement' Charles Passinger (sixth edn 1682)

'Death-bed of Repentance'

'Sinners Sobs'

'Great Assize', *PG*, 17, 335 Thackeray (1681)

'Fathers Blessing', *PG*, 34, 711 Wright, Clarke, Thackeray and Passinger (nd)

'Doubting Christian', *PG*, 30, 623 Wright, Clarke, Thackeray and Passinger (ninth impression 1683)

'Way to Heaven made plain'

'Every man's Duty'

'Posie of Prayers'

'Peter of Repentance', *PG*, 26, 527 Wright, Clarke, Thackeray and Passinger (fourteenth edn 1682)

'Charitable Christian', *PG*, 27, 551 Wright, Clarke, Thackeray and Passinger (1682)

'Andrew's Golden Trumpet'

'Pious Exhortation'

'Dooms-day at hand'

'Lord's-day'

'God's Eye from Heaven'

'Godly man's request'

Small merry books

'St George', *PM*, II (6), 105 Clarke, Passinger and Thackeray

'Gentlewomans Cabinet, or a Book of Cookery', *PM*, II, (5), 81 Thackeray and Passinger (nd)

'Tryal of Wit, or a Book of Riddles'

'Simon and Cicely', *PM*, I (57), 1225 Clarke, Passinger and Thackeray (nd)

'Shepherds Garland', *PM*, II (40), 951 Wright, Clarke, Thackeray and Passinger (1682)

'King and the Tanner'

'Cupids sport and Pastimes', *PM*, I (43), 929 Thackeray (1684)

'Green-Goose Fair'

'Rosamond', *PM*, I (2), 25 Coles, Vere, Wright, Clarke, Thackeray and Passinger (nd)

'Lawrence Lazy'

'Womans Spleen'

'Royal Garland', *PM*, II (39), 927 Clarke, Thackeray and Passinger (1681)

'Guy of Warwick', *PM*, I (44), 953 Clarke, Thackeray and Passinger (1686)

'Robin Hood', *PM*, II (36), 855 Clarke, Thackeray and Passinger (1686)

'Vinegar and Mustard', *PM*, I (48), 1049 Clarke, Thackeray and Passinger (1686)

'Horn Fair'

'Cupid's Masterpiece', *PM*, I (33), 705 Clarke, Thackeray and Passinger (1685)

'Robin the Sadler', *PM*, I (19), 425 Conyers (nd)

'Loves School', *PM*, II (15), 321 Clarke, Passinger, Thackeray and Brooksby (1682)

'John and Kate', *PM* I (10), 209 Clarke, Passinger and Thackeray (1685)

'Tom Long'

'Unfortunate Son', Second part, *PM*, I (28), 609 Printed MW to be sold by J. Clarke (1681)

'Tom Tram', First part, *PM*, I (41), 881 WT to be sold by J. Deacon (nd)

'Tom Tram', Second part, *PM*, I (42), 905 Deacon (nd)

'Queen's Close', *PM*, I (12), 257 Passinger (1682)

'Doctor Faustus', *PM*, I, (54), 1153, Deacon and Dennisson

'Five Wonders', *PM*, II (2), 25 Margaret White (1683)

'Hen-peckt Frigate'

'Jug and Bess'

'Female Ramblers', *PM*, I (26), 569 Wright, Clarke, Thackeray and Passinger (1683)

'Crossing of Proverbs', *PM*, I (53), 1137 Margaret White (1683)

'Tom Hickathrift', *PM*, I (3), 49 Thackeray and Passinger

'Jack of Newbury', *PM*, II (50), 1149 Thackeray (1684)

'Unfortunate Daughter'

'Variety of Riddles', *PM*, I (25), 545 Thackeray (1684)

'Book of Riddles', *PM*, I (24), 521 WT sold by John Back (1685)

'Fryer Bacon', *PM*, I (1), 1 Printed MW sold by Newman and Alsop (1683)

'Tom Thumb', *PM*, II (22), 513 Clarke, Thackeray and Passinger (nd)

'Cupids Sollicitor', *PM*, I (46), 1001 WT sold by John Back

'Jane Shore', *PM*, I (11), 233 Coles, Vere and Wright

'King and the Miller', *PM*, II (7), 129 Clarke, Thackeray and Passinger (nd)

'Robin Conscience'

'Old Woman', *PM*, II (27), 649 WT sold by J. Blare

'King and Northern Man'

'Conscience and Plain-dealing', *PM*, I (29), 633 Wright, Clarke, Thackeray and Passinger (nd)

'Sackfull of News', *PM*, I (6), 113 Clarke, Thackeray and Passinger (1685)

'Distressed Welshman', *PM*, I (30), 657 WT sold by J. Conyers

'Carrols', *PM*, I (22), 481; 'Make Room for Christmas' Thackeray and Passinger (nd)

'Gentle Craft', *PM*, I (36), 761 Clarke, Thackeray and Passinger (1685)

'Cupids Garland', *PM*, II (38), 903 Clarke, Thackeray and Passinger

'Fumblers Hall', *PM*, I (7), 137 Clarke, Thackeray and Passinger

'Tom Potts', *PM*, I (9), 185; 'History of Fair Rosamund of Scotland, Whose Love was Obtained by the Valour of Tommy Potts . . .' WT and Passinger (nd)

'Noble Marquess'

'Diogenes', *PM*, I (55), 1177 Wright, Clarke, Thackeray and Passinger (nd)

'Womans Brawl', *PM*, II (1), 3 (title page missing)

'Valentine and Orson'

'Robin the Cobler'

'The married mans Comfort, and the Batchelours Confession'
'Corydon's Complements'
'A Groatsworth of Wit for a Penny', *PM*, I (49), 1073 WT sold by
  J. Deacon
'Venus Turtle-Dove'
'Welsh Traveller', *PM*, I (40), 857 Clarke, Thackeray and Passinger
  (nd)
'Six pennyworth of Wit'
'Mother Shipton's Prophesies', *PM*, I (56), 1201 Conyers

Double-books

'Christ's first Sermon'
'Christ's last Sermon'
'Christians best Garment'
'Heavens Glory and Hells horror'
'Katherine Stubs'
'School of Grace'
'Kawwood the Rook', *Vulgaria*, IV (10) Wright, Clarke, Thackeray
  and Passinger (1683)
'Golden Eagle', *Vulgaria*, IV (11) Thackeray (1677)
'King Arthur', *Vulgaria*, III (8) Wright, Clarke, Thackeray and
  Passinger (1684)
'The Seven Champions' (a longer version, *Vulgaria*, II (1), three
  parts)
'Reynard the Fox' (a longer version, *Vulgaria*, IV (8))
'Doctor Merryman'
'Christians Blessed choice'
'Warning-piece'
'Patient Grissel', *Vulgaria*, IV (2) Wright, Clarke, Thackeray and
  Passinger (1682)
'Fenner of Repentance'
'Dives and Lazarus'
'Antonius and Aurelius', *Vulgaria*, III (5) Wright, Clarke, Thackeray
  and Passinger (1682)
'Parismus' (a longer version, *Vulgaria*, II (3), two parts)
'Country Farmer'
'Adam Bell', *Vulgaria*, III (16) Thackeray (nd)

Histories

'Dream of Devil and Dives'

'Dutch Fortune-Teller'

'Sport and Pastime', *Vulgaria*, IV (6) Thackeray and Deacon (nd)

'Arcandam'

'Third Part of Seven Champions', *Vulgaria*, II (1) three parts Parts 1
    and 2, *Vulgaria*, II (1) Scott, Bassett, Wootton and Conyers (1687)
    Part 3, Benjamin Harris (nd)

'Jack of Newbury', *Vulgaria*, III (19) Passinger and Thackeray (nd)

'Scoggin's Jest', *Vulgaria*, IV (3) Thackeray and J. Deacon (nd)

'Royal Arbour'

'Markham's faithfull Farrier'

'Markham's Method'

'Garland of Delight'

'Crown Garland'

'Robin Hood's Garland'

'Mucedorus, a Play'

'Speedy Post with a Packet of Letters', *Vulgaria*, IV (16) Thackeray
    (twelfth edn 1684)

'Tom a Lincoln, or the Red-Rose Kt', *Vulgaria*, III (18) Thackeray
    (1682)

'Palmerin of England', three parts, *Vulgaria*, I (1) Thackeray and
    Passinger (1685)

'The Book of Knowledge of things unknown'

'Ornatus and Artesia', *Vulgaria*, III (4) Wright, Clarke, Thackeray
    and Passinger (eighth impression 1683)

'Sir John Hawkwood or the History of the Merchant-Taylors',
    Vulgaria, IV (13) Whitwood (1668)

'History of Montelion', *Vulgaria*, III (1) Thackeray and Passinger
    (1687)

'History of the Gentle-Craft', *Vulgaria*, IV (12) first part only WT
    sold by Gilbertson (nd)

'Albertus Magnus English'

Index

🍃

DATE DUE
